THE NORTHERN CAMINOS

NORTE, PRIMITIVO AND INGLÉS

About the Authors

Dave Whitson is a high-school history teacher in Portland, Oregon, and a graduate of the University of Washington. He made his first pilgrimage in 2002 on the Camino Francés and was inspired to return with a group of his high-school students, which he did in 2004. He has led a total of 11 student pilgrimage trips, including seven on the Camino de Santiago (five on the Francés and two on the Norte) and four on the Via Francigena. In addition, he has made long-distance treks in Norway on the Pilgrim Road to Nidaros, in England on the North Downs Way to Canterbury, and in Turkey on the Lycian Way. All told, he has walked roughly 14,000km on pilgrim roads in Europe. Dave first walked the Camino del Norte and Camino Primitivo in 2008, returned with a student group in 2009, and has since walked them in 2011 and 2013 to ensure up-to-date route information for this guide.

Laura Perazzoli lives in the Pacific Northwest and works in communication and education. She is an avid hiker and climber. She completed her first pilgrimage in 2004 on the Camino Francés. She has since led seven student pilgrimage trips on the Via Francigena in Italy, the Camino Francés, and the Camino del Norte/Primitivo. Laura first walked the Camino del Norte and Primitivo with a student group in 2009 and returned in 2011 and 2013 to rewalk the route and to complete the Camino Inglés in order to provide up-to-date route information for this guide.

THE NORTHERN CAMINOS

NORTE, PRIMITIVO AND INGLÉS

by Dave Whitson and Laura Perazzoli

CICERONE

2 POLICE SQUARE, MILNTHORPE, CUMBRIA LA7 7PY
www.cicerone.co.uk

© Dave Whitson and Laura Perazzoli 2015
Second edition 2015
Reprinted in 2016 (with updates) and 2017
ISBN: 978 1 85284 794 4
First edition 2012

Printed by KHL Printing, Singapore

A catalogue record for this book is available from the British Library.

All photographs are by the authors unless otherwise stated.

Cartographic base 1:50,000 © National Geographic Institute of Spain

Updates to this Guide

While every effort is made by our authors to ensure the accuracy of guidebooks as they go to print, changes can occur during the lifetime of an edition. Any updates that we know of for this guide will be on the Cicerone website (www.cicerone.co.uk/794/updates), so please check before planning your trip. We also advise that you check information about such things as transport, accommodation and shops locally. Even rights of way can be altered over time. We are always grateful for information about any discrepancies between a guidebook and the facts on the ground, sent by email to updates@cicerone.co.uk or by post to Cicerone, 2 Police Square, Milnthorpe LA7 7PY, United Kingdom.

Register your book: To sign up to receive free updates, special offers and GPX files where available, register your book at www.cicerone.co.uk.

Front cover: Hiking near the coast on the walk to La Isla (Norte, Stage 17)

CONTENTS

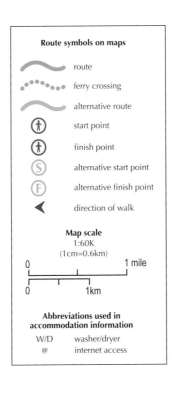

Route symbols on maps

route

ferry crossing

alternative route

start point

finish point

alternative start point

alternative finish point

direction of walk

Map scale
1:60K
(1cm=0.6km)

0 — 1 mile

0 — 1km

Abbreviations used in accommodation information

W/D   washer/dryer
@   internet access

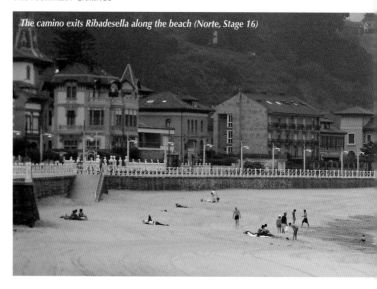

The camino exits Ribadesella along the beach (Norte, Stage 16)

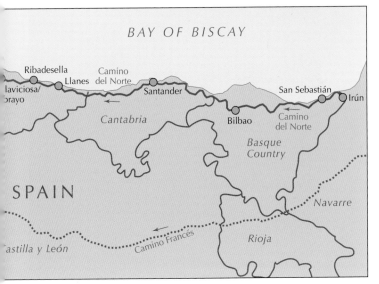

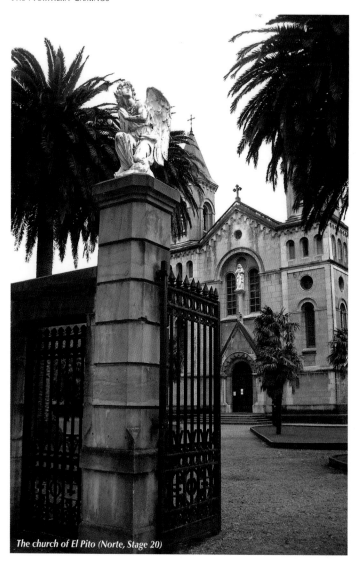

The church of El Pito (Norte, Stage 20)

INTRODUCTION

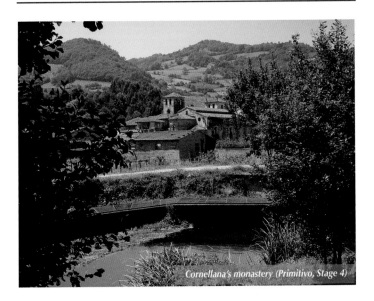

Cornellana's monastery (Primitivo, Stage 4)

The stunning diversity of Spain's Northern Caminos makes them as challenging to classify as they are memorable to walk. While most holidays involve a choice between trekking through mountains, lying in the sun on the beach, or engaging in a more meaningful sort of project, the Northern Caminos allow for all three. Those hungry for mountains may not find a high-level route here, but they will encounter challenging coastal ascents in the Basque Country and rugged rural tracks through Asturias. Beachcombers will find some of Europe's most popular sandy spots, such as San Sebastián, along with more isolated hideaways, accessible in some cases only to walkers. And, all who make the trek will be joined in the great human tradition of pilgrimage, unified in common cause and shared soreness, as they follow these historic pathways to sacred Santiago de Compostela.

Santiago de Compostela, whose cathedral houses the relics of St James, was one of three major centers of Catholic pilgrimage in the Middle Ages, along with Rome and

Jerusalem. Inspired by religious zeal – and particularly the desire to connect more deeply with God through relics, such as the bones of deceased saints – pilgrims from all over the Christian world made the dangerous journey to these celebrated sites. There was no single route to Santiago; the trail began at one's doorstep. But as pilgrims approached Spain, many converged on a handful of particularly popular routes, known historically as the Caminos de Santiago or 'Ways of Saint James'.

Today those pilgrim roads have experienced a popular resurgence and are walked not just by traditional pilgrims, but by people from highly varied backgrounds. In particular, the Camino Francés, which passes through Pamplona, Burgos, and León, draws crowds from all over the world – to the point where it is often referred to as 'the' Camino de Santiago. However, other pilgrim routes, such as the Northern Caminos, have also been rediscovered, and they have a great deal to offer.

The Northern Caminos – the Camino del Norte, the Camino Primitivo, and the Camino Inglés – are located north of the Camino Francés and pass through the Spanish regions of the Basque Country, Cantabria, Asturias, and Galicia. While the Camino Francés has in some ways become a victim of its own success, with huge crowds taking to its trails every year, the Northern Caminos enjoy an ideal situation. They are popular enough to offer sufficient facilities, clear routes, and a community of pilgrims, without the race for beds and lack of privacy that sometimes plagues the Francés.

The Camino del Norte spans 817km, following the coast from Irún, on the French border, to Ribadeo, before cutting inland towards Santiago; the full route takes about 5 weeks to complete. The Camino Primitivo splits off from the Camino del Norte near Villaviciosa and passes through Oviedo and Lugo en route to Compostela. Joining the Primitivo from the Norte, the route is 355km, and takes roughly two weeks to walk. Finally, the Camino Inglés offers a shorter pilgrimage option, starting in either Ferrol or A Coruña the 116km route takes only four to six days to complete. In addition, this book includes an overview of the route to Finisterre, for those who wish to continue there from Santiago.

THE STORY OF ST JAMES

While countless pilgrimage shrines exist within the Catholic world, three cities stand out as major centers of pilgrimage. Two are obvious: Jerusalem is intimately associated with the life of Jesus, while Rome houses the relics of Sts Peter and Paul, not to mention St Peter's Basilica. The third center, situated in an otherwise forgotten corner of Spain, is much more surprising. Santiago de Compostela, in Spain's northwestern

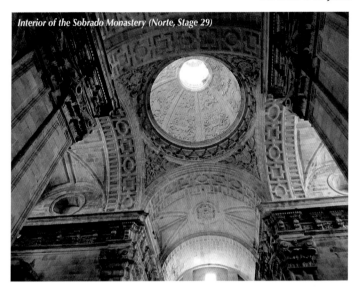

Interior of the Sobrado Monastery (Norte, Stage 29)

region of Galicia, has a history built on equal parts rumor and legend.

Of Jesus's 12 apostles, perhaps less is known about St James (or Santiago) than any other. The brother of John and the son of an assertive mother, James is known for his temper and for being one of Jesus's first followers – and the first to be martyred. However, mystery surrounds James's life between the crucifixion of Christ and his own death. Spanish legend asserts that he brought the good word to the Iberian Peninsula, but with minimal success, winning very few followers. That said, on his subsequent return to the Holy Land he fared worse; he was decapitated by Herod Agrippa in 44AD.

After James's death, the story goes, his disciples smuggled his body to the coast, where it was placed on a stone boat – lacking sails, oars, and sailors – and put to sea. Amazingly, and perhaps under the guidance of angels, this boat maneuvered westward across the Mediterranean and north into the Atlantic, before ultimately making landfall at Padrón on the Galician coast. Once there, two disciples met the boat, took James's body, and eventually buried him in present-day Santiago de Compostela. And then, almost eight centuries passed.

In 813, the hermit Pelayo had a vision in which a star shined brightly on a nearby field. Digging there, Pelayo made a stunning discovery:

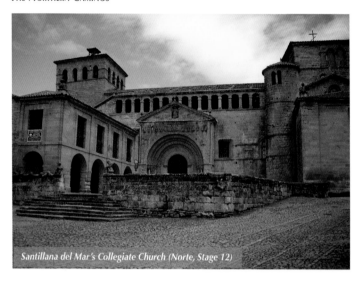

Santillana del Mar's Collegiate Church (Norte, Stage 12)

the very bones of St James, buried and forgotten so many years earlier. The timing couldn't have been better for the local Christians. With the Moorish conquest of the Iberian Peninsula nearly complete, their armies enjoying victory after victory behind the 'arm of Mohammed', the Christian Kingdom of Asturias in northern Spain was in dire straits. However, according to legend, the tide turned at the pivotal Battle of Clavijo. As the Asturian army prepared to face the much larger Muslim force, St James appeared before them on his white horse and led them into battle. So began the legend of Santiago Matamoros ('St James the Moor-killer'), one of the saint's two faces along the camino. In the other, Santiago Peregrino, his pilgrim identity, St James generally appears with a staff and scallop shell.

The cult of Santiago grew gradually over the next two centuries, before two major developments in the 12th century propelled Compostela to the forefront of the Christian world. First, Diego Gelmírez became the bishop of Santiago in 1101 (and archbishop in 1120), and quickly devoted his life to the aggrandizement of Compostela. Second, the 'Codex Calixtinus' emerged sometime in the 1130s. The first 'guidebook' to the Camino de Santiago, it included, among other things, a list of miracles attributed to St James, the history of the route, and a collection of practical advice for travelers, including warnings about 'evil toll gatherers' and the 'barbarous' locals.

The Basque Country

The Basque Country has received significant attention because of the terrorist attacks perpetrated by the Basque nationalist organization Euskadi Ta Askatasuna (ETA). That is, of course, a poor representation of the Basque people and their cultural resurgence over the last few decades. Euskera, the Basque language, is being taught in schools once more and most road signs are bilingual. The striking Basque flag (red background, green X, and white cross) is proudly displayed in houses and businesses. While many Basque people still aspire to having a single Basque state, combining their traditional lands in both Spain and France, the Spanish Basques do enjoy a great deal of control over their community.

For the Spanish-speaking pilgrim, the spread of Euskera should be of little concern. Most Basques – and certainly those in the service sector – also speak Spanish. While towns typically have both a Spanish name and a Basque name (for example, San Sebastián is known as Donostia), both versions are included in this guide. Besides, Euskera is a fascinating language to play with for a few days; it is historically unique, with no identifiable connection to any other language.

The Basques of northern Spain, located in the Atlantic watershed, have traditionally been great seafarers. The opening stages of the Camino del Norte pass through towns closely linked with the Age of Exploration. The seafarer of greatest fame, perhaps, is Juan Sebastián Elcano, who took

San Sebastián (Norte, Stage 1)

17

over command of Magellan's fleet and completed the first circumnavigation of the globe. Elcano is commemorated with a statue in his birthplace, Getaria. In the modern era, the Basque Country emerged as an industrial power, particularly within Spain itself, where it is responsible for nearly half the country's industrial output. Nonetheless, the countryside remains very traditional, with extensive family farms.

The pilgrim's route through the Basque Country begins in Irún, a border town, separated by the Bidasoa river from French Hendaye. The first three stages generally hug the coastline, staying within a kilometer or two of the Bay of Biscay, with sweeping views of the countryside and water.

From Deba, the route turns inland for the next three stages, passing around Mount Arno and through the historical town of Gernika before arrival in Bilbao. After passing through the port town of Portugalete, the camino cuts inland for one more stage before depositing the walker on Pobeña's wonderful beach; this is the last stopping point in the Basque Country.

Cantabria and Asturias

Like the Basque Country, the next two regions, Cantabria and Asturias, also experienced tremendous growth during the Age of Exploration. The influence of 'Indianos', emigrants who returned to Spain after making a fortune in the Americas, remains visible

Picasso's 'Gernika' in the city of Gernika (Norte, Stage 5)

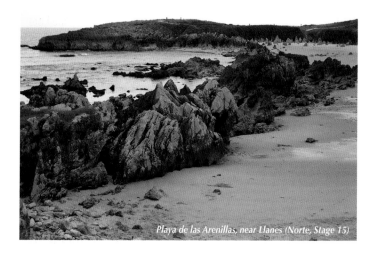

Playa de las Arenillas, near Llanes (Norte, Stage 15)

in the regions' architecture. That said, the story of Cantabria and Asturias goes back much farther. The regions contain some of the finest Paleolithic remains in the world, including some wonderful paintings like those found in the Altamira Caves. Although both regions were conquered by the Romans, the impact of their colonization is not as visible along this stretch as elsewhere on the route. The two regions returned to prominence in the eighth century. As noted, the Kingdom of Asturias became the base for the Reconquest of Spain from the Moors (the Reconquista), and Cantabria joined in common cause soon after. Cantabria emerged as a dominant naval force around this time, behind the combined might of

the Hermandad de los Cuatro Villas ('Brotherhood of the Four Towns'): Castro-Urdiales, Laredo, Santander, and San Vicente de la Barquera.

The coastal route through Cantabria and Asturias moves through a distinctive ecological setting. The ranges of the Picos de Europa and Cordillera Cantábrica press tightly against the Bay of Biscay, leaving only 25–50km between mountain and water. The steep descent and close coastline have resulted in many north-ward-flowing rivers, as well as a climate unique within Spain, with higher humidity and precipitation. The regions have also been indelibly marked by an emphasis on cattle farming, as well as the introduction of eucalyptus and pine trees, which have pushed many

19

Ribadeo (Norte, Stage 24)

native species, such as oak, chestnut, and beech, to the margins.

The Camino del Norte's first major stop in Cantabria is Castro-Urdiales, before it progresses through the town's three brothers. All told, the Norte covers roughly 180 mostly flat kilometers in the region, much of it on asphalt. While the latter detail is unfortunate, it is compensated for by some of the route's finest beaches. The Río Deva marks the border between Cantabria and Asturias, with Unquera wishing you goodbye and Colombres greeting you hello.

For the first 90km of Asturias, the Camino del Norte proceeds in a similar manner to the Cantabrian route, remaining flat and brushing against the coastline with some frequency. Soon after the market town of Villaviciosa, however, the route splits, with the Camino Primitivo forking left and the Camino del Norte continuing to the right. (It is possible for coastal walkers to follow the Primitivo into Oviedo and then return to the Norte later; this route is summarized at the end of the main route description.)

Both options bring ascents that exceed anything encountered over the previous week of walking. Along the Camino del Norte, pilgrims face a 400m climb up the Alto de la Cruz – and, almost immediately after, an equivalent descent. But, after this little challenge, the route gradually flattens out once more, with long stretches on asphalt and two prominent resort towns, Gijón and Avilés. From Villaviciosa to the Ría de Ribadeo, the Norte covers roughly 200km in Asturias; the river crossing into the town of Ribadeo marks arrival in the fourth and final autonomous region, Galicia.

Meanwhile, the Camino Primitivo in Asturias runs just under 190km. As is true on the Norte, the first stage brings an ascent to 400m. However, after a lull around Oviedo, where the Primitivo flattens out, the climb takes pilgrims significantly higher. On three different occasions, the Primitivo tops 1000m (with a fourth coming soon after, in Galicia), reaching 1146m at its high point. Over the same stretch conditions become more rugged, and pockets of civilization become smaller and smaller. Whereas tourists and pilgrims vie for resources along the coast, few travelers other than pilgrims visit many of these villages, making the Camino Primitivo feel more central to the communities.

Galicia

All three of the Northern Caminos – the Norte, Primitivo, and Inglés – follow different trajectories through the final autonomous community, Galicia, to Santiago de Compostela. As in the Basque Country, Galicia features a distinct nationality, the Galego people. The local language, Gallego, is immediately noticeable upon arrival in the region; note that the pilgrimage, for example, is now identified as the 'Camiño' de Santiago. Gallego is often described as a middle ground between Spanish and Portuguese. Those comfortable with either language will have no trouble communicating here.

Geographic isolation protected Galicia from too much interference by Rome (although the Roman walls of Lugo are some of the finest left in the world) and the Moors. It was shaped in many ways, however, by the earlier Celtic presence, as visible in Galicia's very name and the many extant circular hill forts or *castros*. One such fort, the Castro de Chao Samartin, can be visited along the Primitivo, soon after Grandas de Salime.

The discovery of Santiago's remains in the ninth century launched the region into European prominence, of course, transforming it into one of the centers of the Catholic world. But, every rise has its fall. The Protestant Reformation and related decline in the importance of pilgrimage brought about several centuries of regression for Galicia, as it found itself pushed to the margins once more. The 20th century brought an abrupt return to the spotlight, with the emergence of Galicia's own Francisco Franco. Born in Ferrol, the starting point of the Camino Inglés, Franco showered favors on his homeland, including the Camino de Santiago. Franco's death coincided with a resurgent nationalism among Galegos.

The walking conditions in Galicia are, for most pilgrims, delightful: well worn trails, gentle streams with stone footbridges, dense forests offering shade, and traditional villages with homes built out of granite and slate, with old-fashioned hórreos (corn-cribs/granaries) at the front. Galicia experiences more rain than any other region in Spain, but the reward is a pervasive green, even in the middle of a hot summer. Pilgrims will notice two significant changes made to the Galician environment over the last 50 years. Eucalyptus was introduced during the Franco era. Given the rainy climate, it was believed that eucalyptus forests would thrive. And they have – perhaps too much – and now threaten many native species; there is an almost eerie quality to the absolute quiet that reigns within them. In addition, wind turbines line many mountain ridges, looking to translate the region's windy conditions into green energy. Many locals regard these as eyesores and threats to tourism and the local environment.

Galicia is comprised of four provinces. Both the Primitivo and Norte enter Galicia in the province of Lugo, before later moving into A Coruña. The Camino Inglés falls entirely in the province of A Coruña. The routes through Galicia share similar characteristics, particularly as they converge upon Santiago. For the Camino del Norte, this marks the end of the coast and the beginning of a challenging stretch of walking, rising ultimately to 710m in elevation near the provincial border. The Camino Primitivo, meanwhile, has one remaining ascent of significance before descending to Lugo, the last major town before Santiago. Prior to arrival in Compostela, both routes join their more famous sibling, the Camino Francés. The Primitivo intersects it in Melide, while the Norte does

Medieval bridge after El Campu (Primitivo, Stage 2)

so in Arzúa. The sudden change in the number of pilgrims – from a drizzle to a deluge – can be quite jarring! The Camino Inglés, meanwhile, follows an entirely different trajectory than the other caminos, never meeting them until the Praza do Obradoiro in front of the Cathedral of Santiago.

CHOOSING YOUR CAMINO

For those starting their pilgrimage in Irún, the single biggest decision involves whether to fork south in Villaviciosa onto the Camino Primitivo or to remain on the Camino del Norte.

To some extent, this decision can be distilled down to a choice between mountains and coast. The Primitivo cuts inland through the Cordillera Cantabrica and includes some significant ascents and descents between Oviedo and Lugo. Meanwhile, the Camino del Norte between Villaviciosa and Ribadeo follows relatively flat terrain through quiet coastal villages. The Primitivo is better way-marked and has more frequent pilgrim accommodation, but the Norte is not deficient in either area.

There is no clear pilgrim consensus on this point; both routes have their ardent supporters. For those walking from Irún, the authors recommend the Primitivo. After several weeks of hiking on the coast, the mountains bring an exciting change of setting, and the walker is well prepared for the rugged conditions.

That said, there are other considerations worth taking into account.

Time

Those with limited time will have to decide whether arriving on foot in Santiago and receiving the Compostela is a priority or not. If that is a priority, the minimal completion of the last 100km on foot is required. In this case, one would need to begin walking the Camino Primitivo in Lugo (102km), the Camino del Norte in Baamonde (101.5km), or the Camino Inglés in Ferrol (110km). If arrival in Santiago is not essential, there are many worthy stretches of the various routes that could be completed in a week or so, including Irún to Gernika, Santillana del Mar to Ribadesella, and Oviedo to Lugo.

To complete the full Camino del Norte, walking from Irún to Santiago, typically requires at least five weeks, not counting rest days. This is true whether one chooses to remain exclusively on the Norte or transfer to the Primitivo.

Physical challenge

The most physically demanding stretches of the Northern Caminos are the opening stages of the Norte, from Irún to Bilbao, and the Camino Primitivo from Salas to Lugo. The Camino del Norte from Ribadeo to Sobrado dos Monxes also presents a modest challenge. But between Bilbao and Ribadeo the coastal walk is quite forgiving, rarely breaking 200m in elevation. There are some days with frequent ascents and descents, but they are manageable. The Camino Inglés features one significant ascent, gaining roughly 375m from Betanzos to Bruma. However, that is spread over 19km, and thus of minor concern.

Other factors

The first week of the Camino del Norte is the most expensive stretch, passing through popular tourist destinations and offering few *albergues*. It is quite common to spend 15–20€ per night on a bed, and significantly more for a room. On the flip side, most pilgrim lodgings along the Camino Primitivo, the Camino Inglés, and after Gijón on the Camino del Norte continue to operate on donations or a minimal 5€ fee.

The Camino del Norte is the most heavily frequented of the Northern Caminos, attracting two or three times as many pilgrims as the Primitivo. The Camino Inglés offers the most peace and quiet, with only half the traffic of the Primitivo. The Camino Primitivo is the best bet for offroad walking, with very long stretches that avoid pavement. The Camino del Norte, however, has some days on which the majority of the walking occurs on minor roads.

The walk from Irún to Bilbao is, in many ways, the most historically rich section of the Northern Caminos, with a number of important sites and impressive structures. At the same time, it draws heavy tourist attention.

Those seeking parts of Spain that are off the beaten tourist path would be advised to seek out the Primitivo or Inglés.

WHEN TO GO

Summer is the best time for the Northern Caminos for several reasons. First, due to their proximity to the coast, the off-season on the caminos can be quite soggy. Second, some of the albergues are seasonal, open only when local schools are on holiday. Third, even some of the towns are seasonal, thriving with beach-goers when the sun shines, but shutting down completely for the rest of the year. Fortunately, even in the summer, the pilgrim-centric facilities along the Northern Caminos have not yet suffered the same strain as those along the Camino Francés. Although the albergues do begin to fill as the routes approach Santiago, the 'race for beds' is not nearly as intense.

That said, the offseason along the Northern Caminos has its charms. For those in search of solitude, it can be found along the coast in March. Hotels that remain open can be talked into steep discounts. In theory, the Northern Caminos are viable year-round, although winter pilgrims should be prepared for bitter cold and even snow along the Camino Primitivo and on the final stretch of the Camino del Norte as it veers inland towards Santiago.

PREPARATION AND PLANNING

The most important part of your preparation is the physical component, training for the rigors of the trail by doing some walking. Start slowly and build as your body allows, gradually increasing the distances covered. As you become stronger, add weight to your pack until its contents mirror what you will be carrying in Spain. If possible, hike on consecutive days; what might feel easy on fresh legs can be more draining on tired ones.

As you train, monitor three different areas. First, and most obvious, track how much distance you can cover comfortably, how your body responds to breaks, and what kinds of food provide you with the energy that you need. Second, keep a close eye on your feet, watching for blisters or other hot spots. Your goal here is to gradually build up calluses to help prevent blistering on the camino. Third, test your gear and clothing, making sure that your pack fits properly, the weight is manageable, and your clothes don't chafe.

Read about the Camino de Santiago and pilgrimage in general before you go. Knowing some of the history and language of the region will add meaning to your walk. Familiarity with Romanesque and Gothic architecture will help you to know where to direct your eye. Some sense of anticipated highlights will help you to plan stopping points along the route. While there aren't many published narratives

on the Northern Caminos, Michael Gaches' recently published pilgrim diary *Valiant: A Pilgrim on the Camino del Norte* is available via the Confraternity of St James' website; otherwise, there is an overwhelming variety of journals devoted to the Camino Francés, and these will also give you a sense of what is in store (see Appendix C).

That said, unless your time schedule is quite restrictive, try to arrive in Spain without a rigid plan for your daily itinerary. Take it easy early on. Many pilgrims arrive overflowing with energy and excitement, and go too far in their initial stages. It's better to stop too soon than push yourself too far, as the consequences of that exertion can linger in the forms of blisters, tendonitis, or other aches and pains.

In addition, be wary of setting your spiritual expectations too high. Many pilgrims spend their camino waiting for their epiphany, the life-changing moment of enlightenment that they feel is promised to them on pilgrimage, only to be disappointed when it never arrives. Every pilgrim's experience is different.

BEING A PILGRIM

Making a long-distance trek as a pilgrim is a different experience in many ways from that involved in other lengthy walks. Several unique elements of the pilgrim experience are described below.

Pilgrim passport

Known as the credenciál in Spanish, this document identifies you as a pilgrim. It is available in many albergues, including Irún, Santander, and Oviedo, and from many Camino-related groups, such as the UK's Confraternity of St James (CSJ) (paid-up members only). You will get a stamp (*sello*) each day, usually in the a pilgrim hostel, although it is also sometimes possible to get stamps in bars and churches. For most pilgrims, this becomes a treasured memento of the journey.

The Compostela

Upon arrival in Santiago, the Archbishopric will award you the Compostela, a document acknowledging your completion of the pilgrimage, provided that you meet two conditions. First, you must have your credenciál, with stamps documenting your daily progress. Second, you must have walked the final 100km or bicycled the final 200km. Prior to that last stretch, it is acceptable to skip ahead by motorized transportation. But the last 100km must be completed in their entirety.

Albergues

Your credenciál also gives you access to the pilgrim hostels (*albergues de peregrino*). These provide dorm-style accommodation exclusively to pilgrims, and usually include facilities to wash both self and clothes. Some also offer kitchens. Typically, the doors lock and lights are turned off between 2200 and 2300. Pilgrims may spend only one night and are expected to leave by 0800 the next morning. The price varies, typically hovering in the 5–10€ range, although some albergues still operate on a voluntary donation (*donativo*) basis. Unfortunately, there are fewer of these each year, as some pilgrims equate 'donation requested' with 'free'. Pilgrim donations keep many albergues in operation for future pilgrims.

Pilgrim ethic

A popular saying in Spanish is 'Turistas manden; peregrinos agradecen' ('Tourists demand; pilgrims give thanks'). While challenging to remember at the end of a long day, it is an important message to keep in mind. Albergues are typically run by voluntary *hospitaleros*. Often, they are backed by the financial support of the local community. Waymarks are maintained by local organizations. It is easy to find fault with many things along the way, but be cognizant of how many people are giving up their time, money, and energy to make your pilgrimage possible.

Opposite: *Albergues de Peregrinos on the Caminos, clockwise from top L in: Gondán (Norte Stage 25), Sobrado dos Monxes (Norte Stage 29), Bodenaya (Primitivo Stage 4), Pontedeume (Inglés Stage 1) and As Seixas (Primitivo Stage 11)*

The Somo–Santander ferry (Norte, Stage 11)

GETTING THERE AND BACK

Camino del Norte: from Irún

By foot
The Voie Littorale walking route, which originates in Soulac, France, parallels the Atlantic coast for 375km to arrive at Hendaye, across the river from Irún. The CSJ has published a guide to this route online (The Voie Littorale: Soulac to Hendaye, www. csj.org.uk). It is possible to join the Voie Littorale in Bayonne, starting from either St Jean Pied de Port in France or Pamplona in Spain, both of which are on the Camino Francés.

By air
From the UK and Europe budget airlines, including RyanAir and EasyJet, fly into Biarritz airport in France.

From the US, it is generally most economical to fly into London or another major city and transfer to one of those flights. From Biarritz, take the Chronoplus Line C bus to Biarritz train station (10mins) and travel via train to Hendaye (25mins), crossing the border into Irún. Alternatively, Iberia flies into San Sebastián airport, located in Hondarribia, only 3km from Irún. Ekialdebus operates a bus service connecting the airport with Irún.

By train
Irún is well connected to Spain and Europe. Spain's national line, RENFE, offers services to Irún from Barcelona (departs 0730 and 1530, 6hrs, 60€), Madrid (departs 0800 and 1600, 6hrs, 55€), and other major cities. EuskoTren links Irún with San

Sebastián, with a separate train continuing on to Bilbao, although buses are speedier for this route. France's SNCF connects Irún with the rest of Europe, including a daily TGV service from Paris (departs 0630, 6hrs).

By bus

Irún's bus station is located in front of the train station. Spain's major bus company, ALSA, runs a regular service from Bilbao (2hrs, 7€) and Madrid (three daily departures, 6½hrs, 35€). Vibasa operates a convenient overnight bus from Barcelona Nord (departs 2215, 8½hrs, 30€). In addition a wide range of bus companies covers northern Spain, so there are many other options. Check www.movelia.es or the departure bus station.

Other likely points of departure

Both Bilbao and Santander have airports, making them convenient starting points. EasyJet flies to Bilbao, as do many other major airlines. From the airport, take Bizkaibus 3247 to the city center (every 20mins) or the Pesa bus to San Sebastián (hourly). Santander is serviced by RyanAir and Iberia, with a bus linking the airport and the city bus station. ALSA runs buses directly from the airport to other major coastal cities, including Gijón. It is also possible to reach Santander via ferry from Portsmouth

Bilbao (Norte, Stage 6)

and Plymouth in the UK, although this is often much more expensive.

Camino Primitivo: from Oviedo

By foot
The Camino del Salvador links Oviedo with León on the Camino Francés. The route spans roughly 120km and the CSJ has published a guide to this route online (Camino del Salvador, www.csj.org.uk).

By air
Asturias airport is serviced by EasyJet and Vueling, among other airlines, and is located between Oviedo and Gijón. ALSA provides bus services between the airport and both cities (as well as nearby Avilés).

By train
FEVE connects Oviedo with other coastal towns, from Ribadeo in the west (twice daily, 3½hrs, 11€) to Santander in the east (twice daily, 4½hrs, 15€). RENFE provides service to the rest of Spain, including Madrid (three daily, 5hrs, 50€).

By bus
ALSA connects Oviedo with Madrid (hourly, 5hrs, 35€) and most other major Spanish cities. To reach Villaviciosa, take ALSA to Gijón and then transfer to a different ALSA bus to Villaviciosa (1½hrs, total).

Other likely points of departure
The other major city on the Camino Primitivo, Lugo, is accessible by train (RENFE) and bus. For the latter, ALSA again provides the primary connections to the rest of Spain; however other local companies offer more extensive coverage of Galicia. In particular, Empresa Freire links Santiago airport and Lugo (five buses daily, 2hrs).

Hospitales Route (Primitivo, Stage 6)

Camino Inglés: from A Coruña

By air
Vueling, Iberia, and TAP Portugal fly to A Coruña airport. From there, ASICASA provides bus service to the city center (every 30mins).

By train
RENFE connects A Coruña with Santiago de Compostela (hourly, 40mins, 6€), with long-distance services extending to Madrid and Barcelona.

By bus
Once again, ALSA is the company of choice for long-distance connections. Castromil operates hourly buses to Santiago de Compostela (6€), while Arriva offers services to Ferrol (hourly, 1hr, 7€) and Lugo (1¼hrs, 10€).

Getting back from Santiago de Compostela

By air
Lavacolla airport, just outside of Santiago, is well connected with Spain and the rest of Europe, offering multiple routes operated by RyanAir, EasyJet, and Air Berlin. Although Iberia sometimes advertises a special discounted fare for pilgrims with Compostelas, their prices rarely compare with that of a ticket on one of the budget airlines.

By train
RENFE runs a daily service at 0900 from Santiago to Hendaye, on the border between Spain and France; from there, connections to Paris and other European towns are possible. Three trains run daily to Madrid, including a convenient overnight route (departs 2230, 10hrs, 50€ seat, 78€ bed). If you have time, returning along the coast on the FEVE can be a nice way to 'retrace' your steps.

By bus
ALSA is once again the best bet for both domestic and international services. Buses to London operate three times per week (departs 1130, 34hrs, 136€).

EQUIPMENT

Remember that you will have to carry everything you take, every day. The guiding principle is to pack light, focusing on what is absolutely necessary and cutting out everything else. As the caminos pass regularly through towns, it will be possible to restock or acquire new supplies if it becomes necessary.

Footwear
Walkers passionately debate whether shoes or boots are superior. Modern cross-trainers typically provide a great deal of support and comfort, without the weight and bulkiness of boots, and are advisable for most. If you do prefer to wear boots, make sure that they are broken in prior to departure. Outside of summer, it is worth considering waterproof shoes. In addition, bring

a pair of sandals suitable for albergue showers and post-walk strolls around town.

Sleeping bag

Those walking in the summer who don't get cold too easily should consider bringing a sleep-sheet (sheet sleeping bag). Silk liners weigh little and suffice for many. However, if you do not fit in those categories, a sleeping bag will be necessary. Look for an ultra-lightweight +5 degrees Celsius bag.

Rucksack

Pack size will be determined in large part by your sleeping-bag decision. Those who opt for a sleep-sheet could walk the camino with a pack as small as 30l. With a sleeping bag, something in the 45l range will be needed. Regardless, a good fit is critical. Look for a pack that is properly sized for your torso and keeps the weight on your hips.

Clothing

Aim for two or three sets of clothes (shirt/top, socks, underwear) – one or two in your pack and one on you – along with two pairs of pants (trousers)/shorts. Avoid cotton. Synthetic clothing wicks moisture from the body, dries quickly, and packs light. It costs more, but it's worth every penny. Finally, bring a warm outer layer. In the offseason, a long-sleeved/legged base layer is recommended as well.

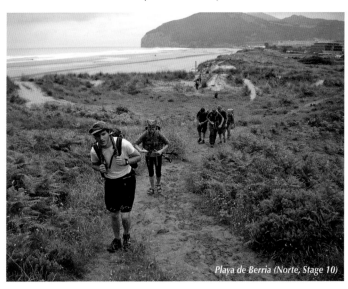

Playa de Berria (Norte, Stage 10)

Poncho

Walking on the coast, the weather can be unpredictable, and rain is more likely than it is inland. A good poncho will cover both person and pack, and can be donned quickly. Otherwise waterproof clothing and perhaps a rain cover for your pack will do. If you're walking outside of summer you may prefer more extensive raingear.

Water

Personal preference will determine the choice of either a bottle or hydration bladder, but make sure to have at least 1l of water with you at all times, and more on certain stretches.

Pack towel

A synthetic, chamois-style towel packs lighter and smaller than a normal towel and dries faster.

Basic first-aid kit

Bring small amounts of most first-aid essentials; it's easy to buy more if you run out. Make sure to carry a good supply of foot-care materials, including Compeed, moleskin or another similar product to cover blisters.

Flashlight/headlamp

Essential for late-night bathroom runs, early-morning packing, and pre-sunrise walking.

Toiletries

Limit these to the essentials.

Other gear worth considering

A hat, sunglasses, camp pillow, notepad/pen, eating utensils and bowl, digital camera, trekking poles, Spanish–English dictionary, and maps.

ACCOMMODATION

Albergues, providing dorm-style accommodation exclusively for pilgrims, are available in many towns and villages along the Northern Caminos, and are usually located a reasonable day's walk from each other. That said, they are not as plentiful as their equivalent along the Camino Francés, and some – especially in the Basque Country – are seasonal, operating only during peak months. Pilgrims walking outside of summer will need to be prepared to make use of other options. Of course, all pilgrims are welcome to stay in any manner of accommodation; some find the albergues to be a

Sign to Miraz Albergue (Norte, Stage 28)

central part of the experience, while others need additional comfort at night in order to regroup for the next day's walk. Whenever possible, a range of options are presented for each stage in this guide, but other possibilities can always be found at the local tourist information office (*turismo*).

While the Spanish classification system for beds is not always on the mark, generally places identified as a *fonda* or *pensión* are designed for travelers on a budget. Furnishings and facilities are often a bit at the scruffier end of things. That said, they can be great deals. Another option for inexpensive lodging, especially in larger towns, is a youth hostel (*albergue juvenil*). Those looking for more amenities will want to target *hostales* or *hoteles*. The distinction between the two is not always clear, although hoteles are typically stand-alone facilities with a receptionist available at all

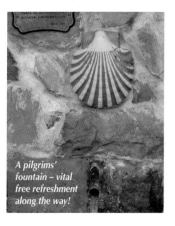

A pilgrims' fountain – vital free refreshment along the way!

hours, while hostales fill only part of the building and provide guests with keys to their room, and the building, so they may come and go. The price is likely to be determined by the number of stars attributed to the facility.

Remember that the Camino del Norte in particular passes through popular holiday areas, so beds can be booked up far in advance in summer, and many places are closed all together in the winter. The Albergues de Peregrinos operate on a 'first-come, first-served' basis, but if you hope to sleep anywhere else, particularly in the summer months, it is wise to reserve ahead, at least a couple of days.

FOOD

A pilgrim's culinary options are shaped in large part by the walking schedule and restaurant opening hours. In the morning, pilgrims can count on finding croissants and *cafés con leche*. Later in the day, those in need of something more substantial can ask for *bocadillos* – large sandwiches filled with a range of options, including ham (*jamón*), sausage (*chorizo*), cheese (*queso*), and omelette (*tortilla*). The *tortilla española* (egg and potato omelette) is a particularly filling snack on its own or in a bocadillo. *Tapas* – bite-sized appetizers, served both hot and cold – can be an excellent option for an evening snack.

A typical sit-down meal will involve a meat dish (pork and lamb are quite common in the north), a side dish, and bread. Vegetables are rarer, generally appearing in salads or soups. Fish is more abundant along the coast and in Galicia. *Paella*, a saffron-infused rice-based dish with seafood can be an excellent option throughout the north. Regional specialties include *marmitako* (fish stew) in the Basque Country, *fabada Asturiana* (white beans, pork, and blood sausage) in Asturias, and *pulpo* (octopus) in Galicia.

The greatest food-related challenge for many can be the Spanish meal schedule. Outside of cities, bars in the north rarely open before 0800, which is late for many pilgrims. Lunch, the major daily meal, is served between 1300 and 1500. Dinner presents the biggest difficulty, as it commonly begins around 2100, making it difficult to finish eating before the albergue curfew. Pilgrim-friendly bars and restaurants will serve earlier, but this varies greatly from town to town.

Some albergues have kitchens, where pilgrims can prepare their own meals. Groceries and supermarkets are accessible on most days, although some planning may be necessary, as they are not always located in the same towns as the albergues. Except in cities, they close during the siesta, so typical opening hours are from 0900 to 1300 and from 1600 to 2000. Almost every supermarket is closed on Sunday.

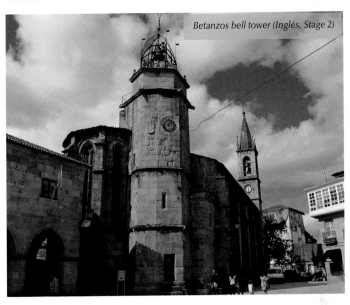

Betanzos bell tower (Inglés, Stage 2)

POSTAL SERVICES

Most post offices (Correos) in Spain are open weekdays from 0830 until 1400. Some reopen in the afternoon and on Saturday mornings. Stamps can also be purchased from tobacco shops. The 'poste restante' system allows pilgrims (and everyone else) to send packages ahead, which comes in handy if you find yourself with unnecessary gear in your pack. While sending the gear home might be very expensive, mailing a package to Santiago is generally quite affordable. It is also an excellent way to receive care packages from home.

To mail a parcel poste restante, ask in the post office about Lista de Correos. If you do not have packing materials, most offices can provide these. On the mailing label, address the parcel to yourself, underlining your surname. Under your name, write 'Lista de Correos', followed by the postal code, town name, and province. Postal codes can be found on the correos.es website. Later, when you go to retrieve your package, make sure to take photo identification. The post office will generally hold packages for one month, but it is wise to reconfirm current policy when mailing.

TELEPHONES

Blue payphones are available in every town. Telephone cards, typically in 6€ and 10€ denominations, can be purchased from tobacco shops; note that different cards are often needed for local and international calls. Instructions for making international calls are provided on each card. To call internationally, dial 00, wait for a new dial tone, and proceed with the country code, area code, and number. Spain's country code is 34; this can be dropped from numbers when you are calling within the country.

More and more pilgrims are bringing their mobile phones with them on the camino. The most expensive way to do this is to activate an international package with your local provider. A more budget-friendly option is to purchase a local prepaid SIM card in Spain. Provided that your mobile phone is unlocked, you can put the Spanish SIM card in and immediately have a local number – and, by extension, local calling rates. Most companies, including Vodafone and MoviStar, have a very affordable starter pack available; credit can later be added online, by phone, or even in many supermarkets and tabacs. International calling cards have a mobile phone access number, so that you can combine the superior rates with the convenience of your own phone.

OTHER LOCAL FACILITIES

Spanish **banking** hours are limited, typically running from around 0900 until 1400, Monday to Friday. Some banks are open on Saturday morning. Almost every town has an ATM for withdrawing euros. Travelers checks can be difficult to cash and are discouraged.

Pharmacies are available in most towns and maintain a similar schedule to supermarkets. Medications, even basic items such as ibuprofen, are not available in supermarkets; they are available only from pharmacies. **Internet** access is somewhat limited along the Northern Caminos, but in each community it is worth checking the local library for public terminals. Churches in most sizable towns hold **mass** on weekday and Saturday evenings, usually around 2000, as well as midday on Sundays. Ask in the albergue or listen for the bells. In some parts of the Northern Caminos, it is possible to **ship your pack ahead**. On the Camino del Norte, try Le P'tit Bag (635 730 852, g.car.trans@gmail.com), the Peregrine Express (644 589 217, christel.langeveld@gmail.com), or contact Jose Luis Pardo Rodríguez in Asturias and Galicia (606 049 858, info@caminodesantiago20120.com.es). On the Camino Primitivo, try Taxi Camino (619 156 730, trastinos@gmail.com) or Jose Luis Pardo Rodríguez (606 049 858, info@caminodesantiago20120.com.es).

WAYMARKING, ROUTE-PLANNING AND MAPS

With occasional exceptions, the waymarking on the Northern Caminos is reliable. Trusty yellow arrows (*flechas amarillas*) painted on trees, signs,

Examples of the waymarks you'll find on the caminos

rocks, and other physical landmarks guide you through the countryside and most towns. In cities, the arrows are often replaced with scallop-shell markers embedded in the sidewalk. In Galicia, concrete markers complement the arrows, appearing at least every 500m. With this reassurance, you should not have to clutch this book tightly each step of the way, nor should you count on it for turn-by-turn directions in all places.

Nonetheless, it is advisable to review each day's route before starting your walk. Look in particular for several potential complications.

First, there are multiple stretches where the camino splits, especially along the coastal route, with two (or three) possible options available. In some cases, only one of these options is clearly marked. In others, the yellow arrows steer walkers towards the most direct route, while the red/white stripes associated with the European GR footpaths offer a more scenic alternative. You will want to anticipate these crossroads to ensure that you follow your desired course.

Second, there are some relatively long stretches without food or water. Plan your day to avoid unnecessary difficulties.

Finally, the Northern Caminos continue to be refined, as efforts are made to move more of the walk from pavement and onto footpaths. Major construction projects have also disrupted many parts of the Camino del Norte. In addition, early 2016

reports indicate minor route revisions throughout Galicia. You may encounter waymarks that lead you in an unexpected direction. Study them carefully, evaluate your options, and make an informed choice. It is always wise to seek updated information from the hospitaleros.

The most useful single overview map of the Northern Caminos is the Northern Spain Adventure Map (#3306) published by National Geographic and available from most online bookstores, including Amazon. The Caminos del Norte and Primitivo routes are highlighted (as is the Camino Francés), but the Caminos Inglés and Finisterre are not. Scaled to 1:350,000, this is helpful for seeing the big picture, but not as useful for turn-by-turn navigation.

The Spanish Mapas Militares (Serie L) are the best bet for more

Camino del Norte 25:4, 24:4, 24:5, 23:4, 23:5, 22:5, 21:5, 21:4, 20:4, 19:4, 18:4, 17:4, 16:4, 15:4, 14:4, 14:3, 13:3, 12:3, 11:3, 10:3, 9:3, 8:3, 8:4, 7:5, 6:5, 6:6, 6:7, 5:7, 4:7

Camino Primitivo 14:4, 13:4, 12:4, 11:4, 11:5, 10:5, 9:5, 9:6, 8:6, 7:6, 6:7, 5:7, 4:7

Camino Inglés 4:7, 5:3, 5:4, 5:5, 5:6, 6:3, 6:4

Camino Finisterre 4:7, 3:7, 2:7, 3:6, 2:6

detailed route-finding assistance, designed on a 1:50,000 scale. The downside is that this is a much more expensive option, requiring you to purchase many individual map sheets to fully cover your route. In the authors' experience, these are not necessary. But, if you want the added security, the sheets needed for each route are shown in the blue box.

The Mapas Militares are available from The Map Shop in the UK, 15 High Street, Upton-on-Severn, Worcestershire, WR8 0HJ, 01684 593146. Those outside the UK can order online.

USING THIS GUIDE

This guidebook has broken the different routes into stages; with rare exceptions, each stage ends in a town or village with a pilgrim albergue. However, these stages are simply recommendations and should in no way be considered the 'official' way of organizing the route. Listen to your body: if you're struggling, stop earlier; if you're flying, enjoy it. Listen to your heart: if the beauty of a place strikes you, stick around. And listen to your fellow pilgrims: they may have excellent advice to offer.

The box at the start of each stage in the guide provides key information to help you assess the day ahead. The 'Difficulty' entry rates two components – difficulty of terrain and quality of waymarks – on a 1–5 scale. The figure for difficulty indicates how physically demanding the stage is, with 1 corresponding to an easy walk and 5 to a very challenging trek. It is important to note that the difficulty rating does not factor in the day's distance. The waymark rating indicates the challenge posed by the day's markers. If you see a 1 or a 2, you can safely put away this book and trust the waymarks. Anything higher suggests that there are at least some problematic stretches. The box also lists all pilgrim albergues on that stage, but not youth hostels or other accommodation. Look through the full stage description for that information.

Key towns and villages along the route are shown in boxes in the route description (the distance from the previous key town/village is given after the heading). The boxes include a short summary of features of interest, as well as information on accommodation and facilities.

With three different languages spoken along the Northern Caminos – Castilian, Euskera, and Galego – it is challenging to achieve a single, consistent approach to place names. In this guidebook, place names in the text have been dealt with as follows (note that spellings on the map may differ). In the Basque Country, both the Castilian and Euskeran versions of town names are included when they are significantly different. In Galicia, names generally follow the Galego spelling to reflect what is seen on street signs and maps. The similarity between Galego and Castilian in most cases makes it easy to draw connections (for example, 'Palas do Rei' and 'Palas de Rey'). Geographical features and other vernacular terms are often presented in both Spanish and English to facilitate not only their identification and but also their use as directional aids.

This guide includes all pilgrim albergues in operation at the time of writing (late 2014), and a range of selected hotels, hostels, and other viable options. All accommodation listings include price, phone numbers, and (when needed) address. Additional information includes the number of beds available, meals served, and the presence of cooking facilities, washer/dryer (W/D), and internet (@). Opening hours are also included if they are much later than normal, and where keys can be obtained if the albergue does not have an on-site hospitalero. Please note that prices, in particular, can change quickly or by season; always confirm in advance.

Each stage of the route in this guide is accompanied by a map, scaled to 1:60,000 and based on Instituto Geográfico Nacional's work. The main route, as followed in the stage description, is outlined in orange, while alternative routes are in blue. All place names in **bold** in the text are also included on the maps.

N followed by a number (eg N-634) denotes a major Spanish highway, while regional roads are identified by the first two letters of the province followed by a number (eg AS-235).

Route summary tables appear in Appendix A, and there is also a glossary of key terms in Spanish and Euskera (Appendix B), some recommended further reading (Appendix C), useful information sources on transport and other practicalities (Appendix D) and an index of principal place names (Appendix E).

HOW LONG WILL IT TAKE?

Timings have not been given for individual stages. The last thing you want as you walk a pilgrim route is a pressure to keep to a schedule imposed by a guidebook! You will quickly discover your own pace and you may well speed up as you get fitter, or slow down as you start to relax and enjoy yourself. (See 'Preparation and Planning' above for how to gauge your own walking pace well before you set off.)

To recap: the **Camino del Norte** takes about 5 weeks, whether via Gijón or Oviedo (shorter but through the hills – add about an hour for every 600m of ascent to your pace on the flat), the **Camino Primitivo** itself about 2 weeks, the **Camino Inglés** 4–6 days from Ferrol (a couple of days less from A Coruña) and the **Camino Finisterre** takes about 3–4 days (one way).

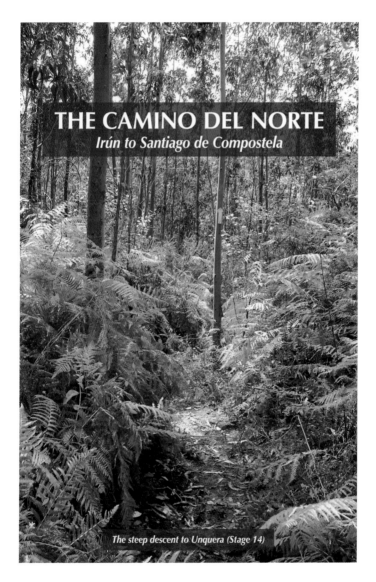

THE CAMINO DEL NORTE
Irún to Santiago de Compostela

The steep descent to Unquera (Stage 14)

THE CAMINO DEL NORTE

The Camino del Norte is the longest route in this guidebook. From the city of Irún, located on the French border, the Norte follows the coast for the better part of 620km. Upon reaching Galicia, it turns inland, with 150km of trails bringing pilgrims to the Camino Francés in Arzúa, 40km before Santiago de Compostela. The highlights are strikingly diverse – hilltop bluffs overlooking the ocean; waymarked walks on sandy beaches; albergues in medieval monasteries; cosmopolitan cities with dramatic cathedrals and stunning art museums... the list goes on, but you'll just have to walk it to see it all. For added variety, pilgrims can consider diverting from the Camino del Norte in Villaviciosa (Stage 18), complementing the coastal walk with the Camino Primitivo's mountainous terrain.

STAGE 1
Irún to San Sebastián

Start	Irún RENFE station
Finish	Albergue La Sirena, San Sebastián
Distance	26.5km
Total ascent	710m
Total descent	720m
Difficulty	terrain: 5; waymarking: 3
Albergues de Peregrinos	Irún, Pasajes de San Juan/Pasaia Donibane, San Sebastián

The Camino del Norte's first stage may also be its most spectacular, offering incredible views of both land and sea. From Irún, there is a walk through a wetland park before the route climbs to the Guadalupe Sanctuary. From there, pilgrims are advised to take the high-level route, which follows a ridgeline high above the Bay of Biscay, passing Neolithic dolmens, medieval towers, and castle ruins before descending to Pasajes de San Juan. A small passenger boat shuttles you across the port. More uphill awaits, leading over another ridge before ultimately – and impressively – San Sebastián appears below.

IRÚN

All facilities; RENFE station. **Albergue de Peregrinos** at Calle Lucas de Berroa 18-1 (donativo, 48 beds, kitchen, breakfast, opens 1600 April–September, credenciáles). Many other accommodation options, including **Albergue Juvenil Martindozenea** (17.30–22.30€, includes breakfast, other meals available, kitchen, @, Calle Elizatxo 18, 943 621 042), **Pensión Bowling** (singles 30–50€, doubles 40–60€, Calle Mourlane Michelena 2, 943 611 452), **Pensión Los Fronterizos** (singles 30–35€, doubles 40–55€, Geltoki Kalea 7, 943 619 205).

The Camino del Norte's starting point, Irún, lies across Río Bidasoa from French Hendaye. As a border town, it has been a frequent site of diplomatic wrangling. Franco and Hitler met across the river at Hendaye rail station. In exchange for Spanish support, Franco demanded significant territorial promises, none of which Hitler was willing to concede. Hitler was bored by the talkative general and skeptical of Spanish military capability; Spain thus remained neutral throughout World War II. However, the dissolution of Franco and Hitler's relationship came too late for Irún, which had seen its historic core obliterated by German bombers (at Franco's behest) during the Spanish Civil War. Because of this, most of Irún today is modern.

From the train/bus station, where the yellow arrows begin, follow Lope de Irigoyen for 400m. Turn left on Calle Lucas de Berroa and keep straight on for 200m. ▶

Take soft right on the main road, Hondarribia Karrika. Keep straight on through a roundabout. After 600m, turn left onto a single-lane road, leading into a park. Turn right on a footpath after 1.7km. Leaving the park, turn left on a road and then fork right. Turn left at a T-junction and then fork left. After 1.3km, fork right onto a gravel road. ▶ Proceed 600m to

Albergue on the left at 18-1.

Fork left for the Aterpetxea Goikoerrota (private albergue), 17–19€, includes breakfast, 943 643 884.

SANTUARIO DE GUADALUPE (4.8KM)

Bar behind church. Fountain water is not potable.

This small 16th-century church offers sweeping views of the Bidasoa valley. When nearby Hondarribia was besieged in 1638, the Virgin of Guadalupe supposedly protected the town for 69 days. Every 8 September, the townsfolk visit this sanctuary to commemorate her.

Map continues on
page 47

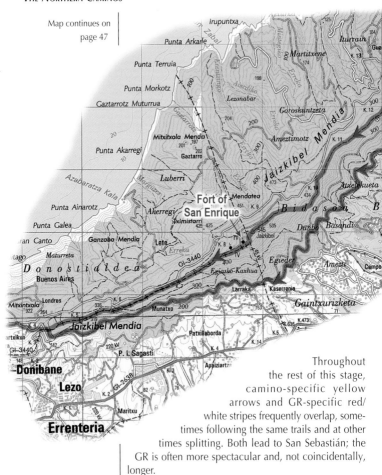

Throughout
the rest of this stage,
camino-specific yellow
arrows and GR-specific red/
white stripes frequently overlap, sometimes following the same trails and at other
times splitting. Both lead to San Sebastián; the
GR is often more spectacular and, not coincidentally,
longer.

The low-level
alternative is
described below.

Turn left uphill on a dirt road. After 200m, the
camino splits, with a sign informing 'Alpinist pilgrims'
to keep straight on, and all other pilgrims to turn left. ◄

For the recommended route, keep straight on, up a
very steep ascent, following red-and-white stripes along
a footpath. While the route is certainly challenging, this

44

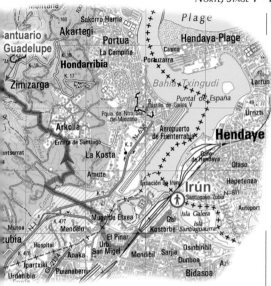

brutal first climb is not representative of the more undulating walk that follows. After 1km, reach the first of Mount Jaizkibel's five (formerly six) towers, built during the 19th-century Carlist Wars. Proceed along the ridge, passing additional towers and an ancient dolmen. After 3.3km, reach the ruined **Fort of San Enrique** atop the mountain. Descend through brambles and pine trees, then join the GI-3440 highway after 4.1km.

Low-level variant
For an easier walk, turn left when the route splits after Santuario de Guadalupe onto the dirt road. Keep straight on, with views of the Spanish interior and frequent tree cover, for 5.1km. Turn right and proceed for 4.2km, ignoring the marked left to Leto. After 1km, join the GI-3440 (and the higher route). This route is 600m longer than the high-level option.

From the GI-3440, fork left onto a single-lane road. After 2.7km, descend steps into Pasajes. Arrows provide an alternative approach towards the albergue.

PASAJES DE SAN JUAN/PASAIA DONIBANE (11.3KM)

Bars, restaurants, pharmacy. **Albergue de Peregrinos Santa Ana** (donativo, 14 beds, open 1600 March 28–October 11 in 2015, 618 939 666), **Lodging Txintxorro** (double 36€, Lezobidea 2, 943 510 083).

Originally two towns, Pasajes and San Juan were founded between 1180 and 1203, and unified in the 19th century. A prominent port for centuries, Pasajes hosted the Spanish naval fleet, the Escuadra Cantabrica, for 400 years and built part of the Spanish Armada. Victor Hugo lived in house #59, near the plaza. The 15th-century Parish Church of San Juan Bautista features a Baroque *retablo* and the image of Santa Faustina Martir, a gift from Pope Leon XII.

Soon after Bar Itxasondo, take the small pedestrian ferry across the port (60c/person). On the other side, the camino splits again. The recommended route turns right, following the promenade to the coast. Turn left and ascend steep steps to the old lighthouse. Take a footpath until turning right onto Faro Pasealekua. Alternatively, it is possible to turn left from the dock, following San Pedro Kalea through town. Turn right up stairs, pass the cemetery, and join Faro Pasealekua, intersecting the other route later. The distances of these two options are roughly equivalent.

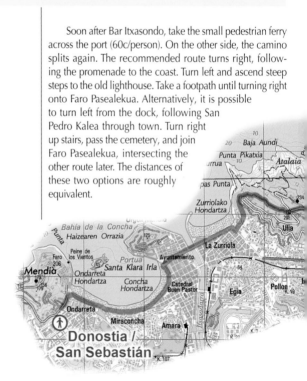

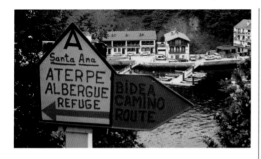

*The descent
to Pasajes*

At 2.6km from Pasajes, turn left onto a footpath and proceed 1.6km. Then, the route splits again. Turn left to follow the yellow arrows on a direct approach (or fork right with the red-and-white waymarks to hug the coastline). Staying with the yellow arrows, turn right after 1.1km into a parking lot, cross it, and veer right onto a footpath. Proceed 1.4km to San Sebastián's outskirts. Join Calle Zemoria and descend the steps. Turn right on Calle Nafarroa, and then left along the beach promenade. After 800m, cross the Puente de Zurriola and keep straight on

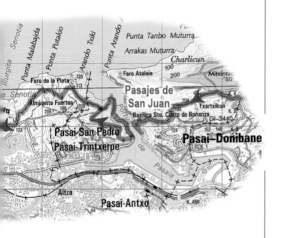

for 600m across the peninsula. Rejoin the promenade and proceed 1.8km. Near the end, turn left on Calle Satrustegi, then fork left on Paseo de Igeldo. Keep straight on for 300m to the Albergue La Sirena in

SAN SEBASTIÁN/DONOSTIA (10.2KM)

All facilities, RENFE and EuskoTren stations, Central Bus Station located on Pio XII Square, small airport near Hondarribia. Seasonal **Albergue de Peregrinos** (donativo, 50 beds, opens 1600, July–August only, credenciáles, Calle Escolta Real 12, 943 427 281), **Albergue Juvenil La Sirena** (13.50–19.80€, kitchen, breakfast, @, W/D, Paseo de Igeldo 25, 943 310 268), **Albergue Juvenil Ulia**, located on the route before the descent into San Sebastián (54 beds, 13.50-16.80€, kitchen, meals available, @, W/D, 943 483 480), **Kaixo Backpackers Hostel** (singles 30–70€, dorms 30–42€, kitchen, @, c/San Juan 9), **Pensión Loinaz** (singles/doubles 50–80€, triples 75–105€, quads 90–120€, W/D, @, Calle San Lorenzo 17, 943 426 714), **Roger's House** (18–20€ low season, 40€ July–November, c/Juan de Bilbao 13, 943 433 856). Many other accommodation options, but book in advance. Internet access possible at Harkochat (c/Fermín Calbetón 36–44) and Puerto Internet Locutorio (c/del Puerto 13).

This is one of Europe's most stunning beach cities. Probably founded by Basques, it later hosted a Roman fort and a monastery before becoming a Navarrese military stronghold. Frequent conflicts between France and Spain left a mark on San Sebastián. The most serious threat came in the Peninsular War, when Napoleon's forces took the town and the Duke of Wellington besieged it for two and a half months. The British finally broke through and celebrated by looting the town for a week. Ultimately, only two churches and 35 houses escaped this clash; the population was halved. San Sebastián has been burned to the ground a dozen times over its history, and thus most buildings date from the 19th century. The oldest section of town, the Parte Vieja, can be found beneath Monte Urgull.

San Sebastián's most impressive sights are natural ones: two fantastic beaches and prominent hills. The larger beach, Playa de la Concha, is capped on its west side by the Miramar Palace. Meanwhile, the Playa de la Zurriola is flanked by the hill Monte Igeldo, with a great park on top (tired pilgrims can ride the funicular). The other hill, Monte Urgull, preserves a rich history, including the Castillo de Santa Cruz de la Mota (1530) and a British cemetery from the Peninsular War.

Human-made highlights include the 19th-century Catedral del Buen Pastor, a Neo-Gothic structure modeled after Cologne's cathedral. Built out of sandstone, it has three large naves and a 75m tower (M–Sa 0800–1230 and 1700–2000; Su 0900–1200). The Church of San Vicente (1507) is a fine Gothic structure with a striking retablo. The Basilica de Santa María del Coro has a long history, but its current exterior is more recent. A legend states that the Virgin del Coro's image was in the church's choir, but a lazy clergyman, tired of the uphill climb to reach it, decided to steal the image. However, he was immobilized as he tried to leave the building. The Naval Museum shares the history of Basque seafaring (Calle Paseo del Muelle 24, T–Sa 1000–1330 and 1600–1930; Su 1100–1400). Finally, the Museum of San Telmo, located in the 16th-century Dominican monastery of San Telmo, contains a number of golden murals documenting Basque history. The museum also includes three works by El Greco and Rubens (T–Sa 1030–1330 and 1630–1930; Su 1030–1400).

STAGE 2

San Sebastián to Zarautz

Start	Paseo de Igeldo, San Sebastián
Finish	Albergue de Peregrinos, Zarautz
Distance	18.5km
Total ascent	520m
Total descent	520m
Difficulty	terrain: 5; waymarking: 2
Albergues de Peregrinos	Orio, Zarautz

After yesterday's brilliant walk, today might feel like a minor let-down. Sea views are not as plentiful and beach access is limited to the start- and end-points, while facilities remain equally limited. However, the comparison is unfair; this remains a wonderful walk, with extensive sections on footpaths stretching across rolling green hills. Short ascents out of San Sebastián and Orio mark the major challenges. These are tamer than yesterday's climb, but may feel harder after yesterday's exertions.

From Paseo de Igeldo, head west on Marbil Bidea, shortly before the youth hostel. Proceed uphill, watching for waymarked shortcuts leading up stairs, including one off a hairpin

Map continues on page 52

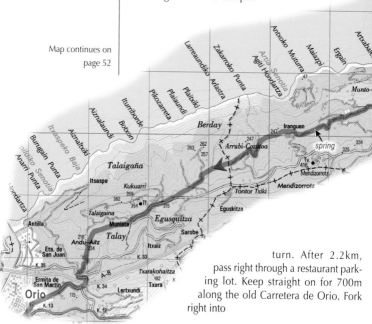

turn. After 2.2km, pass right through a restaurant parking lot. Keep straight on for 700m along the old Carretera de Orio. Fork right into

BARRIO IGELDO (2.9KM)

Pensión/Restaurant Buenavista (singles 40€, doubles 72€, 943 210 600). Camino info, water, and a sello is left by a friend of the camino on the roadside.

Continue straight, following Marabieta Bidea before transitioning to well-marked footpath and dirt roads, with excellent coastal views. After 4.6km, a trailside **spring** offers cool, fresh water. Keep straight on for

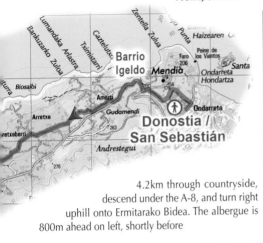

4.2km through countryside,
descend under the A-8, and turn right
uphill onto Ermitarako Bidea. The albergue is
800m ahead on left, shortly before

ORIO (9.6KM)

Well-preserved port town with bars, restaurants, and grocery shops.
Albergue de Peregrinos San Martín (10€, 20 beds, kitchen, meals, open
March–October, 617 118 689), **Youth Hostel Txurruka** (12–13.20€, breakfast included, @, 943 830 887), **Pensión Xaloa** (singles 46–57€, doubles
61–83€, Calle Estropalari 26, 943 131 883).

Orio has long been an important pilgrimage stop; Ferdinand and Isabella
declared in 1484 that pilgrims could not be charged for ferrying across the
Río Oría. Orio's residents were ardent Republicans in the Spanish Civil War
and suffered following Franco's victory. Today, the town is recognized for
its weightlifters and surfers. Its Plateresque Ermita de San Martín de Tours
has a long, covered porch ideal for breaks on a hot day. The 17th-century
Church of San Nicolás de Bari is connected to a neighboring building by a
pedestrian bridge that spans the camino. The Baroque structure replaced an
earlier church from which the graves remain, visible under newer benches.

Descend into the old town, turn left on Ibaiondo
Pasealekua, and then right over the bridge after 800m.
Turn right, following the N-634 for 500m. Fork right on
minor road, past a small *ermita* (hermitage). Continue
1.1km, pass under the A-8, and turn inland. Keep straight

Parish church of San Nicolás de Bari

on for 1.7km to **Gran Camping Zarautz** (bar, **Albergue de Peregrinos**, 5€, 14 beds, limited cooking facilities, 943 831 238). Follow the road, winding 1.2km downhill. Turn right on N-634 and keep straight on for 800m. For the seasonal albergue, turn right on Calle Zinkunegi and left on Calle Zumalacárregui.

ZARAUTZ (6.1KM)

All facilities. **Albergue de Peregrinos** (donativo, 30–50 beds, opens 1600, July–August only, Calle Zumalakarregi 16, 943 830 990), **Youth Hostel Igerain** (15–21€, breakfast, @, 943 132 910), **Galerna Zarautz Hostel** (18 beds, 21.20€, includes breakfast, 943 010 371), **Hotel Ekia Pentsioa** (singles 55–80€, doubles 65–90€, Elizarrure Kalea 3, 943 010 664). Internet at Locutorio Zarautz (Calle Bizkaia).

An important shipping town, historically, home to whalers and great explorers. Magellan's ship, *La Vitoria*, was built here. International attention came in the 20th century with the Belgian royalty's decision to summer here in the Palace of Narros. It has the region's longest beach (2.8km) and, not coincidentally, triples its population during summer months. The Church of Nuestra Señora la Real contains the tomb of 'the pilgrim'. The church was targeted in 1586, when a Genoese pilgrim stole a number of artifacts. However, he was captured, drawn and quartered, and displayed on the camino (nothing remains of the site today). Also worth a visit is the Torre Luzea, a 15th-century Gothic building.

STAGE 3
Zarautz to Deba

Start	Albergue de Peregrinos, Zarautz
Finish	Albergue de Peregrinos, Deba
Distance	24km
Total ascent	640m
Total descent	640m
Difficulty	terrain: 4; waymarking: 3
Albergues de Peregrinos	Zumaia, Deba, Getaria, Akzizu

Today offers a happy balance between beach towns, sea views, and quiet hills. Leaving Zarautz, the pilgrim can choose between a higher inland route and a lower coastal option. After Getaria, the routes rejoin and jut inland, cutting across a hill via Akzizu before returning to the beach in Zumaia. A longer ascent follows, rising 300m only to descend once more – via waymarked elevators! – to Deba, the final taste of Guipúzcoa before entering Vizcaya tomorrow. Enjoy the beach tonight, as you won't return to the coast for several days.

Map continues on
page 57

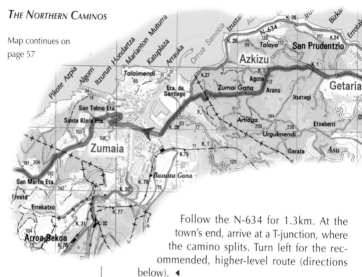

Follow the N-634 for 1.3km. At the town's end, arrive at a T-junction, where the camino splits. Turn left for the recommended, higher-level route (directions below). ◀

Turn right for the coastal option, which follows the N-634 to Getaria.

Shortly after turning left, turn right uphill along a medieval road. The route winds through vineyards overlooking the bay. Join the GI-3391 briefly, then turn left onto a minor road, passing more vineyards. After 5km, pass a restaurant, where there are two options. To visit Getaria, follow the road right downhill for 500m. Otherwise, turn left.

GETARIA (6.3KM)

Bars, grocery stores, and other facilities. **Kanpaia Aterpea** (private albergue, 12€, 30 beds, 3€ breakfast, W/D, 695 711 679, c/San Prudentzio Auzoa, 28-Bajo), **Pensión Getariano** (singles 40–60€, doubles 55–85€, triples 75–100€, 943 140 567).

Another important fishing town with a history of whaling and exploring. Basque navigators were quite popular on Portuguese and Spanish ships. The most famous example, Getaria's own Juan Sebastián Elcano, took over Magellan's fleet after Magellan was killed and completed the globe's first circumnavigation. He is still honored today; every four years, townspeople re-enact his heroic return. The 13th-century **Church of San Salvador** hosted Elcano's baptism and contains his (empty) tomb. It has several distinctive and curious elements, including a tilted floor, a menorah on the back wall, and a chapel and crypt accessible by the alley.

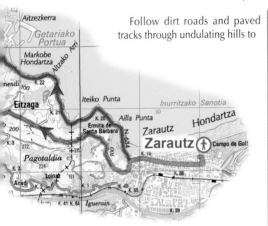

Follow dirt roads and paved tracks through undulating hills to

AKZIZU (1.9KM)

Agote Aundi has a pilgrim menu and beds available (private albergue, 15€, includes breakfast, 943 140 455).

Azkizu has one of the oldest Christian churches in Guipuzcoa, the **Church of San Martín de Tours**, noted for its Gothic masonry. Key obtainable from a neighbor.

Descend 2km to N-634. Follow pedestrian track across the bridge and descend steps to the dock. Turn left and continue straight across a second bridge into

ZUMAIA (3.5KM)

All facilities. Seasonal **Albergue-Convento San Jose** (8€, 25 beds, open June–September, W/D, San Jose Kalea 1, 600 280 375), **Pensión Goiko** (singles 30–45€, doubles 45–57€, 943 860 078), **Santa Klara** (private albergue, 20€ for B&B, 35–55€ for rooms, located 1.3km after town, 943 860 531).

Set on the Ría Urola, Zumaia developed around a 13th-century monastery, and was a frequent target for piracy in the Middle Ages. By the 16th century, the town had 136 houses, 70 within the walls. Zumaia's beaches are set on the longest continuous rock strata in the world, which is over 100 million

Zumaia

years old. The **Museo Zuloaga**, former home of the Basque painter Ignacio Zuloaga, includes pieces by Goya, El Greco, and Zurburán (and, of course, Zuloaga). The 15th-century **Church of San Pedro** features a gargoyle-lined entrance and Juan de Antxieta's Romanist retablo (note the monumental, energetic human figures, including St Peter in his chair). The building exemplifies the late Gothic, with pointed arches and a star vault over the apse.

Continue straight uphill. Turn right at Eroski super-market (easily missed), following a single-lane road that becomes a gravel track. After 2.7km, pass through a park with bathrooms. Follow the grassy footpath to

ELORRIAGA (3.2KM)

Toki-alai Taberna.

Small village founded in the 10th century. **Hermitage of San Sebastián** features a Romanesque baptismal pool.

▸ Proceed along quiet country roads, crossing the N-634 twice. Fork right off the N-634 downhill onto a footpath. Then, ascend sharply to the N-634 for a third time. Continue straight into

An alternative route – more strenuous, very scenic and 7.6km – is possible from here, following the GR-121's red/white markings along the coast into Deba.

ITZIAR (5.1KM)

Bars, grocery store. **Hotel Kanala** (singles 56–69€, doubles 76–89€, triples 83–96€, 943 199 035).

The 16th-century **Sanctuary of Nuestra Señora of Itziar** preserves the image of the Virgin of Itziar – one of the Basque region's most important – in its niche.

Follow a generally flat cement track for 3.4km, ending with a steep descent. Turn right at bottom of elevator and proceed 300m to the Turismo. Check in here for the Albergue, which is located near the top of the first elevator.

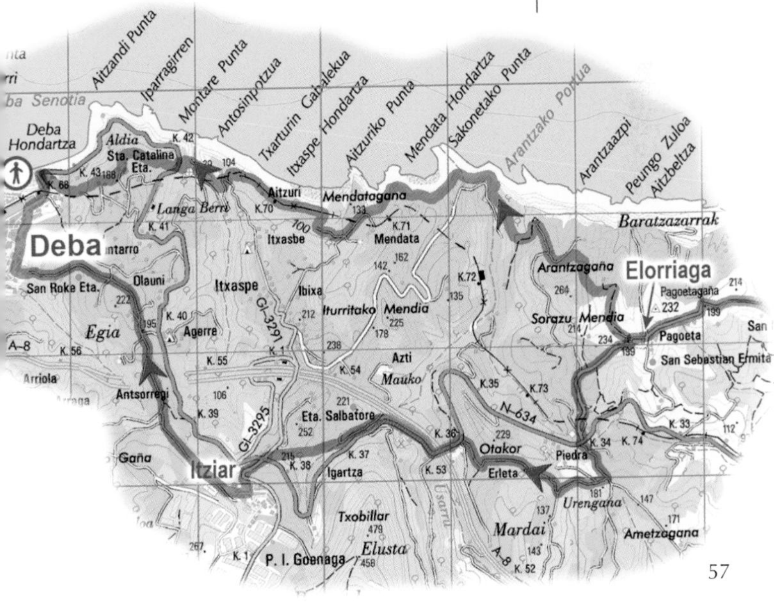

DEBA (4KM)

All facilities. **Albergue de Peregrinos** (5€, 56 beds, W/D, registration and keys in turismo, or with Policia Municipal when the tourist office is closed, 943 192 452), **Albergue Naparrenekua** (private albergue, 16€, 943 199 090) located 10km from Deba in Lastur; the albergue drives pilgrims to and from the lodging. **Pensión Zumardi** (singles 45–55€, doubles 55–75€, pilgrim discounts, Marina Kalea 12, 943 192 368). Internet in the Biblioteca Municipal.

Founded in 1343 by Alfonso XI, Deba maintains its original layout. Like its neighbors, its past was devoted to whales and trade, while its present focuses on tourism. At its peak, Deba had three pilgrim albergues. Its must-see **Church of Santa María** is a National Monument and one of the region's finest churches. The Gothic entrance is the highlight. Six apostles flank each side, while 38 angels, virgins, and martyrs adorn the frieze. The Annunciation, Visitation, Birth, and Epiphany are narrated on the tympanum. The cloister is also a masterpiece designed to perfect classical proportions.

The Iglesia de Santa María in Deba

STAGE 4
Deba to Markina-Xemein

Start	Albergue de Peregrinos, Deba
Finish	Albergue de Peregrinos, Markina-Xemein
Distance	23km
Total ascent	915m
Total descent	830m
Difficulty	terrain: 5; waymarking: 2
Albergues de Peregrinos	Ermita del Calvario, Markina-Xemein
Note	Leaving Deba is no longer well-marked because of vandalism. Get instructions from the turismo

Say goodbye to the coast for a few days. From Deba, the camino heads for the interior of Vizcaya, climbing en route over the Collado de Arno, some 500m higher than Deba. With extensive stretches of dirt roads and footpaths passing through densely forested hills, this stage's scenery and climate differ dramatically from those of the preceding days. Markina-Xemein also offers a much less touristed stopping point. Alternatively, consider walking a little farther where the monks of Zenarruza (Stage 5) provide hospitality. Plan ahead: it is rarely possible to buy food or drink along this route.

Cross the Río Deba and turn right. The well-marked route begins on

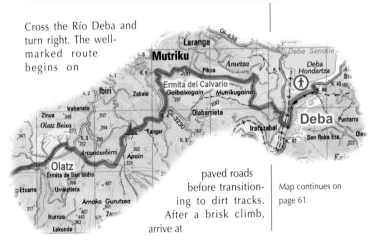

paved roads before transitioning to dirt tracks. After a brisk climb, arrive at

Map continues on page 61

59

ERMITA DEL CALVARIO (4.9KM)

Fountain behind church, restaurant (open nights). **Izarbide Aterpetxea**, 450 meters beyond the restaurant (private albergue, 12€, 32 beds, meals available, W/D, 655 459 769).

Across from the restaurant is the old *probadero*, where oxen tested their strength by dragging rocks over cobblestones.

Keep straight on for the paved road, which again becomes an unpaved track. Follow the dirt road into

OLATZ (2.9KM)

Taberna (erratic hours). Fountain at town entrance.

Picturesque village with small church.

Continue straight along the road for 3km. Transition to a footpath, running uphill through a lovely forest to

COLLADO DE ARNO (5.7KM)

Covered fountain on left.

A small cluster of houses, located on border between Guipúzcoa and Vizcaya.

Turn right at the T-junction, following the dirt road. Proceed 7.5km along a mix of dirt roads, footpaths, and occasional paved stretches. Finally, a long, rocky downhill leads 2.1km into Markina-Xemein. Arrive first at the **Iglesia de Santa María de la Asunción** and proceed through a neighborhood into the historical center. The albergue is located shortly before the end of town.

The camino as it approaches Olatz

61

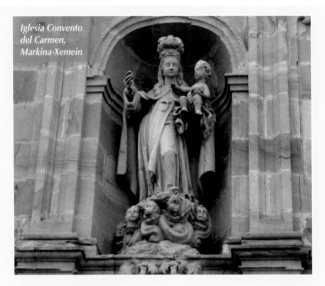

Iglesia Convento del Carmen, Markina-Xemein

MARKINA-XEMEIN (9.6KM)

All facilities. **Albergue de Peregrinos** in the Convento de los Padres Carmelitas (donativo, 28 beds, open May–September, Calle Carmen 5, 630 536 137), **Albergue Intxauspe** (12€, 20 beds, open April–October, meals available, 652 770 889) located outside of Markina's center but the hospitaleros will pick pilgrims up at the soccer field near the entrance to town), **Albergue Augusto** (12€, includes breakfast, 17 beds, c/Okerra 24, 667 967 555), **Albergue Pitis** (12–15€, 12 beds, Karmengo Plaza 11, 657 727 824), **Hostal Vega** (Abesua Kalea 2, 946 866 015).

Paleolithic remains have been found in the area. The town coalesced around a fort in 1355, reflecting its strategic value as a border post. Born of conflict, it enjoyed little peace, with Napoleon, the Carlist Wars, and the Spanish Civil War all wreaking havoc on the region. However, today Markina-Xemein is called the 'University of Pelota' because of the town's many *pelota* (court games) champions. It features several notable churches, including the **Church of the Assumption**, the **Church of Santa María**, and the hexagonal **Sanctuary of San Miguel de Arretxinaga**, founded in the 11th century around three Megalithic stones.

STAGE 5

Markina-Xemein to Gernika

Start	Albergue de Peregrinos, Markina-Xemein
Finish	Youth hostel, Gernika
Distance	25km
Total ascent	440m
Total descent	515m
Difficulty	terrain: 4; waymarking: 3
Albergues de Peregrinos	Zenarruza, Gernika

The route from Markina meanders alongside a small creek before turning towards the village of Bolibar and the picturesque Monastery of Zenarruza. From there, it proceeds parallel to the highway, but with sufficient separation from the noise to allow for quiet walking. The tree cover thins the farther west you travel, as do the stopping points, and the final stretch into Gernika is paved and a little monotonous. But arrival in Gernika makes the trek well worthwhile, as it is one of the most historically significant towns on the camino.

Proceed straight from the albergue
towards the BI-633. Turn left
on a pedestrian track.
Cross under the

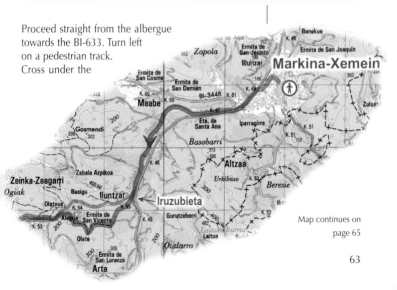

Map continues on
page 65

highway and keep straight on along the other side for 1.4km. Turn right at km47 sign and then left onto a footpath. Follow the Río Artibai into

IRUZUBIETA (3.8KM)

Two bars/restaurants.

Turn right on minor road. Join a footpath, crossing the tree-covered hillside. Descend the hill, cross the BI-2224, and fork right into

BOLIBAR (2.2KM)

Bar, grocery, bakery.

Founded in the 11th century, and the ancestral homeland of Simón Bolívar. Although his ancestors departed Spain four generations before his birth, he is commemorated with the **Casa-Museo de Simón Bolívar** (open 1000–1300). The name 'Bolibar' is Basque for 'windmill valley'. The **Church of Santo Tomás** is a typical fortress-temple.

The medieval road to Zenarruza

Map continues on
page 66

Re-cross the highway and
return to the hillside. Follow the
medieval road 1.6km to the monastery.
Join the paved road and continue 200m
to

MONASTERIO DE ZENARRUZA (1.8KM)

Medieval monastery with **Albergue de Peregrinos** (donativo, 11 beds,
meals provided, 946 164 179). Shortly before the monastery is the
Albergue Privado Ziortza Beitia (12€, 42 beds, bar/restaurant, W/D, 946
165 722).

Legend holds that an eagle brought
a skull here from the Gerrikaitz
ossuary, prompting the monastery's construction. It was first
documented in 1082, although the
14th-century Gothic church came
later. Cistercians took over the
monastery in 1994. It is a serene
spot for rest or reflection, with a
large covered porch, impressive

The Monastery of Zenarruza's cloister

65

altar, and evocative cloister. The tympanum and retablo are impressive; the former features El Salvador between two trumpet-bearing angels, while the latter details the Virgin's life with a Santiago Peregrino towards the bottom.

Shortly before the monastery is the **Albergue Privado Ziortza Beitia** (12€, 42 beds, bar/restaurant, W/D, 946 165 722).

◀ Leaving the monastery, return to the hills once more, following a rocky footpath with a couple of steep drops. Descend a series of steps to the rural road leading into

MUNITIBAR (3.4KM)

Two bars, grocery shop, pharmacy.

Follow the BI-2224 for 100m. Turn left on a minor road uphill. After 2.4km, turn left onto a footpath for the Mendata Albergue Municipal (7€, 36 beds, closed Monday and Tuesday, open April–October, 946 257 204). Those continuing should remain on the road. After 6km, ascend to an impressive church in **Elexalde** before looping back to the river. Proceed 1.5km along footpaths. Join the

BI-3224 in **Marmiz** and follow it 3.5km to a T-junction in Gernika. Turn right for the youth hostel, 150m away. Turn left to follow the camino into the center of

GERNIKA (13.7KM)

All facilities. **Albergue de Peregrinos** (donativo, 35 beds, **August only**, 609 031 526, Zeharreta 11 (in the Colegio Allende Salazar)), **Youth hostel** (16–20€, includes breakfast, kitchen, W/D, Kortezubi Bidea 9, 944 650 775); the Polideportivo may serve as an Albergue de Peregrinos in the summer (Calle Zeharreta 11, 630 536 137), **Hotel Boliña** (singles 33€, doubles 39–48€, Calle Barrenkale 3, 946 250 300), **Hotel Akelarre** (singles 33–43€, doubles 43–55€, Barrenkalea 5, 946 270 197). Internet at cyber café on San Juan Kalea and many other places.

For centuries, the Lords of Viscaya gathered under Gernika's oak tree to swear loyalty to the nation's *fueros* (charter). Later, when the Basques joined Spain, Spanish kings made the trek there to reiterate their commitment to protecting Basque liberties. However, Gernika is known internationally primarily because of two men: Franco and Picasso. As the Spanish Civil War languished in a bloody stalemate, Franco faced heavy pressure to produce results. He shifted focus to the Basque country. Although Franco's military was outdated, he had Hitler and Mussolini's modern air forces available, carrying with them a brutal new kind of war. On a market day in 1937, the German Condor Legion introduced saturation bombing, pummeling the town with incendiary explosives before passing a second time to strafe the fleeing townspeople. The town was destroyed and thousands were killed. Aghast, Picasso took up the brush and produced one of his most famous works, which shares the town's name. Intended as a warning to the world of the destructive power of new technology and the savagery of the fascist militaries, its message went largely unheeded.

As a result of the bombing, today's Gernika is a modern city, with few historic buildings. However, a sapling of the old oak survives in the park surrounding the **Casa de Juntas**, the seat of the Viscayan Provincial General Assembly. It includes an exhibit on Basque government and culture (daily 1000–1400 and 1600–1800). Even more compelling is the **Gernika Peace Museum**, which goes beyond the bombing to examine 20th-century efforts at peace and transitional justice (4€, T–Sa 1000–1400 and 1600–1900; Su 1000–1400).

STAGE 6
Gernika to Bilbao

Start	Youth hostel, Gernika
Finish	Albergue de Peregrinos, Bilbao
Distance	35.5km
Total ascent	835m
Total descent	825m
Difficulty	terrain: 4; waymarking: 3
Albergues de Peregrinos	Lezama, Bilbao

This is a long stage, connecting two of the Camino del Norte's more famous stops. The first half is quite enjoyable. Warm up by climbing 300m in the first 5km. Descend to the highway, then steel yourself for more uphill, leading to the Alto de Morga and Aretxabalgane. Arrival in Goikolexea spells the end of the day's most pleasant walking, as it is followed by a long, straight, flat stretch of highway. From Zamudio, one more ascent awaits, the completion of which promises impressive views of Bilbao – and a long, paved downhill into the dynamic city.

Map continues on
page 71

▶ From the albergue, return to the T-junction and keep straight on Kortezubi Bidea. Turn left on Calle Portu, then right towards the *ayuntamiento* (town hall). Proceed upstairs through the ayuntamiento, turn left past the Escuelas Publicas, then turn right around the Casa de Juntas. Fork right, then turn left at a T-junction. Pass through a residential neighborhood, before an ermita signals Gernika's abrupt end, 2.6km from the hostel. A pleasant 4.6km walk follows, along wooded tracks. Cross under the BI-2121 to arrive at

Brown street signs, labeled 'Donejakue Bidea', mark the camino through Gernika.

MEAKAUR TURN-OFF (7.2KM)

No facilities. To reach **Albergue Meakaur** (16€, 62 beds, meals, W/D, @, 944 911 746) turn right on the BI-2121 and walk 2km.

The small **Church of San Esteban** contains Roman remains.

The next section involves multiple sharp climbs, crossing the **Altos de Morga** and **Aretxabalgane**. A house in Eskerika, 2.7km from the Meakaur turn-off, offers water to walkers, the only chance to refill before Goikolexea. ▶ Keep straight on for 2.5km, join the BI-2713, and continue 2.2km farther. Turn left onto a footpath, descend a steep hill, and curve right along a minor road into

Turn right here for **Albergue Eskerika** (15€, 20 beds, includes breakfast, kitchen for 1€, open April–October, 696 453 582).

GOIKOLEXEA (8.9KM)

Bar, pharmacy.

Like Gernika, Vizcayan lords gathered here for loyalty oaths. The Gothic **Church of Santos Emeterio and Celedonio** honors two Roman legionnaires martyred for their Christian faith. In 1991, routine restoration work revealed several murals of great artistic significance.

Keep straight on the BI-3713 to

LARRABETZU (1.4KM)

Bar, grocery. **Albergue de Peregrinos Larrabetzu** (donativo, 30 beds, July–August only, microwave, W/D, in school facilities on c/Lehendakari Agirre, 609 031 526.

Founded in 1376 by Prince Juan and ravaged by fire in 1830, today's town is largely the post-fire Neoclassical incarnation. The 18th-century **Church of Santa María** includes a Greek cross and a 15th-century statue of Our Lady.

Continue along the BI-3713 to

LEZAMA (3.5KM)

Bars, restaurants, supermarket. **Albergue de Peregrinos** (donativo, 20 beds, open June–September, W/D, in Centro Civico), **Casa Rural Matsa** (singles 44–52€, doubles 51–61€, Calle Aretxalde 153, 944 556 086).

Lezama is known for its three famous towers – Basabil, Arechavaleta, and Lezama – which speak to its medieval military significance. **Church of Santa María de Lezama** is a good rest stop.

Map continues on page 72

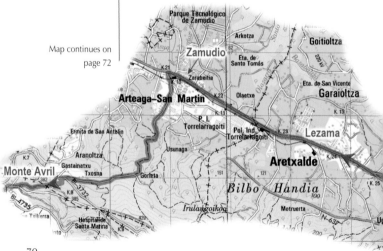

And, yet again, follow the BI-3713 to

ZAMUDIO (2.9KM)

Bars, restaurants, supermarket. **Pensión Udondo** (singles 45€, doubles 55–60€, Calle Mungialde 3, 946 564 909).

Turn left at the end of town, proceeding uphill. Cross the roundabout, fork right, and cross the expressway, 1.1km later. From there, dirt tracks and minor roads lead uphill to

MONTE AVRIL (4.8KM)

An enjoyable park offering excellent views of Bilbao.

Continue downhill. Cross the BI-631 and wind around the Basilica de Nuestra Señora de Begoña after 2.1km. Proceed 800m down the Calzada de Mallona, following a long series of steps into the Plaza de Unamuno. For a scenic alternative route through the city center, see below.

Keep straight on through the plaza on Calle de la Cruz, looking for bronze scallop shell waymarks in the road. Keep straight on Calle Tendería. At a T-junction, turn left on

Bilbao's Casco Viejo

Calle de la Ribera, then turn right across the Puente de San Antón, after 550m. Turn right on Calle Bilbao la Vieja (also the N-634), which becomes Calle San Francisco. After 850m, cross the railroad, and then continue straight through Plaza Zabálburu. The road is now Calle

Autonomía. Fork left onto Carretera Basurto. After 2.4km, turn left up stairs. Turn right on Calle Kobetas. Seasonal Albergue de Peregrinos on right. Alternatively, to reach Youth Hostel Aterpetxea, continue straight on along Carretera Basurto instead of turning. The hostel is on your right. Both accommodation options are 300m from the bottom of the steps. This route largely bypasses central Bilbao.

Scenic Bilbao variant

It is possible to walk instead through the center of Bilbao. From Plaza de Unamuno, turn right on Sombrereria Kalea. Then, turn right on Calle del Correo. After 450m, cross the Puente del Arenal. Follow Gran Vía for 800m, passing the RENFE station. Turn right in Plaza Eliptica onto Alameda Recalde and proceed 650m to the **Guggenheim Museum**. Turn left on the riverfront walkway. Cross the next pedestrian bridge, turn left, and continue straight for 1.5km. Fork right on Morgan Kalea, just before Puente Euskalduna, skirting the roundabout. The Akelarre Youth Hostel is 400m further, on the right. This route is 300m shorter than the other, although it ends at a different accommodation option. ▶

It is possible to continue walking directly from here tomorrow – see 'East Nervión variant' (Camino del Norte Stage 7)

BILBAO (7KM)

A major city with all facilities and services. RENFE and EuskoTren stations, Termibus bus station located near San Mames. Bilbao airport is 9km from the center and can be reached by Bus A3247. Seasonal **Albergue de Peregrinos** (donativo, 40 beds, kitchen, open May–September, breakfast available, Calle Kobetas 60, call to confirm it is open, 609 031 526). Many youth hostels have popped up here over the past few years, providing many options for affordable accommodations near the center. Options include: **Ganbara Hostel** located in the heart of the old town (17€, 62 beds, kitchen, breakfast included, W/D, @, 944 053 930), **Bilbao Central Hostel** (17€, 40 beds, kitchen, breakfast included, W/D, @, 946 526 057, c/Fernández del Campo 24) and **Moon Hostel** (10€, 92 beds, kitchen, @, 944 750 848, c/Luzarra 7). **Youth Hostel Aterpetxea** is a massive structure on the outskirts of town (17€, 142 beds, breakfast, W/D, @, 944 270 054), while the new **Youth Hostel Akelarre** is closer to the center (14€, 42 beds,

breakfast, kitchen, @, 944 057 713).
Pensión Manoli (singles 36€, doubles
42€, Calle Libertad 2, 944 155 636),
Pensión Mendez (doubles 35€, Calle
Santa Maria 13, 944 160 364), **Hotel
Petit Palace Arana** (doubles 120–140€,
Bidebarrieta 2, 944 156 411).

Today, Bilbao is a center of Spanish
industry, insurance, and banking, which
has inspired a significant influx of non-
Basques. From its founding in 1300, it
was destined to be a place of economic
importance, given its strategic position
on the Río Nervión, connecting the
Basque country with Castille. Despite a

The Guggenheim flower dog

sound thumping from Napoleon's forces and during the Carlist Wars, 19th-
century Bilbao was changed most markedly by the industrial revolution.
Given the region's extensive natural resources, including iron mines, forests,
and the potential for abundant water power, Bilbao enjoyed a boom in shipbuilding and steel mills.

The Gothic **Basilica of Begoña** was the first landmark seen by sailors as
they approached the city, and feels more monumental than Bilbao's cathedral, given its three naves, massive entryway, and bell tower (containing 24
bells, one of which weighs a ton). Vibrantly restored paintings on the life
of the Virgin line the walls. The basilica was damaged in the Spanish Civil
War, when a bomb exploded in one of the building's doorways; speculation
places the blame on a Franco supporter.

The historic center, known as the Seven Streets, radiates out from the
Cathedral of Santiago. The original cathedral was largely destroyed by fire
in 1571; its replacement features a variety of styles, including a Renaissance
porch, Gothic cloisters and main doors, and a Neo-Gothic façade and tower.

Bilbao's **Guggenheim Museum** is undeniably the city's major highlight,
although the building – wonderfully designed by Frank Gehry and built in
1997 – exceeds in quality anything on display within it. The eclectic con-
temporary collection is still primarily comprised of temporary exhibits on
loan from other Guggenheim holdings (July–August: M–Sa 1000–1900, Sun
1000–1800; Sept–June T–Su 1100–1800, closed M).

STAGE 7
Bilbao to Pobeña

Start	Albergue de Peregrinos, Bilbao
Finish	Albergue de Peregrinos, Pobeña
Distance	22km
Total ascent	230m
Total descent	250m
Difficulty	terrain: 2; waymarking: 5
Albergues de Peregrinos	Portugalete, Pobeña

As you slog through the first half of today's stage, remind yourself that by day's end you will be in a beautiful place. If only you could get there faster! Sometimes bleak, often forgettable, the walk from Bilbao to Portugalete – regardless of the option you choose – is poorly waymarked and best finished quickly and put behind you. Several route options are outlined; find the one that suits you. From Portugalete the route slowly sputters to life, transitioning gradually to a peaceful bicycle track. Finally, mercifully, this track deposits you on the coast, where the soothing Playa de la Arena offers a place to relax, and the comfortable albergue in Pobeña a place to sleep.

From Bilbao to Portugalete, there are three routes to consider. ▸ For those staying in the Aterpetxea Youth Hostel or the Albergue de Peregrinos, the recommended route follows the west side of the Río Nervión. Backtrack along the Carretera Basurto towards Bilbao. After crossing the A-8, take the second left (unmarked), following a minor road as it curves left through a parking lot and then right around some houses. Pass under the railroad, cross the N-634, and turn left. Keep straight on for 2.8km; the road becomes Calle Fray Juan. Make a soft right after the bridge onto Calle Zumalacarregui (BI-3739). Fork right on Calle Olaetzke, pass under the N-637, and fork right on Avenida de los Altos Hornos, skirting **San Vicente de Baracaldo** after 2.8km. Fork right across the water

There is even a fourth possible option – if you are not a stickler about walking every step, consider taking the metro from Bilbao to Portugalete. It's quick, cheap, and easy.

on Avenida de Kaiku, then follow the BI-3739 for 3km through **Sestao**. Rejoin the yellow

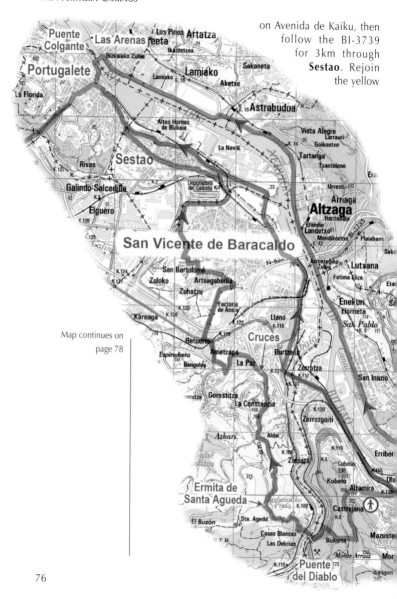

Map continues on page 78

arrows in **Portugalete**, turning right downhill towards the church. After 1.7km, turn left on Avenida de Carlos VII, and proceed into the town center.

'Official camino' variant
This lies to the west of the recommended route, and is the least appealing option, combining industrial sub-urbs with the most walking. But, if following the yellow arrows wherever they lead is important to you, here's the route. From the Albergue de Peregrinos, proceed 2.6km on roads and footpaths to the 15th-century **Puente del Diablo**. The nicest part of this walk follows, with a well-preserved section of medieval road leading 1.2km uphill to the **Ermita de Santa Águeda**. From there, follow Basatxu Bidea 3.1km into **Cruces**, where food is available. Navigate a series of minor roads and tracks until turning right on Calle Ametzaga. Turn left on N-634 and keep straight on for 1.3km. Turn right at the Iglesia del Sagrado Corazón in **San Vincente de Baracaldo**, where all facilities are available. Continue straight to the Bilbao Exhibition Center and turn left. Fork right at the rounda-bout, then left at the next roundabout, joining a cycling track. Keep straight on for 5.7km to **Sestao**. From there, follow Gran Vía de José Antonio de Aguirre. Turn right on Calle Aizpuru, then join the BI-739, leading into **Portugalete**. This route covers 16.4km.

East Nervión variant
This route is advisable for those staying in the Akelarre Youth Hostel, as the route proceeds directly past it, and for those who get lost easily, because the route is straightforward. From the hostel, cross Calle Morgan and turn right. Keep straight on the BI-711 for 9km. Upon reaching **Las Arenas**, take the famous **Puente Colgante** across the river. On the other side, turn left on the riverfront, then right on Calle Doña

Casilda Iturrizar. Continue uphill on Avenida de Carlos VII, into the center of **Portugalete**. This covers 9.4km.

PORTUGALETE (10.3KM)

All facilities. Last supermarket before Castro-Urdiales. Seasonal **Albergue de Peregrinos** (donativo, 28 beds, open July–August, Calle Casilda Iturrizar 8, 630 536 137), **Pensión la Guía** (singles 22€, doubles 32€, Calle Virgen de la Guía 4, 944 837 530), **Hostal Santa María** (singles 20–35€, doubles 25–42€, Calle Salcedo 1, 944 722 489). Internet at Locutorio Nallestel on Calle Araba 9.

A thriving suburb, with an active commercial center. First documented in 1249, but undoubtedly much older, Portugalete contains the remains of early walls and a tower. Its highlight is the **Church of Santa María**, built as Columbus set sail for the New World and then gradually expanded over the years. Although a prototypical Gothic building, the Renaissance is visible in the central retablo. The Santiago Chapel has a bold Santiago Matamoros.

Map continues on page 80

Proceed uphill along Avenida de Carlos VII (enjoy the moving sidewalks!). Keep straight on out of town and over the A-8 expressway. The route splits 1.5km from Portugalete. Continue straight

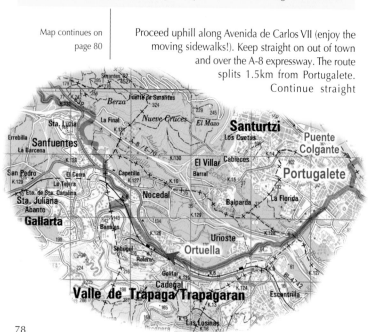

along the cyclist/pedestrian track to go directly to Pobeña (saving 500m in the process). Alternately, turn L and continue 600m into

ORTUELLA (2.1KM)

Bars/restaurants.

A sprawling town that boomed in the 19th century due to local mining deposits.

Continue through town, eventually reaching Bar Luis after 2.1km. Soon after, join a cyclist/pedestrian track, winding gradually downhill to

PLAYA DE LA ARENA (8.6KM)

Bars/restaurants. **Apartamentos La Arena** (singles 35€, doubles 55€, triples 70€, kitchen, 946 365 454).

Turn left along the road, continuing through a beachside park. Alternatively, it is possible to disregard the waymarks and follow the beach. Regardless, keep straight on

Playa de la Arena

towards and across the pedestrian bridge. After 800m, the camino splits. Fork right up a flight of stairs to continue walking, or continue straight for the albergue in

POBEÑA (1.1KM)

Bars/restaurants. **Albergue de Peregrinos** (donativo, 22 beds, breakfast, open May–September, W/D, 609 031 526), **Apartamentos Mugarri** (doubles 60€, kitchen, meals, Plaza de Pobeña, 617 038 292).

STAGE 8

Pobeña to Castro-Urdiales

Start	Albergue de Peregrinos, Pobeña
Finish	Albergue de Peregrinos, Castro-Urdiales
Distance	17.5km
Total ascent	235m
Total descent	235m
Difficulty	terrain: 3; waymarking: 4
Albergues de Peregrinos	Castro-Urdiales

This stage begins – following a surprisingly long flight of steps – with a stunning walk along the coastal hillside. From Pobeña, a recreational path follows the trackbed of the former railroad that carried iron ore to waiting ships. Towards the end of the path, you can still see the old *descargadero*, where the ships were loaded. Soon after, choose between two possible routes to Castro-Urdiales, either a direct approach via the highway (with an exciting new off-road stretch with coastal views) or a longer trek along quieter roads.

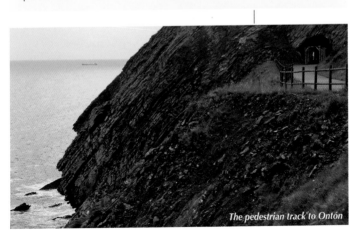

The pedestrian track to Ontón

Backtrack to the waymarked steps and begin the ascent. Follow the pedestrian track, offering impressive beach views. Shortly after a tunnel, curve inland, pass under the A-8, and descend into

ONTÓN (5.9KM)

Although older Norte guides mention an albergue and a bar here, neither exists. No facilities.

Map continues on page 84

After 4.3km, 500m before arriving in **Mioño**, where there are bars, a grocery store, and

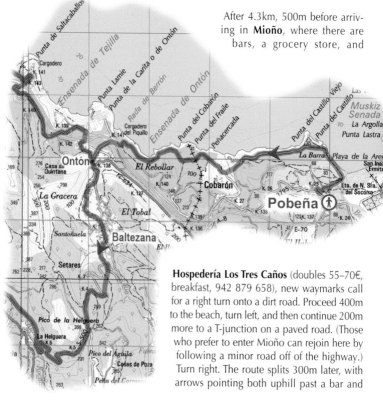

Hospedería Los Tres Caños (doubles 55–70€, breakfast, 942 879 658), new waymarks call for a right turn onto a dirt road. Proceed 400m to the beach, turn left, and then continue 200m more to a T-junction on a paved road. (Those who prefer to enter Mioño can rejoin here by following a minor road off of the highway.) Turn right. The route splits 300m later, with arrows pointing both uphill past a bar and along the coastline. Both routes work, but the coastal approach is preferable.

Continue on a gravel pedestrian track, then pass through a long tunnel. After 500m, emerge from the tunnel and climb uphill. Shortly thereafter, turn right at a T-junction (rejoining the other track here). The next 1.5km follow trails and dirt roads, with outstanding coastal views. Finally join the beach promenade outside **Castro-Urdiales** and follow it 1.3km to the center.

'Official camino' variant

From the N-634 in Ontón, follow yellow arrows left onto CA-523, towards Baltezana and Otanes. This route mixes highway walking, occasional dirt roads, and a long stretch along a paved cycling track, although there is little to see. From the fork, it proceeds: 1.1km to **Baltezana** (bars), 5.1km to the old train station of **Otañes** (the route does not enter the town proper), 2.4km to **Santullán** (bar, panaderia), 1.9km to **Sámano**, and 3.3km to the edge of **Castro-Urdiales**. This route is 5.3km longer than the highway approach.

The two routes converge on the promenade in the center of Castro-Urdiales, but the albergue is still 3km away. Continue along the promenade towards the church and castle. ▸

Small blue Camino stickers on lampposts mark the way through town.

Castro-Urdiales

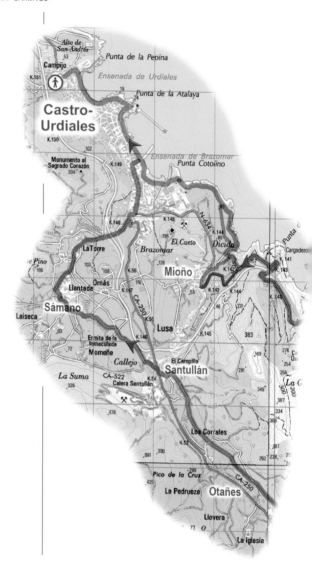

Fork left uphill towards the **Church of Santa María de la Asunción**. Descend to the other side of town, continuing to the last beach. Fork left along the adjacent plaza, turn left at the end, and then left again on Calle del Sable, leading towards the Plaza de Toros. The albergue is behind the bullring.

The promenade leading through the center of Castro-Urdiales

CASTRO-URDIALES (11.7KM)

All facilities. **Albergue de Peregrinos** (6€, 16 beds, kitchen, 608 610 992/942 871 512), **Pensión La Mar** (singles 35–45€, doubles 47–60€, triples 60–72€, Calle la Mar 27, 942 870 524), **Hostería Villa de Castro** (singles 35–45€, doubles 50–65€, triples 60–75€, quads 70–95€, kitchen, Calle Los Huertos 2, 650 483 650). Internet in the Biblioteca Municipal.

A long-inhabited area, with human remains dating to 12000BC and a Roman milestone outside the Church of Santa María. A Templar castle stood here, although little remains; its ruins serve as the lighthouse's base. The town suffered at the hands of the French in the Peninsular War.

The **Parish Church of Santa María de la Asunción** is the must-visit sight. It holds a dominant position overlooking town and water, accessible by an old stone staircase. One of the Norte's finest Gothic churches, its exterior is spectacular, with buttresses flying in all directions. Strange iconography on the main entrance's frieze harkens back to Templar time, with rabbits kissing oxen, dragons eating serpents eating birds, and so on. Inside, a cross from the Battle of Las Navas de Tolosa – the turning point in the Reconquista – is on display (1030–1330 and 1600–1900).

STAGE 9
Castro-Urdiales to Laredo

Start	Albergue de Peregrinos, Castro-Urdiales
Finish	Plaza Capuchín, Laredo
Distance	30km
Total ascent	410m
Total descent	410m
Difficulty	terrain: 3; waymarking: 3
Albergues de Peregrinos	Islares, El Pontarrón de Guriezo, Liendo

For those with the time and energy, today's longer route offers some of the greatest variety of the Norte's first half. From Castro-Urdiales to Islares, the route meanders along gentle hills with sweeping coastal vistas. After a short and unavoidable stretch along the N-634, the route turns inland, and the sea is replaced by craggy hilltops and wide green valleys. It is terrain that simultaneously uplifts and makes one feel very small! Finally, the route rises back out of the valley of Liendo, before depositing tired walkers on Laredo's sandy beach. A highway variant offers walkers a more direct alternative.

On leaving the albergue continue uphill, following a minor road. Keep straight on for 2.1km to **Allendelagua** (bar) then 2.2km to **Cerdigo**. Follow a footpath 3.1km through excellent coastal terrain to

ISLARES (7.4KM)

Bar/restaurant. **Albergue de Peregrinos** (8€, includes breakfast, 18 beds, kitchen, Calle Escuela, 643 311 758), **Camping Playa Arenillas** offers beds to pilgrims (10€, restaurant and grocery, 942 863 152), **Hotel Aisia Islares** (singles 60–80€, doubles 69–86€, 942 862 212).

16th-century **Iglesia de San Martín** and ruins of 16th-century **Hospital de la Vera Cruz.**

Rejoin N-634, and follow it 3.5km towards **El Pontarrón de Guriezo**. Before town, but immediately

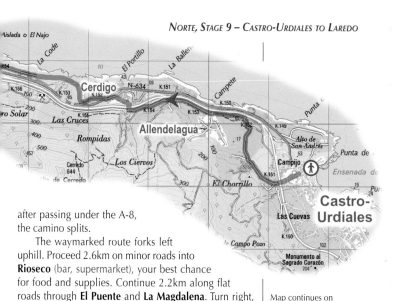

after passing under the A-8, the camino splits.

The waymarked route forks left uphill. Proceed 2.6km on minor roads into **Rioseco** (bar, supermarket), your best chance for food and supplies. Continue 2.2km along flat roads through **El Puente** and **La Magdalena**. Turn right, soon transitioning to dirt roads, which lead most of the way to Liendo. (This route is sufficiently marked, but note that yellow/white stripes do not correspond to the camino, although they sometimes overlap. Follow the yellow arrows, even when they have been crossed out by white/yellow Xs.) The walk spans 8.4km, but it is also beautiful, and far preferable to the highway alternative. Arrive in **Liendo**, where the new albergue is immediately after the church.

Map continues on page 89

The descent towards Liendo

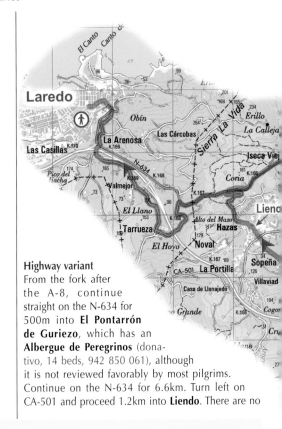

Highway variant
From the fork after the A-8, continue straight on the N-634 for 500m into **El Pontarrón de Guriezo**, which has an **Albergue de Peregrinos** (donativo, 14 beds, 942 850 061), although it is not reviewed favorably by most pilgrims. Continue on the N-634 for 6.6km. Turn left on CA-501 and proceed 1.2km into **Liendo**. There are no

LIENDO (16.7KM)

Bars, restaurants, supermarket. New **Albergue de Peregrinos** (8€, 16 beds, kitchen, W/D included, 682 074 723), **Posada La Torre De La Quintana** (doubles 68–86€, Barrio de Hazas 25, 942 677 439), **Hospedaje Valle de Liendo** (singles 30–45€, doubles 45–75€, Barrio Iseca Vieja 58, 942 677 581). Internet across from Bar Villamar.

A sprawling community set in a valley; dense fog is common in the morning.

waymarks, but this route is 4.9km shorter than the recommended approach.

Pass the church and keep straight on for 1.2km. Turn left on N-634. After 800m, turn left onto a single-lane road, through the suburb of Tarrueza. ▶ Remaining on the highway might be preferable, as this detour adds distance without saving you from pavement.

After 2.9km, veer right through the roundabout, away from the highway. Finally, descend many steps into town. After 800m, turn left

Accommodation in **Casa de Acogida de Tarrueza**, donativo, 15 beds, open April–October, kitchen, W/D, 686 655 204.

on Calle Emperador and proceed 300m into the Plaza Capuchín in

LAREDO (6KM)

All facilities. Two **Albergue Privados**: El Buen Pastor (13€, 20 beds, kitchen, Calle Fuente Fresnedo 1, 942 606 288) and Casa de la Trinidad (10€, 12 beds, kitchen, Calle San Francisco 24, 942 606 600), **Hotel El Cortijo** (singles 40–52€, doubles 62–68€, Calle González Gallego 3, 942 605 600), **Hostal Ramona** (offers significant discounts for pilgrims: singles 18–32€, doubles 26–45€, Calle Alameda de España 4, 942 607 189). Cyber café on corner of Calle Marqués de Comillas and Ignacio Ellacuría.

An important Roman site, known as Portus Luliobrigensium, and the location of a naval clash with the Celtiberians. The town grew around the Monastery of San Martín, receiving its charter and walls from Alfonso VIII. Allison Peers noted in 1928 that the church featured the following sign in three different locations: 'It is forbidden to spit in the House of God.' Today, it is Cantabria's biggest resort town. The 13th-century **Church of Santa María de la Asunción** features five naves. A gift from Charles V, two eagle-shaped lecterns, is on display.

Note that the next stage of the route involves taking the Laredo–Santoña ferry, which makes its first run at 0900; in the off-season, it might start later. Early risers might prefer sleeping in Santoña (see next section).

STAGE 10
Laredo to Guemes

Start	Plaza Capuchín, Laredo
Finish	Albergue de Peregrinos, Guemes
Distance	29.5km
Total ascent	280m
Total descent	200m
Difficulty	terrain: 2; waymarking: 4
Albergues de Peregrinos	Santoña, Colindres, Gama, Guemes

Start your morning on the beach in Laredo before catching the small ferry across to Santoña. After a short walk through town, return to the coast for one of the Norte's nicest stretches, crossing the Playa de Berria, cutting over the scrub-covered hill, and then continuing across yet another beach, the Playa de Trengandín. The second half of the day moves from sand to pavement, following quiet country roads until arriving at the finest albergue on the Camino del Norte. Alternatively, pilgrims can consider an inland variant, bypassing the ferry and the coast.

In Laredo's Plaza Capuchín, the camino splits. ▶ Look for small blue waymark stickers in front of Snack Bar Rivera, on Calle Jose Maria Pereda. Turn right from Plaza Capuchín on Calle Pereda. Cut diagonally through the next plaza and turn right towards the coast. Turn left on the beach promenade and keep straight on. At the peninsula's end, follow signs to the **Santoña ferry** (1.7€). The boat pulls directly up to the beach, close to a small shelter, and takes you to the center of

The recommended coastal option is described below; the inland variant is summarized at the end of the stage.

SANTOÑA (5.4KM)

All facilities. **Albergue Privado La Bilbaina** (private albergue, 10€, 24 beds, W/D, 942 661 952, Plaza San Antonio), **Youth hostel** (7.50€, 68 beds, meals available, W/D, @, Crta Santoña-Cicero, 942 662 008), **Hospedaje La Tortuga** (singles 48–70€, doubles 65–108€, Calle Juan de la Cosa 39, 942 683 035).

Map continues on
page 95

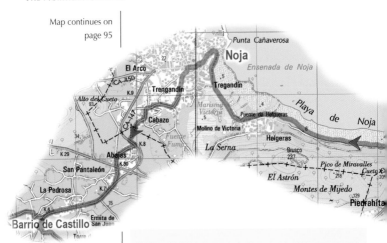

Another town with monastic origins, although only
the **Church of Nuestra Señora del Puerto** remains.
Santoña dates to the ninth century and was under
the abbot's control throughout the Middle Ages.
Columbus's *Santa María* was built here, and the
town was also the home of his second trip's cartog-
rapher, Juan de la Cosa. Towards the quay's end, a
large fort remains from the Peninsular War.

Continue straight from Santoña's dock, first along
Calle Santander and then Calle Cervantes. Cross two
roundabouts and the highway. After 900m, curve left on
Calle Sanjurjo. Keep straight on for 1.1km, passing the
prison, and join the CA-907. Proceed 1.9km to the end
of **Playa de Berria**; turn right onto the beach. It is possible, however, and probably preferable, to instead take the
second right after the prison and then turn left along the
beach, thus escaping the road.

At the end of the beach, climb the hill. Descend to
more impressive beaches; once again, it is possible to
proceed along the beach or the road into

NOJA (8.8KM)

All facilities. **Hotel Las Olas** (doubles 75–140€, Playa Trengandin 4, 942 630 036), **Hostería Los Laureles** (doubles 55–80€, Calle Las Viñas 14, 942 630 000), **Youth Hostel Noja Aventura** (11€, 70 beds, open April–October, kitchen, W/D, 609 043 397) located near the beach before town.

A modern beach town with a number of restaurants, great views, and a pleasant central plaza.

The beach leading to Noja

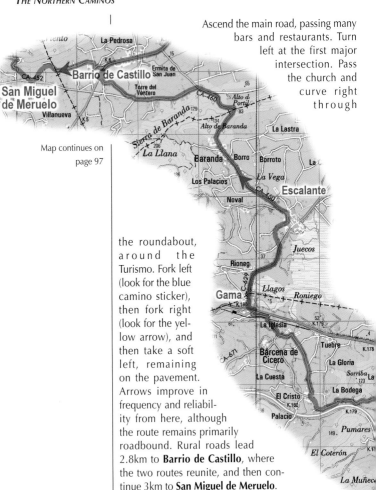

Ascend the main road, passing many bars and restaurants. Turn left at the first major intersection. Pass the church and curve right through

Map continues on page 97

the roundabout, around the Turismo. Fork left (look for the blue camino sticker), then fork right (look for the yellow arrow), and then take a soft left, remaining on the pavement. Arrows improve in frequency and reliability from here, although the route remains primarily roadbound. Rural roads lead 2.8km to **Barrio de Castillo**, where the two routes reunite, and then continue 3km to **San Miguel de Meruelo**.

Inland variant
This option avoids the ferry and has two very good albergues. Unfortunately, it is almost entirely on highways, not scenic, and longer. From the Plaza Capuchín

in Laredo, follow the N-634 3.6km to **Colindres**, which has all facilities, including an **Albergue de Peregrinos** (6€, 18 beds, Calle Heliodoro Fernández, 942 674 000). Keep straight on along the N-634 and then follow yellow arrows 2.4km to **Adal-Treto** (bar, hostal) and an additional 6.6km to **Gama**, which has bars, a supermarket, and an Albergue de Peregrinos (4€, 14 beds, keys from Bar El Yugo, 942 642 065). Take the **CA-148** for 1.7km to **Escalante** (all facilities), and then the CA-460 for 4.5km to Barrio de Castillo, rejoining the coastal route. Finally, follow rural roads 2.6km to **San Miguel de Meruelo**. This route is 1.4km longer than the coastal option.

SAN MIGUEL DE MERUELO (5.8KM)
Bars and grocery store located off-route.

After passing the Iglesia de San Miguel, proceed downhill and join CA-454. Towards the town's end, watch for a cement waymark in the sidewalk and turn left. Descend to the Puente de Solorga, after 2.1km. Cross the bridge, turn right, continue past the **Albergue de Meruelo** (private albergue, 12€, 36 beds, meals available, W/D, open March–October, 699 486 444), and keep straight on for 1.4km into **Bareyo**. Fork right through town, then turn left onto CA-447 towards **Camping Los Molinos** (bar/grocery).

95

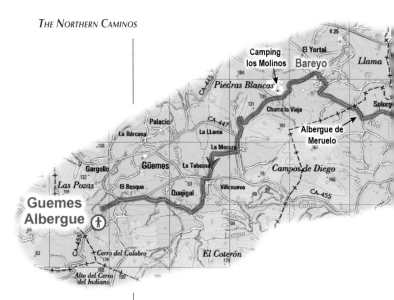

Follow a combination of highways and minor roads 5.3km towards Guemes. Turn left and proceed 800m to

GUEMES ALBERGUE (9.6KM)

The magnificent **Albergue La Cabaña del Abuelo Peuto** offers excellent hospitality (donativo, 68 beds (with overflow space on the floor), communal meals, 942 621 122). Make sure that your camino includes an overnight in this wonderful place. The hospitalero, Ernesto Bustio, is fascinating and generous, and the community has joined with him to care for pilgrims and other wanderers. The facilities are excellent, pilgrims are welcomed with cookies and drinks, and the post-dinner gathering often leads into storytelling and song.

The Guemes albergue

STAGE 11

Guemes to Santander

Start	Albergue de Peregrinos, Guemes
Finish	Albergue de Peregrinos, Santander
Distance	17km
Total ascent	80m
Total descent	160m
Difficulty	terrain: 1; waymarking: 4
Albergues de Peregrinos	Santander

Arrival in major cities generally presents a problem on pilgrimage, as industrial sprawl and unconstrained urban growth combine to produce unpleasant walking conditions that can span more than 10km. Santander offers a rare, enjoyable exception. From Guemes, the recommended route leads straight to the coastline, where a footpath proceeds along the cliff's edge, eventually delivering you straight into Somo. From there, the ferry takes you the rest of the way, offering a refreshing capstone to the walk. Pilgrims seeking a more direct route have the option to bypass the coast and follow the highway directly from Galizano to Somo.

Return to the CA-443 and continue straight for 3km. Turn left on the CA-141 and proceed 500m. Turn right on the CA-440 and proceed 500m into

GALIZANO (4KM)
Bar and grocery store. **Posada El Solar** (doubles 50–85€, meals, 942 505 292).

A pilgrim hospital was documented here in 1620.

From Galizano, there are two possible routes to Santander. The longer, more scenic approach (described here) is recommended, and the variant is described below. Turn right onto the CA-441 in Galizano, which leads 1km to the coast. From there, follow dirt roads and minor footpaths along the coastline all the way to **Somo**, enjoying incredible views. ◄ As you approach the center of Somo, leave the beach past a bar and proceed inland along Calle las Quebrantas. Turn right on Avenida Trasmiera and then fork right on Calle Peñas Blancas, joining the other route (description below).

Although there are no camino waymarks, the route is intuitive and a pleasure.

'Official camino' variant
Soon after passing the church in Galizano, follow yellow arrows back towards the highway. After 1.1km, merge with a bike track running parallel to the road. Keep straight on the CA-141 for 5.3km into **Somo**. As you approach

Map continues on page 100

Isla de Santa Marina

La Canaleta

29

Playa de los Tranquilos

Las Quebrantas

Los Abades

Pinar de Arna

Nuestra Señora de Latas

Somo

Arna

El Cruce de Ru

Las Ventas

K 13

K 14

CA 434

La Herrería

K 12

La Tejera

Puente de Somo

53

K 1

CA 443

Ría

Ribera del Mar

Casa Alta

the town, ignore waymarks calling for a left turn. This leads to an optional route, via El Astillero, that bypasses Santander entirely. Instead, follow signs towards the port, forking right downhill. Curve left through the intersection and then join Calle Peñas Blancas. Turn left at the waterfront; the ferry dock will be on your right after 600m. This route is 5.1km shorter than the recommended option.

SOMO (12.1KM)

Bars, restaurants, and grocery stores. **Hotel Alemar** (doubles from 40€, Calle Regunil 44, 942 510 601), **Hotel Las Dunas** (singles 40–60€, doubles 50–80€, Avda las Quebrantas 5, 942 510 040).

A comfortable port town, Somo might be worth a little quiet time before bustling Santander.

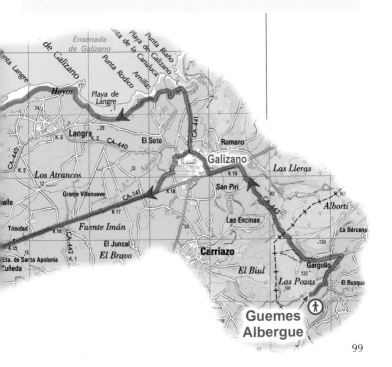

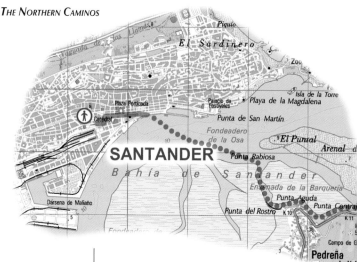

Take the ferry to
Santander, which runs every half-hour
and costs 2.70€. From Santander's dock, turn
left along the waterfront, watching for cement waymarks
in the sidewalk. Turn right, crossing into the Jardines de
Pereda. Turn left and proceed out the far side onto Calle
Somorrostro. Pass the cathedral, descend the steps, and
continue straight on Calle Emilio Pino, ignoring conflicting waymarks. Ascend a flight of steps to Calle Rúa
Mayor and turn left. The albergue is on your left.

SANTANDER (0.8KM)

Albergue de Peregrinos (8€, includes breakfast, 40 beds, kitchen, W/D,
opens 1500, credenciáles, Calle Ruamayor 9–11, 942 219 747), **Plaza
Pombo B&B** (doubles 35–80€, triples 65–95€, includes breakfast, Calle
Hernan Cortes 25, 942 212 950), **Pensión Plaza** (singles 30-38€, doubles
40–61€, triples 57–73€, 942 212 967, c/Cádiz 13), **Hostal Cabo Mayor**
(singles 35–65€, doubles 45–65€, Calle Cadíz 1, 942 211 181), **Hostal del
Carmen** (singles 29–39€, doubles 39–55€, triples 57–75€, c/San Fernando
48, 942 230 190). Internet in many places, including Ciberlope (Calle Lope
de Vega).

Santander's Palacio de la Magdalena

The third major city on the Camino del Norte and the capital of Cantabria. Founded by the Romans, it became a major medieval port, exporting wine, olives, fish, and wool. Santander emerged as an important Catholic destination, as pilgrims gained indulgences by visiting the relics of Sts Emeterio and Celedonio. Like San Sebastián, Santander gained prominence for beached royalty – in this case, Queen Isabel II chose to summer here in the 1860s, hoping the sea air would improve her health. After World War I, it became *the* fashionable summer spot for Madrileños.

Santander knows disasters. In 1893, a ship full of dynamite exploded in the harbor, killing 500 and destroying the surrounding area. A fire broke out in 1941, starting in the Archbishop's Palace and consuming much of the old center. The result is a modern waterfront, certainly enjoyable but perhaps lacking in atmosphere. Most vacationers and locals make a beeline for the Sardinero district, which features two excellent beaches and the Belle Epoque casino.

The **cathedral** is comprised of two 13th-century Gothic churches. The upper church has a 14th-century cloister that was rebuilt after the 1941 fire. The lower church of El Santísimo Cristo serves as the crypt and contains the original furnace box that held the patron saints' skulls. They have since been encased in silver and are now carried in festival processions. A glass floor covers Roman remains.

The **Museum of Prehistory and Archeology** holds a collection of prehistoric artifacts from across the region. The highlights are copies of regional cave paintings and a small collection of Roman *stellae* (T–Sa 1000–1300 and 1600–1900; Su 1100–1400). In addition, the **Museo de Bella Artes** houses a collection of European art from the last five centuries, headlined by Goya's portrait of King Fernando VII (Calle Rubio 3, M–F 1015–1300 and 1730–2100; Sa 1000–1300).

STAGE 12
Santander to Santillana del Mar

Start	Albergue de Peregrinos, Santander
Finish	Albergue Municipal, Santillana del Mar
Distance	32.5km
Total ascent	180m
Total descent	100m
Difficulty	terrain: 1; waymarking: 4
Albergues de Peregrinos	Santa Cruz de Bezana, Boo de Piélagos, Requejada, Santillana del Mar

While the walk into Santander is lovely, the same cannot be said of the exit. Indeed, this is one of the drearier legs of the Camino del Norte – flat, paved, and with little to see. Two significant shortcuts are recommended, cutting unnecessary kilometers from the official route, in order to reach Santillana del Mar sooner. Santillana's perfect medieval center and nearby prehistoric cave art make the trek well worthwhile.

Turn left out of the albergue and proceed uphill on Calle Alta. The route generally proceeds in a straight line out of

town, following N-611. The sidewalk waymarks (bronze scallop shells) point back towards the cathedral until you exit Santander; walk against the waymarks, heading west

Horses in the countryside outside Santander

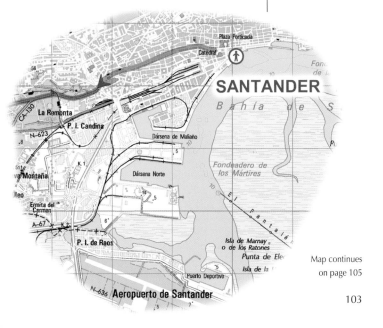

Map continues on page 105

from the cathedral and out of town. After 4.8km, arrive in **Peñacastillo** (bar) and turn right off the N-611.

Walk 200m, cross the railroad, and turn left after it. Follow dirt tracks to the CA-301, continuing 3.1km into

SANTA CRUZ DE BEZANA (8.1KM)

Bar, grocery store. **Albergue La Santa Cruz** (donativo, 14 beds, communal meals, 659 178 806), **Albergue Nimon** (12€, includes breakfast, 10 beds, kitchen, 635 451 714, c/Ramón Ramírez 2, keys from Cafetería Nimon). **Hotel Alcamino**, soon after town, offers a special deal for pilgrims: single room, dinner, and breakfast for 42–59€, depending on the season (942 020 659).

The **Church of Santa Cruz** is worth a quick visit, if open.

Follow Avenida de la Mompia for 1.6km. Turn left on Avenida de los Condes and proceed 700m, over the railroad. Fork right through a major roundabout and follow the CA-304 for 900m. Fork right on minor road, re-cross the railroad, and arrive at the train station in

BOO DE PIÉLAGOS (5.6KM)

Albergue Piedad (12€, 16 beds, breakfast and W/D included, kitchen, 680 620 073), **Hostería de Boo** (Barrio San José 1, 942 586 231). FEVE station.

The next section poses a dilemma. The nearby river, Ría de Mogro, looming just past the town, was traditionally a minor concern for pilgrims. A ferry shuttled walkers from one side to the other, and while the boat operators were irreputable fellows, no unnecessary kilometers were added to the trek. Today, the ferry is long gone and the nearest pedestrian-friendly bridge is 6km

Map continues on page 107

south, in Puente Arce. There are two options to consider, along with a third that is no longer recommended. The first is the 'official' camino route, described below.

If you don't need to walk every step of the way, we suggest taking the train across the bridge, from the Boo train station to Mogro. Trains run every 30 minutes or so on weekdays and hourly on weekends, and the total journey just takes two minutes. Leaving the Mogro station, turn left and yellow arrows immediately reappear.

The third option is to walk across the railroad bridge. To do this, follow the camino out of Boo, proceeding along a minor road parallel to the railroad line. As the road curves left, away from the tracks, 600m after Boo's station, transfer from the camino to the railroad. From here, carefully follow the tracks across the bridge, arriving at the Mogro train station after 900m. Pass through the parking lot, past a bar, and then turn left. This route is 1.5km, compared to over 9km for the 'official' camino route. However, whereas five years ago when this approach was encouraged by locals, it is now actively

discouraged. Beyond the safety concern, bridge-crossers may be fined by the police.

'Official' camino route

The yellow arrows curve south from Boo towards **Puente Arce**, following suburban roads, before turning right back around on the other side of the river and giving back all of the distance just earned. The 16th-century bridge and surrounding neighborhoods are pleasant, with bar/restaurants and a supermarket available, but all told, the walk is a frustrating 9.3km to the **Mogro** train station.

The two routes converge along the CA-232, the highway running in front of the Mogro train station. Those coming from Puente Arce will turn left uphill along a footpath, soon after passing under the A-67. Those walking from the train station will fork right uphill on the CA-322. Both arrive at the small ermita, where another decision looms.

The authors recommend disregarding the waymarks and continuing straight on the CA-322,

Map continues on page 109

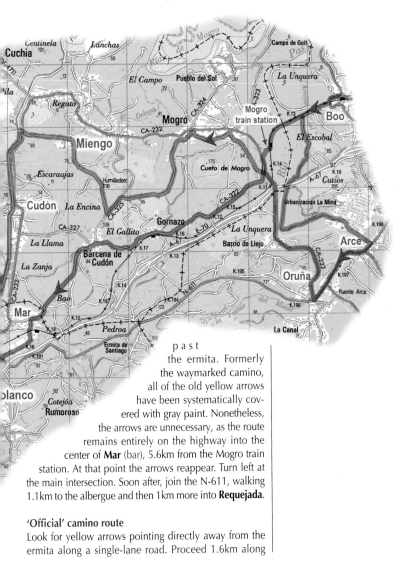

past the ermita. Formerly the waymarked camino, all of the old yellow arrows have been systematically covered with gray paint. Nonetheless, the arrows are unnecessary, as the route remains entirely on the highway into the center of **Mar** (bar), 5.6km from the Mogro train station. At that point the arrows reappear. Turn left at the main intersection. Soon after, join the N-611, walking 1.1km to the albergue and then 1km more into **Requejada**.

'Official' camino route

Look for yellow arrows pointing directly away from the ermita along a single-lane road. Proceed 1.6km along country roads into the minor town of Mogro and then over minor hills towards the Río Saja Besaya, turning left before reaching it. Pass through **Cudón** (bar) 4.6km later and follow the pipeline trail. On the approach to **Polanco** the camino splits. Turn left for the albergue or continue straight for the center of **Requejada**. If you stay in the albergue, you will not have to backtrack to this point. Instead, follow the N-611 and rejoin the camino soon after. Those continuing to Requejada will proceed parallel to the river, turn left uphill, cross the railroad, and continue into the town center. This route is 2.4km longer than the alternative.

REQUEJADA (9.2KM)

Bars, grocery store, bakery. **Albergue de Peregrinos Clara Campoamor** (5€, 12 beds, 942 583 708 (keys from Bar El Puerto)), **Albergue Regato de las Anguilas** in neighboring Polanco (4€, 6 beds, keys from house A-19, 50m down the highway).

Follow the N-611 to

BARREDA (1.4KM)

Bars, supermarket. **Hotel Husa Wuppertal** (doubles 47–73€, Avda Solvay 99, 942 803 858).

St Francis is said to have stayed in the House of Calderón on his rumored pilgrimage to Santiago.

Turn right and proceed 800m, crossing the railroad and river, then fork right through the roundabout. Curve left 300m later, following the CA-340 through the hills. After 4.5km, turn left to stay in the **Albergue Privado Arco Iris** (9€, 60 beds, meals, W/D, 942 897 946), located on the outskirts of **Queveda**. Otherwise, keep straight on for 2.6km into Santillana. After passing the church, turn left into Museo Jesús Otero. The albergue is located behind it.

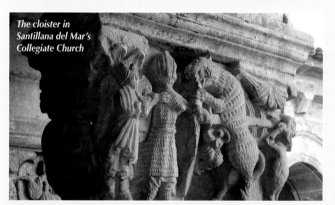

The cloister in Santillana del Mar's Collegiate Church

SANTILLANA DEL MAR (8.2KM)

Many bars and restaurants, small grocery store. **Albergue Municipal Jesús Otero** (6€, 16 beds, opens 1600, 942 840 198) located behind the museum. **Casona Solar de Hidalgos** has a dorm set up for pilgrims (15€ August, 12€ July/September, 10€ rest of year, private rooms available, Plaza de Santo Domingo 5, 942 818 387). **Camping Santillana**, located at the end of town, has bungalows available to pilgrims (10€, restaurant and grocery, W/D, 942

818 250). **Hospedaje Santillana** (singles 30–60€, doubles 40–70€, Calle Los Hornos 14, 942 818 803), **Casa del Organista** (singles 49–76€, doubles 60–92€, Calle Los Hornos 4, 942 840 352). Internet in Museo Jesús Otero.

One of the most picturesque stopping points on the Camino del Norte, this wonderfully preserved medieval village is all cut rock and tourist kiosks. In the Middle Ages, Santillana experienced great financial success thanks to wool and linen production, making nobles out of its residents. It has since enjoyed a string of celebrity residents and visitors, including the Marqués de Santillana, the Archduchess of Austria, and even Jean-Paul Sartre, who called it the most beautiful village in Spain. It also gained acclaim as pica-resque hero Gil Blas's home. Its transformation into a popular tourist stop is quite recent. Only 20 years ago cows filled the ground floor of local homes; now souvenir shops have taken their place.

The 12th-century **Collegiate Church** is a must-see. The cloisters are spectacular, finely crafted Romanesque works. One section even has pre-served its paint. The impressive capitals depict biblical and hunting scenes. Inside the church, highlights include the altar made of Mexican silver and the sepulcher of St Juliana, who was martyred by Diocletian and whose remains have been protected in Santillana since the sixth century. That said, the church's back wall does not inspire a great deal of confidence.

The famous **Altamira Caves**, a UNESCO World Heritage site featuring Paleolithic cave art, are located 2km from the town center. The real cave has been closed to tourists, but a near-perfect replica has been built to accom-modate visitors. It is well worth a visit, but reservations are necessary (T–Sa 0930–2000; Su 0930–1500; shorter hours in offseason).

STAGE 13

Santillana del Mar to Comillas

Start	Albergue Municipal, Santillana del Mar
Finish	Albergue de Peregrinos, Comillas
Distance	23km
Total ascent	320m
Total descent	380m
Difficulty	terrain: 3; waymarking: 2
Albergues de Peregrinos	Cóbreces, Comillas

While you will rarely escape pavement today, there is much to enjoy. Grassy fields yield sprawling vistas, broken periodically by church towers. San Martín de Cigüenza is a pleasant surprise – a small town with a stunning church and peaceful river. The next stop, Cóbreces, lights up with color, a true novelty after so many stone buildings. Finally, Comillas signals your return to the coast, and features some of the most impressive architecture on the Camino del Norte.

▸ From the albergue, walk to the Parador hotel, located in the Plaza de Ramón Pelayo. With your back to the Parador, proceed straight away from town and past the camping on Calle Hornos. The route transitions from paved roads to dirt tracks, taking you 2.4km to **Arroyo** (bar), 1km to **Oreña** (bar, **Hospedaje Oreña** (doubles 35–50€, 657 339 794)), and then 2.4km to **Caborredondo** (bar). Keep straight on the CA-352 through town, cross the CA-131, and fork right on a country road. Descend into

Waymarks are limited in Santillana.

SAN MARTÍN DE CIGÜENZA (9KM)

Bar. **Posada Cigüenza** (doubles 50–70€, 942 890 759).

The 18th-century **Church of San Martín** features a Baroque façade, comprised of two massive symmetrical towers flanking a central arch.

The route outlined below is now labeled the 'alternate route,' while a new 'official route' leads pilgrims to the coast, passes a bar in Playa Luaña, on the edge of Cóbreces, and then continues along the beach and a minor lane to Comillas.

On leaving Cigüenza, rejoin the CA-353 after 1.4km, and follow the highway 1.2km to Cóbreces. Before town, turn right onto a minor road. This final 1.2km stretch is a bit wiggly, with frequent turns, a sharp descent, and an abrupt climb. Finally, return to the CA-353 in

CÓBRECES (3.8KM)

Bar, grocery store, bakery. **Albergue de Peregrinos** in the Cistercian Abbey (5€, 30 beds, 942 725 017), **Posada Las Mañanitas** (beds 20€, Calle Antoñan 88, 942 725 238), **Albergue Privado El Pino** (15€, includes breakfast, 12 beds, open April–October, kitchen, 620 437 962, c/El Pino 1).

A comfortable stopping point, dominated by two large pastel-colored buildings – the red **Church of St Peter ad Vincula** and sky-blue **Cistercian abbey of Viaceli**. The former is a striking Neo-Gothic structure with two prominent towers and an octagonal dome. A monument to pilgrims stands behind it.

Map continues on page 114

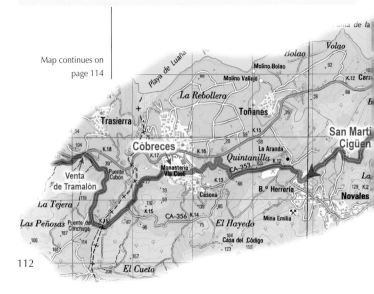

The abbey, one of Spain's first concrete buildings, is distinctive for its rows of pointed windows. Those staying in the monastery's albergue are invited to evening vespers. All facilities are located off the camino; from the CA-353, turn left for the grocery, and turn right for everything else.

Cross the CA-353, pass behind the church, and transition to medieval tracks, which make for a very pleasant 3.7km into tiny **Venta de Tramalón** (bar). In Venta, briefly join the CA-131 before promptly forking left off it. Dirt roads and a paved pedestrian track lead 1.3km to a camping/bar and then continue 600m into

LA IGLESIA (5.6KM)
Bar, **Youth Hostel Gargantia** (5.6€, 40 beds, meals available, 942 207 407).

Keep straight on for 1km to the monastery of **Pando** and then 1.1km to the village of **Concha**. In Concha, turn left on Calle Mayor, turn right at the street's end, and

then turn left. The minor country road quickly becomes a dirt track. Proceed 1.4km to the CA-131. Turn left 200m later onto Calle Calvo Sotelo. Continue 700m into the pedestrian center. At the

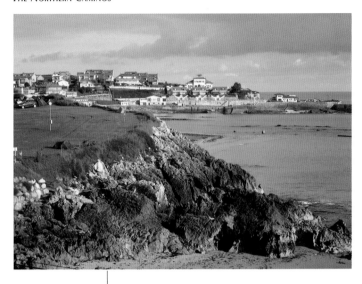

The approach to Comillas	T-junction, turn right uphill 100m for the albergue or left to continue through

COMILLAS (4.5KM)

All facilities. **Albergue de Peregrinos** (5€, 20 beds, kitchen, open April–September, Calle Barrio la Peña, 942 720 033), **Pensión La Aldea** (doubles 35–50€, Calle La Aldea 5, 942 721 046), **Hostal Esmeralda** (singles 40–60€, doubles 50–80€, Calle Antonio López 7, 942 720 097).

Comillas hit its stride in the 19th century, when the Barcelonan aristocracy started summering here – and brought their architects along. The local shipping magnate, Antonio López, made a fortune from the Cuban slave trade, bought the title of Marquis de Comillas, and married the daughter of Barcelona's richest man. With money to burn, the marquis became Antoní Gaudí's primary patron, and Gaudí left his mark in Comillas.

The **Capricho de Gaudí** was entirely his own creation. Built as the marquis's summerhouse, it is a stunning combination of iron, brick, and pottery, displaying both Spanish and Arabic influences. Sunflowers stand out as the central image on this surrealist structure. Gaudí assisted with the general design and furnishings of the **Palacio de Sobrellano**, which is more properly attributed to Joan Mortorell. An impressive Neo-Gothic building, this dominates the left hill as you follow the camino out of town. The interior is considered even finer than the exterior, particularly the grand salon. Regular tours run daily (3€). Gaudí also contributed to the **Capilla-Pantéon**, which holds the crypts of the marquis's two sons, designing the pews, confessionals, and royal seats.

Opposite the Palacio de Sobrellano is the equally impressive **Pontifical Seminary**, which was founded in 1883 for the training of priests and quickly was acclaimed for its music school and choir. Sadly, this building has remained vacant since 1964, when the papal university was moved to Madrid. Check out the gargoyles carved over the main stairway.

Although easily reached today, Comillas enjoyed its isolation for many years. Its residents reveled in that timelessness, noting: 'Comillas will be Comillas / For ever and ever. Amen.'

STAGE 14
Comillas to Colombres

Start	Albergue de Peregrinos, Comillas
Finish	Central Plaza, Colombres
Distance	28.5km
Total ascent	440m
Total descent	345m
Difficulty	terrain: 3; waymarking: 2
Albergues de Peregrinos	San Vicente de la Barquera, Serdio, Colombres

The last stage in Cantabria, this is a day of great variety, mixing roads and trails, small villages and a major town (San Vicente de la Barquera), and several river crossings. With a wide range of possible stopping points – for food, drink, or sleep – you can break this day up in a lot of different ways. Arrival in Colombres marks your entry into Asturias, a region that feels a little more rugged and wild than the others on this route. Enjoy the evening in your choice of several different types of pilgrim-friendly accommodation.

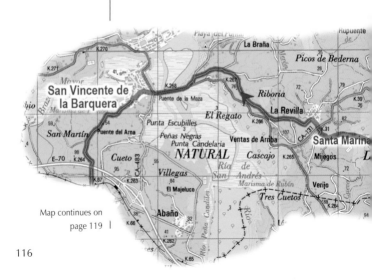

Map continues on page 119

Keep straight on the CA-135 for 2.8km, passing Comillas's many great architectural sights as you leave. Cross the Ría de la Rabia and continue straight on the highway. After 1.1km, shortly after rejoining the highway, waymarks call for a sharp left in front of a cemetery. This detour leads abruptly downhill to an ermita and almost immediately back up to the highway. Consider this an optional jaunt. Proceed 800m to

SANTA ANA (4.7KM)

Bar, **Posada El Teju** (doubles 30–50€, 942 709 639).

Keep straight on for 1.7km to the **Santa Marina golf course**. Cross the small bridge and turn left. Leave the golf course, forking left at the exit. ▶ Fork right across the CA-131. Proceed 4.6km along minor roads, crossing a modest hill before descending towards San Vicente. Join the N-634 and cross the Ría de San Vicente. Turn right immediately after the bridge for bars/restaurants. Proceed

For **Albergue VA Aventure** (10–12€, 60 beds, W/D, meals available, 942 712 075) fork right.

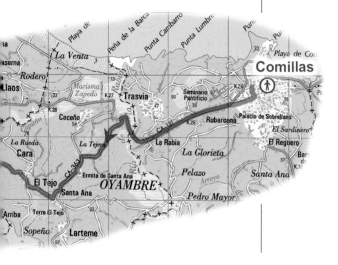

117

uphill to find the albergue or continue walking. 300m later, the waymarks split. Fork right for the albergue in

SAN VICENTE DE LA BARQUERA (6.6KM)

All facilities. **Albergue de Peregrinos El Galeón** (10€, includes breakfast, 46 beds, W/D, @, Calle Alta 12, 942 715 349), **Pensión Liebana** (doubles 27–42€, Calle Ronda 2, 942 710 211), **Hotel Cantón** (doubles 35–70€, Calle Padre Ángel 8, 942 711 560).

Another fishing/resort town, San Vicente is dominated by the ruins of its eighth-century **castle** (1.2€, T–Su 1100–1400 and 1700–2000). Although the town boomed in the Middle Ages, it was devastated by fires; its prominent Jewish Quarter was wiped out in 1483, and a 1636 blaze devoured most of what remained. The 13th-century Gothic church of **Santa María de los Angeles** holds the tomb of Inquisitor Antonio del Corro. The statue of del Corro is regarded as one of the finest pieces of Renaissance funerary art. Classical music aficionados will recognize Schubert's 'Ave María', played in the church's bell tower every quarter-hour (exhausted locals suggest this was the work of a town enemy).

The sixth-century Monastery of Santo Toribio is said to house the largest piece of the True Cross. The pilgrimage route is roughly 55km and there are albergues along the way.

Proceed uphill from the bridge, along the Camino de las Calzadas. Cross the A-8 expressway and railroad tracks before reaching a T-junction in **La Acebosa**, 2.2km from San Vicente. Turn left, leaving the road soon after, and wrap around the hillside before joining the CA-843. In tiny **Hortigal**, 2.6km later, waymarks for the local pilgrimage to Santo Toribio de Liébana call for a left. ◄ Ignore these and continue along the highway for 1.9km to the 12th-century **Torre de Estrada**. Turn right and proceed 1km along minor roads into

SERDIO (7.7KM)

Bar, **Albergue de Peregrinos** (5€, 16 beds, kitchen, 619 044 026), **Posada La Torre** (doubles 42–55€, 942 718 462).

Pesués

Nansa

El

Muñorrc

La Tesna

Fork right at the church and keep straight on for 3km. Turn right on the CA-181 and proceed 800m into **Pesués** (bars). Turn left, cross the Ría de Tina Menor, and turn left again, winding uphill through a small neighborhood. After 1km, cross the N-634 and transition soon after to a difficult 1.4km following footpaths with thick brambles and a steep, rocky downhill. Pass under the A-8

Departing San Vicente de la Barquera

Map continues on page 120

expressway, cross straight through the next roundabout, and then follow the main road as it curves right into

UNQUERA (7.5KM)

FEVE train station. **Hostal Río Deva** (singles 19–29€, doubles 32–38€, Calle San Felipe Neri, 942 717 157), **El Rincón de Bustio**, located across the river (doubles 80–100€, 985 412 525).

A small town with few sights, but the best opportunity to resupply between San Vicente and Llanes.

Continue straight across the Río Deva, arriving in the autonomous region of Asturias. Cross the highway and climb an easily missed cement track. Pass a private albergue before sloping downhill into the central plaza in

COLOMBRES (2.1KM)

Bars, restaurants and supermarkets. **Albergue Privado El Cantu** (12€, 120 beds, meals, 985 413 026), **Hotel San Angel**, located on the N-634 on the way out of town, offers special pilgrim prices (985 412 000).

While Indianos architecture – a style popular with locals who made fortunes in the New World – is prevalent throughout Asturias, Colombres features some exemplary cases of it. Of particular interest is **La Quinta Guadalupe**, a marvelous blue edifice that houses the **Museo de la Emigración**.

STAGE 15
Colombres to Llanes

Start	Central Plaza, Colombres
Finish	Albergue La Estación, Llanes
Distance	23.5km
Total ascent	180m
Total descent	285m
Difficulty	terrain: 2; waymarking: 4
Albergues de Peregrinos	Buelna, Pendueles, Llanes

From Colombres to Pendueles, the camino largely follows paved roads, including one prolonged stretch on the N-634. After Pendueles, however, the route leaves the camino and joins the E-9 long-distance footpath, and remains near the coast for the remainder of the day, not always within view but certainly close enough to feel the sea breeze. With natural marvels vying for your attention – the Picos de Europa to your left and the sea to your right – it's easy to lose track of the route, so be careful! Llanes is the trendiest, hippest stop along this stretch of the Norte, with many highlights to enjoy.

With your back to the church at Colombres, walk out of the back-right corner of the plaza, fork right, and then turn right at the next roundabout, proceeding along Calle del Badalan. When the road makes a 90° curve to the right, continue straight along a footpath. After a short off-road stretch, join the N-634, 1.9km from Colombres. Follow the highway 1.1km into **La Franca** (bar, **Albergue Renacer** (14€, includes breakfast and W/D, 10 beds, 678 169 939), **Camping Playa de la Franca** (cabins available for pilgrims (10€, 985 412 222)). ▸

Fork left after town, eventually transitioning to a footpath. Descend to a small river, then climb the other side. The camino is interrupted here by signs announcing a provisional detour. Turn right along a dirt road, backtracking for a short stretch before rejoining the N-634 after 2.2km. Turn left onto the highway. Keep straight on for

A new coastal route alternate was waymarked and established in summer 2013, leaving the highway in La Franca and proceeding off-road to Pendueles, bypassing Buelna.

In Asturias, the waymarkers indicate the direction you should turn based on where the lines in the shell converge. But this is reversed when you reach Galicia!

2.4km into **Buelna** (bar, **Albergue de Peregrinos** (15€, includes dinner and breakfast, 60 beds, W/D, 985 411 218)), then fork right on a minor road towards Pendueles.

The 1.8km walk to central Pendueles is not well marked. Proceed under train tracks and turn right at the scallop shell. Turn left at a yellow arrow. ◀ Stay on the same road as it curves through the scattered houses, until it finally arrives at the town's church. Turn right, following the road as it curves left, finally reaching the center of

PENDUELES (9.4KM)

Bar, grocery store, **Albergue Aves de Paso** (donativo, communal meals, W/D included, reservations accepted, open March–November, 617 160 810), **Albergue Casa Flor** (7€, 21 beds, W/D, 650 431 982). **Bar Castiellu** has rooms available (doubles 25€, 639 881 604).

Only the church remains from the **Monastery of St Aciscio**.

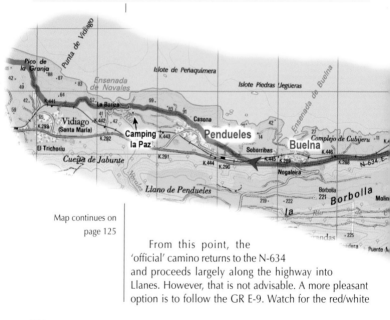

Map continues on page 125

From this point, the 'official' camino returns to the N-634 and proceeds largely along the highway into Llanes. However, that is not advisable. A more pleasant option is to follow the GR E-9. Watch for the red/white

*A bridge en route to
Bufones de Arenillas*

stripes, which appear near the bar/grocery in Pendueles, and turn accordingly.

This route leads towards the coast, almost exclusively along dirt roads. Walk 1.4km to **Camping La Paz** and its tiny beach, then an additional 3.7km to

BUFONES DE ARENILLAS (5.1KM)

An impressive geological feature: cracks have formed within the rock cliff, allowing for eruptions of seawater as high as 20m when the waves are strong. Proceed with caution through the *bufones* and remain on the trails.

Follow the footpath for 3.4km. Join a paved road in **Andrín** (bar, **La Casona de Andrín**, doubles 70–80€, 985 417 250). Cross the small town, ascend to the highway, and turn right, passing a scenic viewpoint. From here, you have two options – a highway approach or a more scenic route along the GR E-9 (see below). The former follows the LLN-2 into **Cue** (bar), then turns right along the LLN-1 towards the beach, 2.6km from Andrín. Turn left, and keep straight on for 2.6km along the coast to the outskirts of **Llanes**. Turn right onto the AS-263, cross the small river, and curve left. After 300m, turn left on LLN-7 towards the train station. **Albergue La Estación** is on your right.

GR E-9 variant

From the scenic viewpoint above Andrín, follow the red/white stripes back across the highway and proceed 3km to the **Ermita del Cristo del Camino**. Turn right and return to paved roads. After 750m, turn left for Albergue La Portilla, or continue straight into **Llanes**. 850m later, rejoin the other route on the AS-263. This route is 600m shorter than the highway approach.

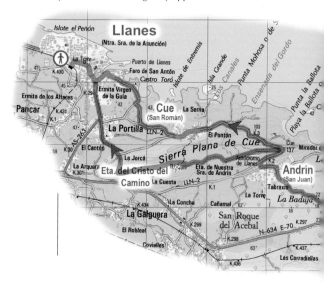

LLANES (8.9KM)

All facilities and a wide range of accommodation are available. **Albergue La Estación** sets aside a couple of rooms for pilgrims and is centrally located (13.50–19.50€, 34 beds, open March–December, kitchen, W/D, 985 401 458). In addition, Llanes has two other youth hostels: **Albergue Juvenil Juventudes** (13€, 70 beds, meals, Calle Celso Amieva 15, 985 400 770) and **Albergue La Portilla** (15€, 48 beds, open March–September, located in 'La Portilla' neighborhood outside the center, 616 460 183). **Pensión Los Pinos** (doubles 40–70€, Avda Las Gaviotas 28, 985 401 116), **Hotel Posada del Rey** (singles 35–85€, doubles 50–103€, pilgrim discounts, Calle Mayor, 985 401 332). Internet at Ciber Traveling (Calle Genaro Riestra 2).

A lively town, popular with tourists thanks to its wonderful location, nestled between the coast and the Picos de Europa. Llanes has enjoyed a long history, as evidenced by the surviving remnants of its 800-year-old city walls. The town celebrates two major events from the 16th century with commemorative plaques: the visit of Emperor Charles V in 1517 and the contribution of 65 men and three ships to the Spanish Armada. Beaches are the major attraction, but find time for a look at the **Cubos de la Memoria**, which honor the city's seafaring tradition, located in the port. These are visible on the walk from Cue.

STAGE 16
Llanes to Ribadesella

Start	Albergue La Estación, Llanes
Finish	Church of Santa María Magdalena, Ribadesella
Distance	30km
Total ascent	150m
Total descent	160m
Difficulty	terrain: 1; waymarking: 2
Albergues de Peregrinos	Villahormes, Piñeres de Pría

Today provides more evidence that monastery builders had excellent taste in building sites. First in Celorio and then again near the Playa de San Antolín monasteries lurk within range of beaches, close enough to enjoy the fresh sea air but with sufficient distance to allow for grassy fields and a quiet sentry of tall trees. The latter monastery is particularly intriguing, abandoned and yet accessible to the curious pilgrim. The rest of the walk offers a mix of road and trail, small villages and open countryside, and generally flat conditions that make for easy going. Ribadesella promises more great beaches and spectacular prehistoric cave paintings.

Map continues on page 129

Keep straight on the AS-263 for 1km. Fork left away from the highway, walk 1.7km, and rejoin it in

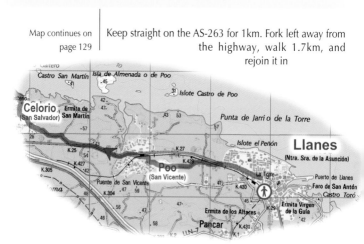

PLAYA DE POO (2.7KM)

Bar, grocery store. **Albergue Llanes Playa de Poo** (11–15€, 26 beds, W/D, @, Calle de la Playa 36, 985 403 181).

Continue on the AS-263. Fork right, near the km25 sign. Proceed into

CELORIO (2.3KM)

Bars/restaurants, grocery store, pharmacy. **Pensión Costa Verde** (doubles 20–35€, 648 277 347), **Hotel Moran Playa** (singles 40–65€, doubles 50–90€, Avda de la Playa 5, 985 401 107).

The **Monastery of San Salvador** had a pilgrim refuge in the 12th century.

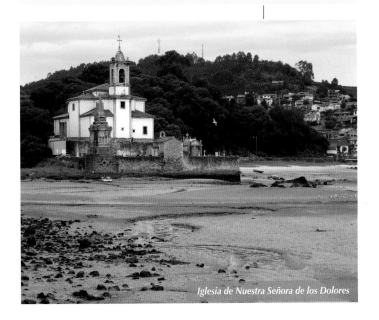

Iglesia de Nuestra Señora de los Dolores

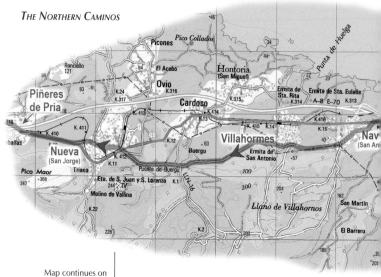

Map continues on
page 131

Turn left along the beach, cross
the promenade, and walk across a sec-
ond beach. Turn left after the bar. Keep straight on for
1.6km into **Barro** (bars). After crossing the Ría de Barro,
and before reaching the picturesque **Iglesia de Nuestra
Señora de los Dolores**, turn left onto a footpath. After
2km turn left at a T-junction, away from the red/white
markings. Proceed 2.2km, passing the ruined **Monasterio
de San Antolín** and the beach of the same name. Cross
under the expressway and follow a mix of single lane
and dirt roads, walking 1.9km through **Naves** (bar) and
1.1km to **Villahormes** (**Albergue Privado Punta Pestaña**
(10–15€, 24 beds, W/D, 671 692 095)). Keep straight on
for 3.1km more, descend to the AS-263, and cross to the
bar's right into

NUEVA (11.9KM)

Bars/restaurants, grocery stores. **Pensión San Jorge** (doubles 40–50€, pilgrim
discounts, 985 410 285), **Hotel Cuevas del Mar** (doubles 50–70€, Plaza de
Laverde Ruiz, 985 410 377).

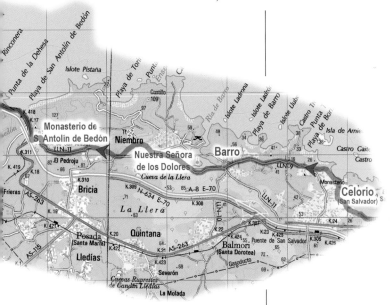

Rejoin the highway, cross under the expressway, and continue straight into

PIÑERES DE PRÍA (2.3KM)

Bar (no food). **Casa Rural La Llosa de Cosme** (10€, 8 beds, kitchen, W/D, 609 861 373), **Albergue Casa Rectoral** (5€, July–August only, kitchen).

Join a dirt road running parallel to the railroad and expressway. After 2.5km, make a hard right on the road, then a hard left, leading uphill towards the **Iglesia de Pría**. Pass through tiny **Cuerres** (**Albergue Casa Belén** (donativo, 8 beds, communal meals, open May–October)) 1.3km later (which has a 15th-century pilgrims' fountain), cross the railroad after 300m, and follow the road for 4.5km. Join the AS-263, then turn left soon after, passing a soccer field before returning to the highway. After

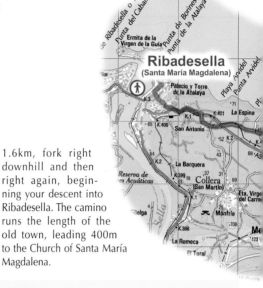

1.6km, fork right downhill and then right again, beginning your descent into Ribadesella. The camino runs the length of the old town, leading 400m to the Church of Santa María Magdalena.

RIBADESELLA (10.6KM)

All facilities. **Youth Hostel Roberto Frasinelli** (12.50–14.50€, 50 beds, meals, W/D, @, Calle Ricardo Cangas, 985 861 105), **Pensión Arbidel** (singles 30–40€, doubles 40–60€, triples 60–85€, Calle Oscura 1, 985 860 141), **Hotel Marina** (singles 35–58€, doubles 55–83€, triples 65–98€, Calle Gran Via 36, 985 860 050). Internet at Unitec (Plaza Nueva). The nearest Albergue de Peregrinos is 5.3km further on, in San Esteban de Leces.

Conquered by Romans during Augustus's rule, Ribadesella traditionally marked the border between the Astures and Cantrabras tribes. Today's town, however, was founded in 1270 by Alfonso X and developed around the whaling industry, with a whaling factory constructed on the beach. Like other strategically significant locations, Ribadesella suffered badly during the Peninsular War, the Carlist Wars, and the Spanish Civil War. The highlight of this port city, the **Tito Bustillo Caves**, echoes the region's more distant past. Unlike Santillana del Mar's Altamira Caves, where tourists can visit only a replica cave, these are the real thing. Regular guided tours lead deep underground, through the stalactites, to a room filled with paintings 15,000–20,000 years old depicting deer, horses, bison, and more. Reservations are essential (7€, open April–October, 1000–1700, 985 861 255).

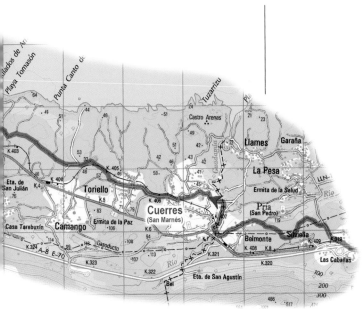

Countryside near Ribadesella

STAGE 17
Ribadesella to Sebrayo

Start	Church of Santa María Magdalena, Ribadesella
Finish	Albergue de Peregrinos, Sebrayo
Distance	31.5km
Total ascent	420m
Total descent	400m
Difficulty	terrain: 3; waymarking: 3
Albergues de Peregrinos	San Esteban de Leces, La Isla, Sebrayo

After briefly cutting inland to San Esteban, the camino returns to the coastline early today, leading past three excellent beaches – a final burst of sandy glory before Primitivo-bound pilgrims take leave of the sea. The second half of the walk begins in the cheerful market town of Colunga before passing through a series of small, long-standing villages, one of which contains one of the oldest churches along the Norte. Sebrayo has no facilities other than the Albergue. If you plan to stay the night in Sebrayo, be sure to stock up in Colunga beforehand.

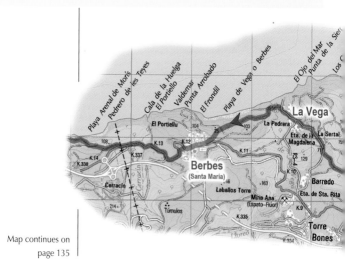

Map continues on
page 135

From the church, proceed to the waterfront and cross the Río Sella. Turn right along the promenade and follow it 2.3km. Turn left at the end of the beach on Calle Ramon y Cajal, then turn right on Carretera San Pedro. At the roundabout, 900m later, continue straight along the lower road towards San Pedro, proceeding gradually uphill for 2.1km. At a marked intersection, the camino splits. Keep straight on to continue walking, or turn left for the albergue in

SAN ESTEBAN DE LECES (5.3KM)
Albergue de Peregrinos (6€, 38 beds, kitchen, 985 857 611), take-away food available.

Keep straight on, curving eventually towards the coast and the small town of

LA VEGA (1.9KM)
Bar.

Capilla de Santa María Magdalena.

The camino near
La Vega

Turn left immediately before the beach, joining a medieval road leading uphill. After a pleasant, coastal walk, join the N-632 in

Map continues on
page 137

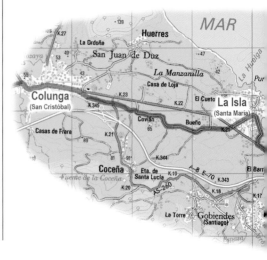

BERBES (2.8KM)

Bar.

The hassles of local government are not a new phenomenon; an attempt to run a pilgrim hospital here was undermined by scheming, bickering town officials in the Middle Ages.

Keep straight on for 1.3km. Turn right onto a footpath, the Camino Real, for an abrupt ascent followed by an equally jarring drop. After 3.9km, reach the lovely **Playa de la Espasa** (bars). Follow the N-632 1.8km away from the beach, zigzagging off on both sides, before arriving in

LA ISLA (7KM)

Bars, grocery store. **Albergue de Peregrinos** (5€, 24 beds, kitchen, 985 852 005), **Hotel Monte y Mar** (doubles 35–45€, @, 985 856 561), **Youth Hostel El Furacu** (13€, 42 beds, meals available, open all year, but must be reserved outside of summer, 985 856 661).

Fork left off the N-632 onto a footpath running parallel to the highway. This is a bit dicey at first, often overgrown with brambles.

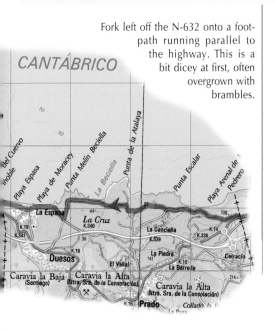

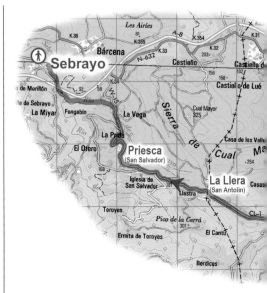

However, the narrow path widens into a proper dirt track, then a paved road, and then finally joins the N-632 for the final approach into

COLUNGA (3.5KM)

All facilities. Buy food here if you plan to sleep in Sebrayo. **Confiteria Las Palmeras** has rooms (singles 15€, 985 856 560), **Hostal El Mesón** (Calle Santa Ana 4, 985 856 335).

The remains of the Romanesque Church of San Cristóbal serve as the cemetery chapel.

Fork right off the N-632 after the church onto a pedestrian-friendly, red-brick street. At end of town, return to the highway and turn left. Follow the CL-1 5.1km to **Pernús**, then proceed on minor roads 1.9km to **La Llera**, and 1.4km to

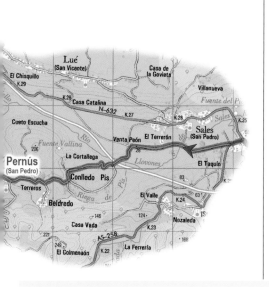

PRIESCA (8.4KM)

The Pre-Romanesque Church of San Salvador, built in 921, is one of the oldest churches on the camino. Amazingly, some of the original painting is still visible in the apses and on the walls. Keys are available from a nearby house.

Descend an often muddy trail, pass under the A-8 expressway, and proceed into Sebrayo. The albergue is on your right.

SEBRAYO (2.8KM)

Albergue de Peregrinos (4€, 20 beds, kitchen, key from house #7, open March–November, 985 996 012), but no shops or restaurants, aside from a nightly food truck. Check with the hospitalero.

STAGE 18
Sebrayo to Gijón

Start	Albergue de Peregrinos, Sebrayo
Finish	Iglesia de San Jose, Gijón
Distance	35.5km
Total ascent	660m
Total descent	680m
Difficulty	terrain: 4; waymarking: 5
Albergues de Peregrinos	Tornón, Villaviciosa, Cabueñes

Today brings great changes. First, the caminos split, with Primitivo-bound pilgrims saying their goodbyes and forking south. Second, the Norte hits its sharpest ascent in many days, with a 400m climb to the Alto de la Cruz. Finally, the stage ends in Gijón, the first big city in a week. With little traffic and few distractions, the route is surprisingly peaceful, making for a quiet day before the hustle and bustle of Gijón. But be prepared for only limited opportunities for food or drink along the way.

For pilgrims taking the Primitivo, today's route from Sebrayo is described in The Camino Primitivo, Stage 1.

◀ The first few kilometers on small roads and tracks are well marked, passing through the village of

TORNÓN (2.9KM)
Albergue de Peregrinos La Llamarga
(donativo, 8 beds, communal dinner and breakfast, 985 892 501)

The walk to Villaviciosa is a bit wiggly, twice crossing the A-8 before joining Calle Cervantes into

Map continues on page 141

VILLAVICIOSA (3KM)

All facilities. Stock up on food here. **Albergue Villaviciosa** (11–15€, 18 beds, kitchen, W/D, c/ Marqués de Villaviciosa, 985 891 555), **Hotel Carlos I** (doubles 30€, pilgrim discounts, breakfast, Plaza Carlos I, 985 890 121), **Hostal Café del Sol** (singles 25€, doubles 35€, pilgrim discounts, Calle Sol 27, 985 891 130), **Hotel Casa España** (singles 38–53€, doubles 48–66€, Plaza Carlos I, 985 892 030). Internet in Hotel La Ria.

Although its best years are long past, Villaviciosa is a pleasant commercial town and the 'apple capital' of Spain. Many of those apples end up in the town's dozen cider distilleries. It was the first Spanish town to welcome the new king Charles V when he arrived from Flanders in 1517. The 13th-century **Church of Santa María de la Oliva** is worth a visit.

The marker at the split of the Camino del Norte and Camino Primitivo

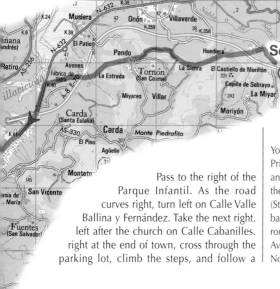

Pass to the right of the Parque Infantil. As the road curves right, turn left on Calle Valle Ballina y Fernández. Take the next right. left after the church on Calle Cabanilles. right at the end of town, cross through the parking lot, climb the steps, and follow a

You can follow the Primitivo to Oviedo and then return to the Norte at Avilés (Stage 19/20) without backtracking. For the route from Oviedo to Avilés see 'Primitivo–Norte Link'.

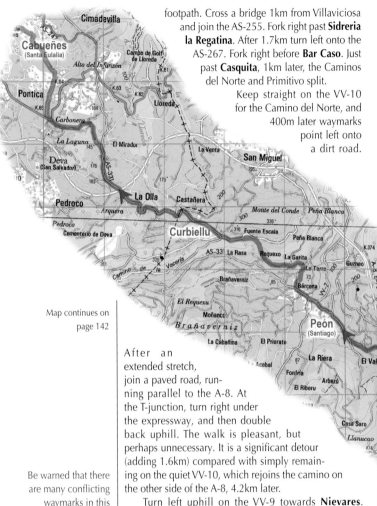

footpath. Cross a bridge 1km from Villaviciosa and join the AS-255. Fork right past **Sidreria la Regatina**. After 1.7km turn left onto the AS-267. Fork right before **Bar Caso**. Just past **Casquita**, 1km later, the Caminos del Norte and Primitivo split.

Keep straight on the VV-10 for the Camino del Norte, and 400m later waymarks point left onto a dirt road.

Map continues on
page 142

After an extended stretch, join a paved road, running parallel to the A-8. At the T-junction, turn right under the expressway, and then double back uphill. The walk is pleasant, but perhaps unnecessary. It is a significant detour (adding 1.6km) compared with simply remaining on the quiet VV-10, which rejoins the camino on the other side of the A-8, 4.2km later.

Be warned that there are many conflicting waymarks in this stretch, related to the local pilgrimage to Covadonga.

Turn left uphill on the VV-9 towards **Nievares**. ◀ Ignore an arrow calling for a right turn as you ascend. Instead, turn left after 400m, away from the main road. Turn right up a concrete road, and then fork right uphill.

A long ascent follows. Turn left on the VV-8 towards the **Alto de la Cruz** before descending the other side. Waymarking is poor in this area. Watch carefully on the descent for a small yellow arrow and some yellow camino tape marking a left onto a footpath. Turn right at a T-junction and then fork left immediately.

Return to paved roads after 5.4km. The descent into Peón is poorly marked and can be very frustrating, with many conflicting arrows pointing you in exactly the wrong direction. Proceed downhill and to the right, eventually joining the VV-8 at Casa Pepito after 1.4km in

PEÓN (15.5KM)

Bar Casa Pepito serves meals.

Iglesia de Santiago, restored in 1929.

Continue straight along the AS-331. Turn right at house 17. Turn left at the T-junction. Follow a mix of footpaths and single-lane roads 2.4km through peaceful countryside, eventually joining the AS-331 in

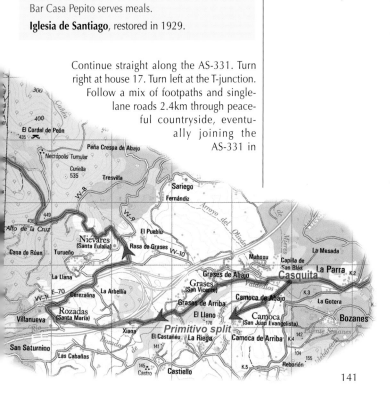

El Curbiello. Turn right at the km25 sign, beginning the descent towards Gijón. After 3.8km, join the N-632 in

CABUEÑES (6.2KM)

Bar/restaurant. **Albergue de Peregrinos** in Camping Deva (5€, 36 beds, W/D, 985 133 848). **Warning** There is no Albergue de Peregrinos in Gijón.

Turn right off the N-632, towards **Somió** (bars). One of the Norte's most frustrating stretches follows. It feels like an endless left turn, with cement walls blocking all views. Waymarks are limited, but the route primarily follows a single road. After 5km, when you finally reach the roundabout announcing the transition from Somió to Gijón proper, it feels more like liberation than arrival.

Bronze scallop shells in the sidewalk serve as waymarks through the city.

Proceed straight across the roundabout, towards the 'Centro Urbano' sign. Fork left along the bicycle track. ◄ Unlike in most other cities on the Camino del Norte, the route here does not follow the coastline. Instead, it follows Avenida de la Costa to the central train station (currently closed for repairs) and the Iglesia de San Jose, 2.8km from the roundabout.

It is easy and perhaps preferable to disregard the waymarks and head to the beach instead. To do this, turn right at the roundabout, following the Río Piles. Walk the length of the Playa de San Lorenzo, cut across the Cimadevilla, and then proceed along Calle Rodriguez San Pedro, where you will eventually rejoin the waymarks.

The Revillagigedo Palace in Gijón

GIJÓN (7.8KM)

Youth Hostel San Andrés de Cornellana is the only hostel option, but it is located 3km from the center (15€, 120 beds, meals, @, 985 160 673). **Pensión Brasas** (singles 36€, doubles 70€, Calle San Antonio 12, 985 356 331), **Hospedaje Don Pelayo** (doubles 30–60€, Calle San Bernardo 22, 985 344 450), **Hospedaje Cimavilla** (doubles 38–80€, Calle Vicaria 29, 985 349 932), **Hotel Costa Verde** (singles 31–41€, doubles 41–51€, Calle Fundición 5, 985 354 240).

A major city with all facilities and two lovely beaches. Gijón has prehistoric origins, but it became far more organized and established under Roman rule. As the Via de la Plata's northern outpost, Gijón was a major economic link in the empire's Iberian operations. The town still preserves its **Roman baths**, dating from Augustan rule (2.5€, T–Su 0930–1400). The city's most profound transformation occurred during the Industrial Revolution, when it became a major manufacturing center. Part of that development is documented in the **Railway Museum** (2.5€, T–Sa 1000–1900 in summer).

For something completely different, consider the **Museo de la Gaita**, devoted to the inimitable bagpipe (2.35€, hours vary by season). For nightlife and a historic feel, head for the **Cimadevella**, the tiny peninsula dividing the town's beaches that was formerly the fishermen's quarter.

STAGE 19
Gijón to Avilés

Start	Iglesia de San Jose, Gijón
Finish	Albergue de Peregrinos, Avilés
Distance	24.5km
Total ascent	220m
Total descent	210m
Difficulty	terrain: 2; waymarking: 2
Albergues de Peregrinos	Avilés

First, the bad news: this is probably the least enjoyable stage of walking on the Camino del Norte. The departure from Gijón passes through an ugly industrial district, and the final third of the walk is highway-bound. But now, the good news: even on its worst day, the Norte still delivers some highlights. The ascent from Gijón brings you into the Monte Areo recreational area, which features a prehistoric dolmen. And Avilés, the day's final destination, is a lively, fashionable town with an excellent albergue. Stock up before leaving town, because resources are limited, and treat yourself to a picnic on Monte Areo.

Those not committed to walking every step of the way might consider taking Bus 24 from the center of Gijón through the industrial district to Camin Rebesosu – ask for the 'Poago Alto' stop.

◀ From the Iglesia de San José, proceed to the waterfront. The route moves in a generally straight line, via Calle Rodriguez San Pedro, Avenida de Juan Carlos I, Calle Mariano Pola, Avenida de Galicia, and the AS-19. After 3.8km, cross one railroad line and proceed 300m, ignoring a damaged shell waymark that seems to call for a right turn. Before reaching a second set of rail tracks, fork right onto a dirt road. Cross the railroad and turn right. At the roundabout, fork right under the

A colorful hórreo

AS-19 overpass, then turn right onto the footpath running parallel to the highway. At the next roundabout, fork right under the overpass once again, following the AS-19. Turn left before the railroad overpass. Cross the railroad then double back uphill, finally escaping the city's industrial outskirts. ▶

Turn right uphill on Camin Rebesosu. Fork left on a cement road, ignoring red/white stripes, then fork right uphill. Turn left on the Camino Real. After 3.7km, finally arrive at the top, entering the **Monte Areo Park**. Keep straight on dirt roads. After 1.8km, waymarks offer a possible

Those taking Bus 24 can disembark at this point.

Map continues on page 147

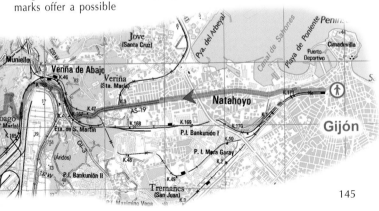

detour to the prehistoric **Dolmen de San Pablo**. Continue 2.1km through the park and descend the other side, arriving in modest

EL VALLE (11.7KM)

17th-century **Iglesia de Santa Eulalia**.

Follow minor country roads towards Tamón, passing under a tunnel at the entrance. Turn right at the church onto AS-326, and continue into

TAMÓN (4KM)

Two bars.

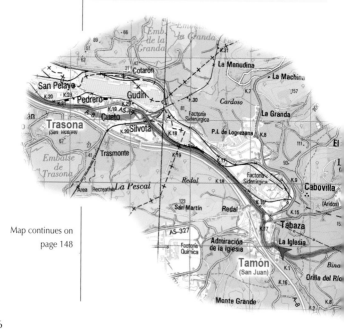

Map continues on page 148

Turn left shortly before the roundabout. Walk around the guard-rail and turn left on the highway. Very soon after, cross the highway and climb the embankment. Follow the AS-19 into

TRASONA (3KM)

Bars/restaurants, supermarket.

Keep straight on through the next roundabout, passing along the right side. About 5km before Avilés a new route forks off of the highway and onto a pedestrian track that follows the river into town. When the camino turns right on Calle Rivero, look for the albergue across the street in

AVILÉS (5.6KM)

All facilities. **Albergue de Peregrinos** (5€, 76 beds, kitchen, credenciáles, W/D, Calle Magdalena 1, 669 302 676), **Pensión La Fruta** (doubles 40€, Calle La Fruta 19, 985 512 288), **Hotel Don Pedro** (singles 60–75€, doubles 70–95€, Calle La Fruta 22, 985 512 288), **Hotel El Magistral** (doubles from 43€, Calle Llano Ponte 4, 985 561 100), **Hostal Puente Azud** (singles 25€, doubles 35–45€, Calle Acero 5, 985 550 177).

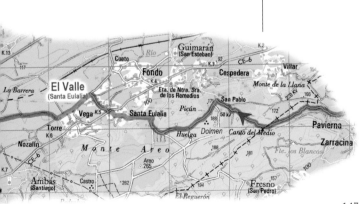

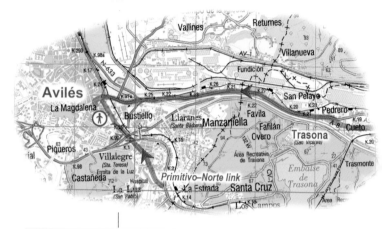

A prominent naval town in the Middle Ages, with an economy built around shipbuilding and trade with France. Pedro Menéndez de Avilés, the founder of St Augustine, Florida (the first permanent European settlement in the US), was born here. Like Gijón, Avilés has become an industrial center, but its preserved pedestrian center feels more relaxed. Architecture buffs can anticipate a full range,

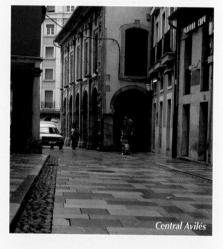

Central Avilés

from the 12th-century Romanesque **Iglesia de los Padres Franciscanos** to the stunning **Óscar Niemeyer International Cultural Center**. The **Plaza de España** is home to the monumental *ayuntamiento* (town hall) and Palacio de Llano Ponte.

148

STAGE 20
Avilés to Soto de Luiña

Start	Albergue de Peregrinos, Avilés
Finish	Albergue de Peregrinos, Soto de Luiña
Distance	39km
Total ascent	670m
Total descent	640m
Difficulty	terrain: 3; waymarking: 4
Albergues de Peregrinos	Muros de Nalón, Muros de Nalón, El Pito, Soto de Luiña

This is a long walk, with few opportunities to break it into shorter stages. Departure from Avilés follows a circuitous route, remaining primarily on minor roads through a series of suburbs. The middle of the stage passes through a mix of more interesting towns, beginning with El Castillo's fortress and concluding with El Pito's Renaissance gardens. The final stretch drags a bit, and has been shaken up by road construction, but it moves through a lush, expansive valley and concludes in pilgrim-friendly Soto de Luiña.

▶ From the albergue, proceed 500m on Calle Rivero, a pedestrian-only route, into the **Plaza de España**. Skirt the edge of the plaza, and continue straight on Calle la Ferraria, passing the Parque del Muelle and the Plaza de la Merced. Depart the city on Avenida de Alemania after 800m. Proceed straight through the roundabout. From here, the route is frustrating, with lots of backtracking. Take care, as waymarks are patchy and some turns are counter-intuitive.

In **San Cristóbal** (bar), 2.6km later, turn right at the bar. Follow the road as it curves right. Turn left onto a dirt road. After 1.5km, cross the N-632a, then keep straight on for 400m. Turn left at a T-junction onto Calle Doctor Fleming and proceed 600m. Turn right on Calle Piñole and then turn left on Calle Ramón y Cajal. At the T-junction 400m later, turn left and then take the sharp right on Calle Torner. Continue straight into

Waymarks in Avilés are a mix of arrows and blue/yellow scallop shells.

The Quinta de Selgas in El Pito

SALINAS (6.9KM)

Bars/restaurants, supermarket, pharmacy. **Hotel Castillo de Gauzon** (singles 45–65€, doubles 69–93€, Avda Campón 22, 985 502 634).

Map continues on page 153

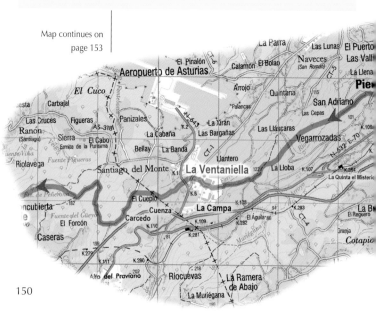

Proceed uphill on Avenida San Martín. Turn left onto a cement track, followed by another steep ascent in **Barrio El Cueto**. Turn left in **San Martín de Laspra**, 900m later. After a long descent, turn right at the T-junction, then left at the next T-junction. Continue straight across the highway, proceeding 2.2km into **Barrio de la Cruz**. Fork right onto a dirt road; a beautiful walk follows, along a tree-lined track. A short climb and a longer descent lead 3.4km into **La Ventaniella Santiago del Monte**. Fork left after the chapel, cross the N-643, and follow steps down and back up.

After 1.4km, cross the A-81

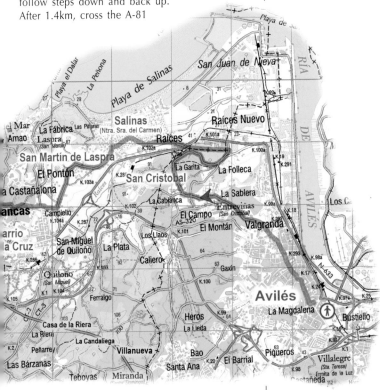

Mining activity in this area has caused minor route changes and some old waymarks remain. Nonetheless, the route is fairly clear.

expressway and curve left. ◄ Turn right onto a waymarked dirt road and continue straight, ignoring potential turns. Fork right. Two more critical right forks follow; watch carefully for the markers. Proceed 3.8km downhill through a eucalyptus grove, eventually emerging at a road running parallel to the highway. Cross the medieval bridge and ascend 200m into

EL CASTILLO DE SAN MARTÍN (11.9KM)

Built over the ruins of a Roman fort, this medieval castle dates to Alfonso III's rule. This also used to be the embarkation point for pilgrims crossing the Río Nalón.

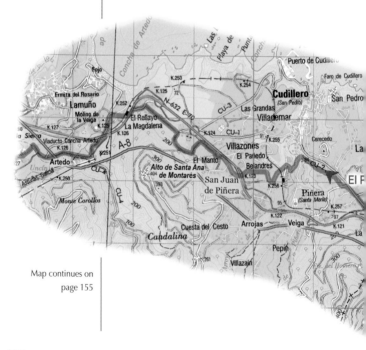

Map continues on page 155

Proceed uphill through the old town. Turn left onto the N-632. Make a sharp right in the roundabout, leading into

SOTO DEL BARCO (0.8KM)

Bar, supermarket. **Hotel Palacio de la Magdalena** (doubles 80–150€, breakfast, 985 588 899). The camino skirts the town and most facilities are off-route.

A town shaped in many ways by trade and emigration to the Americas, as displayed in the many examples of Indianos architecture.

Follow the old N-632 for 1.8km as it swings widely out of town. Join the N-632 and cross the Ría de San Esteban. After 500m, fork left up a steep dirt road, and keep straight on for 1.8km through a small neighborhood.

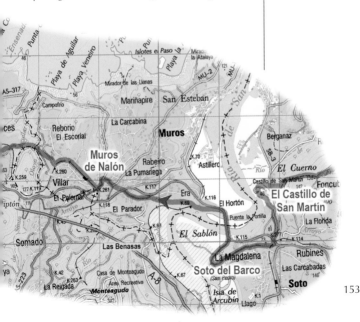

153

Cross back over the highway and proceed 300m to the small central plaza in

MUROS DE NALÓN (4.4KM)

Bars, grocery store. **Apartamentos Turísticos La Flor** (doubles 40–60€, kitchen, pilgrim discount, Calle Arango 28, 985 583 106), **Albergue Turístico Casa Carmina** (16€ (bunks), 30–45€ (private rooms), 20 beds, kitchen, meals available, W/D, 985 583 137, Avda de Riego 21–23).

The 16th-century **Plaza del Marqués de Muros**, in the center of town, includes the Iglesia de Santa María.

Keep straight on the road out of Muros, transitioning to a picturesque footpath that winds through densely forested hills into

EL PITO (3.8KM)

Bar, grocery store. **Hotel Álvaro** (doubles 40–55€, pilgrim discounts, 985 590 204) also operates Albergue Cudillero (12.50–20€, 8 beds, kitchen). **Hotel Aguilar** (singles 36–52€, doubles 45–65€, 685 162 882).

A small town shaped by the powerful Selgas family and quite a surprise. The 19th-century **Quinta de Selgas** palace and its adjoining gardens are styled after the Italian Renaissance, and the palace is home to an art collection that includes works by Goya and El Greco. It may be possible to arrange a tour (985 590 120). Nearby, the **Escuelas Selgas**, one of the family's many gifts to the town, remain open as a museum.

Keep straight on along the CU-2. Fork left after the church onto a road that quickly becomes a dirt road, and then a footpath. Turn right on a paved road, then fork left. Before reaching **Hotel Lupa** (singles 25–30€, doubles 45–55€, breakfast, 985 590 973), 1.6km later, watch for a poorly marked right turn. Soon after, join the N-632. While the camino has traditionally gone to the south side of the highway, major construction projects have forced a detour, which will probably be in effect for the

foreseeable future. Follow the N-632 for 600m. Fork right on the N632a. Keep straight on for 3km, pass the **Hotel/ Restaurant Mariño** (singles 25–30€, doubles 45–55€, 985 590 186), then make a sharp right downhill. Proceed 600m to the bottom of the hill, where arrows point in three different directions.

The official camino proceeds straight, but construction once again interferes. Detour signs point left. Follow the detour 1.1km, joining the N-632a into **Artedo** (bar). After 600m, fork right onto

Past meets present near Soto de Luiña

155

a dirt track shortly before a small bridge. Wind along the hillside for 900m until arriving in small **Mumayor**. Fork right at the end of town, then left along a footpath. Return to the N-634a for the final stretch into

SOTO DE LUIÑA (11.3KM)

Bars, restaurants, grocery store. **Albergue de Peregrinos** (5€, 22 beds, keys from Café Bar Ecu, 985 597 257), **Hostal Paulino** (singles 15–20€, doubles 25–30€, Calle Los Quintos, 985 596 038).

A pleasant, small town where a former pilgrim's hospital is now used as a cultural center. The 18th-century **Iglesia de Santa María** contains a Baroque retablo dedicated to Nuestra Señora de la Humilidad.

STAGE 21
Soto de Luiña to Cadavedo

Start	Albergue de Peregrinos, Soto de Luiña
Finish	Albergue de Peregrinos, Cadavedo
Distance	20.5km
Total ascent	370m
Total descent	320m
Difficulty	terrain: 3; waymarking: 4
Albergues de Peregrinos	Cadavedo

While today's route may appear discouraging at first, given how much of it follows the wiggly N-634a, there are numerous highlights. The highway itself is quite peaceful, with very little traffic and many trees. More importantly, old footpaths have been recovered over the last decade, allowing pilgrims not only to escape the highway on multiple occasions but also to visit some secluded, gorgeous beaches. It makes for a relaxing, pleasant walk, necessary after yesterday's long trek!

Map continues on
page 159

From Soto de Luiña to Albuerne, the route generally follows the N-634a, although it frequently veers onto parallel tracks. After turning left past the **Hotel Cabo Vidio**
(singles 40–50€, doubles 50–60, breakfast included, 985
596 112) the camino splits. ▶

Continue straight along the N-634a, brushing against
Albuerne after 3km and then continuing into

The left fork, labeled
'Camino', is not
recommended, as
it is poorly marked
and maintained.

NOVELLANA (6.4KM)

Bar, **Hotel El Fernón** (doubles 40–60€, pilgrim discounts, breakfast, 985 598 082).

*The split near
Albuerne*

Fork right off the highway and then left, off road.
The footpath proceeds 1.8km across the wooded hillside and into **Castañeras**. Turn right along the road
towards the beach. Look carefully for a small purple
arrow spray-painted on the road 300m later, before a
white house on your left. Turn left and proceed 1.3km
along the footpath into

SANTA MARINA (3.4KM)

Bar, **Pensión Prada** (doubles 30–40€, pilgrim discounts, 985 598 184).

The beach near Ballota

Fork right at the town entrance, then fork right before Pensión Prada, immediately after the bar. Continue straight through the next intersection, ignoring an old arrow, then curve left uphill. Fork right on a dirt track. Turn left onto a paved road, then turn right onto the N-634a. Keep straight on to the edge

of Ballota, 3.5km from Santa Marina, reaching the bar 500m later.

BALLOTA (4KM)

Hotel/Restaurant Casa Fernando (singles 25–30€, doubles 44–50€, 985 598 291).

Continue along the highway. Take a sharp right onto a dirt road, beginning a 3.5km off-road stretch. Turn left before the beach, past the site of the former **Puente que Tiembla** ('the bridge that trembles'). The old wooden bridge was a well-known pilgrim hazard; today, a stone structure has taken its place. Follow the footpath up and down the hill, ignoring possible turns. Turn left on a small road in **El Ribón**, then right on the N-634a, and keep straight on 1.4km. Turn right before the km153 sign. Proceed straight through two intersections, rejoin the highway, and enter Cadavedo. The albergue is at the town's end, 1.8km further on, just off the highway.

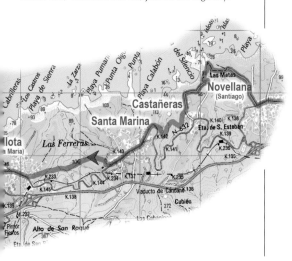

CADAVEDO (6.7KM)

Bars/restaurants, grocery store. **Albergue de Peregrinos** (5€, 13 beds, 985 645 320), **Hotel Astur Regal** (doubles 45–70€, breakfast, Calle Millares 985 645 777), **Casa de Peregrinos Covi y Peter** (private albergue, donativo, 10 beds, 660 147 482, Barrio Las Corradas 7).

A prominent medieval whaling port, Cadavedo is today focused more on agriculture and livestock. A thoroughly decentralized town, with some 300 structures scattered across 10km², one-third of which predate the 20th century.

STAGE 22
Cadavedo to Luarca

Start	Albergue de Peregrinos, Cadavedo
Finish	Paseo de Gómez, Luarca
Distance	15.5km
Total ascent	140m
Total descent	230m
Difficulty	terrain: 2; waymarking: 4
Albergues de Peregrinos	Almuña, Luarca

Today's walk is a quick jaunt through the Asturian countryside. Unfortunately, it is a day spent too close to the highway and too far from the coast, with persistent road construction problems along the way. On the plus side, you can maintain a leisurely pace and still be finished before lunch, enjoying the traditional port town of Luarca. Luarca has a brand new and centrally located Albergue de Peregrinos, making the stay here even more pleasant.

Map continues on page 163

Proceed straight along the N-634a. Turn right after crossing the railroad. Follow a footpath running parallel to the highway, arriving in **San**

Cristóbal after 2.9km. Fork left (looking for the arrow on a rock), then immediately fork right. Keep straight on the road, then continue on the highway towards

QUERUÁS (5.1KM)

Bar, grocery store.

Construction once again causes route problems. ▶ From the highway, fork right towards the church. Then, near a shop, fork left. Turn left at the T-junction. At the roundabout, turn left under the highway, ignoring conflicting waymarks. At the next roundabout, turn right on a dirt road, and then fork left. Cross the N-634 and descend steps. Cross the highway again and climb to a church. Curve right across the parking lot and proceed along a footpath. Rejoin the highway and cross the Río Esva. After 2.9km, arrive at the **Hostal/Restaurant Canero** (doubles 35€, 985 475 036), which offers a pilgrim menu. Turn right on the dirt road immediately before the hostal. Fork left into the woods. Rejoin the highway, cross it, turn left, and fork uphill. Emerge on a road running parallel to the N-632, cross over it, and eventually join the N-634.

After 3km, the camino splits, near the turn for La Rampla. For the albergue, continue straight along the highway. It is 3.5km away in **Almuña** (bar, **Albergue de Peregrinos** (5€, 22 beds, located on the AS-220). ▶

Take great care through this next stretch, and be aware that the course of the camino may change again in the future.

Those who stay at the albergue will rejoin the camino tomorrow by walking 1.7km to Luarca via a waymarked series of roads.

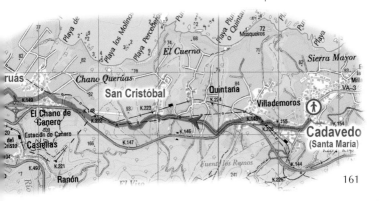

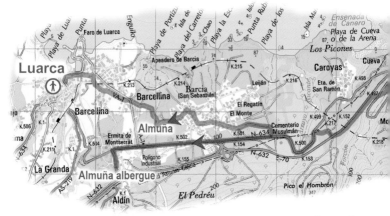

To continue along the camino, fork right, then turn left along a footpath. The approach to Luarca is deceptively long, spanning 4.3km, briefly joining Carretera Lugar 1 before forking left onto unpaved tracks. The steep, final descent, involving many steps, delivers you to the bridge over the Río Negro in

The port of Luarca

LUARCA (10.2KM)

All facilities. ALSA bus station. **Albergue Privado Villa de Luarca** (10€, 22 beds, 660 819 434, c/Álvaro de Albornoz 3), **Hotel Villa de Luarca** (doubles 50–96€, pilgrim discounts, 985 470 703), **Hotel Báltico** (doubles 45–75€, Paseo del Muelle 1, 985 640 991).

A small fishing town that packs its white and gray buildings tightly around the rectangular harbor. Luarca was founded in the 13th century as an administrative center. Threats from the English and French in the 16th century necessitated the establishment of fortifications, some of which are still visible. Emigration to Cuba and Argentina reshaped the town once again in the 19th and early 20th centuries. The attractive cemetery is perched in a stunning location above the town.

STAGE 23

Luarca to La Caridad

Start	Paseo de Gómez, Luarca
Finish	Albergue de Peregrinos, La Caridad
Distance	31km
Total ascent	340m
Total descent	280m
Difficulty	terrain: 2; waymarking: 2
Albergues de Peregrinos	Piñera, La Caridad

As has been true for the last several stages, the walk from Luarca to La Caridad is generally level (although the climb out of Luarca will break a sweat), passes primarily through quiet countryside, and offers few interesting sights. It has one energetic market town, Navia, along the way, and several minor possible stopping points. Near the midway point, Piñera has an Albergue de Peregrinos, which can be particularly useful for those hoping to go farther than Luarca in one day. La Caridad is a pilgrim-friendly place to end your day, with a shiny new albergue.

Those who stayed at the albergue in Almuña will start their day by walking 1.7km to Luarca via a waymarked series of roads.

◀ Leaving Luarca, cross over the Río Negro, bend left into the small plaza, and turn right uphill on Calle La Peña. After 1.3km, turn right at T-junction, then fork left 200m later. Proceed 2km, then cross the railroad and N-634. Turn right and continue straight for 2.5km through **Otur**. Before reaching a small ermita, construction necessitates another provisional detour. This is well marked, with large white signs. After crossing the Río Barajo, 4km later, make a sharp left. Wind uphill through a small community before returning to the highway in

VILLAPEDRE (12.2KM)

Two bars. **Hotel El Pinar** (singles 28–32€, doubles 36–45€, 985 472 221).

The 13th-century **Iglesia de Santiago** features a retablo of Santiago Matamoros.

Map continues on page 167

Pass the church, loop under the railroad, and cross the highway. Proceed 1.9km into Piñera, passing

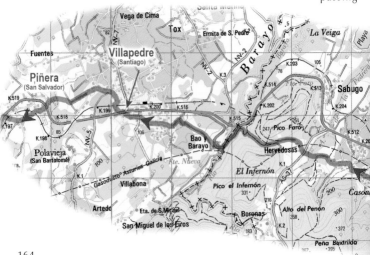

The church in Piñera

a grocery store and the marked home of Pili the hospitalera. ▶ Cross the railroad twice, curve around the church, and return to the N-634. The albergue is located here, on the outskirts of

PIÑERA (3KM)

Grocery store. **Albergue de Peregrinos** (5€, 20 beds, 985 472 171).

To stay in the albergue, 1.1km further on, you must check in here. Pili will also cook meals (the only option in town), and these should be booked at check-in.

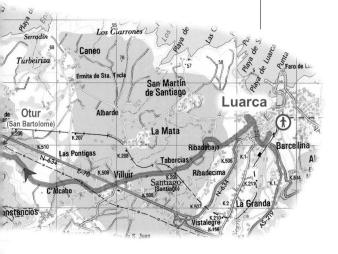

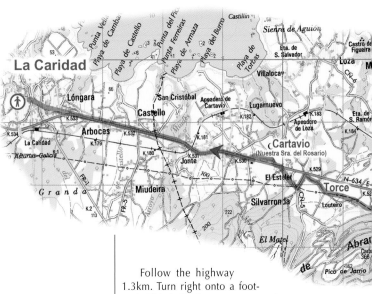

Follow the highway
1.3km. Turn right onto a footpath. This is badly overgrown and
poorly marked. Look uphill across the field
to see the small town of **Villaoril**. If the official path is
unclear, navigate towards the town as well as possible.
The camino runs 1.5km into Villaoril, then 1.3km along
the road into

LA COLORADA (4.1KM)

Bar, **Hotel Blanca** (doubles 65–70€, 985 630 775).

Turn left after the Hotel Blanca and then right onto
a footpath. Keep straight on past the cemetery. Wind
downhill to the Ría de Navia and the center of

NAVIA (2.2KM)

All facilities, including a thriving weekly market. **Hotel Palacio Arias** (doubles from 35€, Avda de los Emigrantes 11, 985 473 671), **Pensión Cantabrico**
(doubles 30–40€, 985 474 177).

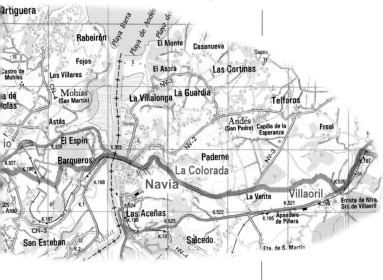

First documented in the 10th century, although Celtic remains have been found in the area. Alfonso X ordered the construction of walls in the 13th century, and parts of these remain. The town's architectural highlights are more recent, including the Baroque **Iglesia de Santa Marina de Vega** and the Neo-Gothic parish church.

Cross the river on the N-634. Take the second left, then turn right for Jarrio. Turn right onto a footpath, cross the railroad, and continue straight, arriving in **Jarrio** after 1.9km. Follow a footpath out of town, cross the A-8, and join a country road running parallel to the expressway. After **Torce**, fork right at an unmarked intersection (construction in the area may be affecting waymarks here), then fork right again. Arrive in **Cartavio** (bar) on the N-634 after 3.4km. Between Cartavio and La Caridad, the route generally follows the N-634, but it frequently shoots off to the left for brief stretches. The old albergue, which now serves as overflow space, is located well before town, left

167

off the highway, after 2.8km. However, a brand new albergue is 1.2km ahead, much closer to the center, so keep straight on. Fork right and descend to the albergue. From there, proceed 200m uphill into

LA CARIDAD (9.5KM)

Bars/restaurants, grocery stores. **Albergue de Peregrinos** (5€, 18 beds, 685 154 405), **Pensión Sayane** (doubles 40–50€, Avda de Asturias 6, 985 478 229).

STAGE 24
La Caridad to Ribadeo

Start	Albergue de Peregrinos, La Caridad
Finish	Albergue de Peregrinos, Ribadeo
Distance	21.5km
Total ascent	70m
Total descent	85m
Difficulty	terrain: 1; waymarking: 4
Albergues de Peregrinos	Tapia de Casariego, Tol, Ribadeo

Today is your last day on the coast. As has been the trend in recent days, the bulk of the walking occurs inland, with arrival in Ribadeo coinciding with the first prominent sea views. That said, there is an alternative route, via Tapia de Casariego, that offers extra time near the water. Ribadeo represents a major landmark along the pilgrimage. On crossing the river into town, with the wind whipping your face and ripping into your pack, you enter Galicia, the final region of the trip. And you can plan on sleeping well, with an albergue offering million-dollar views.

Proceed straight through La Caridad, following the new sidewalk waymarks. At the end of town, fork right downhill onto a footpath. Turn right onto a road, walking to the left side of the N-634. Cross the highway, loop around a small park, and return to the N-634, proceeding into

VALDEPARES (3.1KM)

Two bars.

Nearby is the **Castro del Cabo Blanco**, an excavated Celtic settlement from the fourth century BC.

At the bar, cross the highway, and follow a minor road 1.1km into **El Franco**. Curve right and then left, joining a footpath that leads across the highway, past an ermita, and over the Ría Porcia. In **Porcia**, after 1.1km, fork right uphill. The camino splits 700m later.

The direct, inland option forks left, across the N-634. On the other side, follow the middle of three roads, which quickly becomes a dirt road, leading 5.6km into **Brul**. Fork left near a palm tree. ▶ Leaving Brul, join a paved road soon after passing soccer fields. Turn left at the intersection, joining the AS-31 soon after. Follow this 2.1km to the church in **Tol**.

The camino after La Caridad

The coastal route rejoins the camino here.

Map continues on page 171

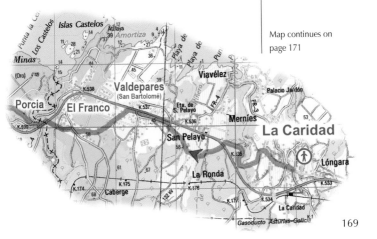

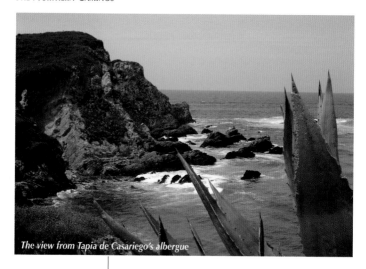
The view from Tapia de Casariego's albergue

Coastal variant

This route adds 4.5km to your walk.

◄ A more scenic option, particularly for coastal views, is to keep straight on at the fork, towards Tapia de Casariego. This well-marked route (shown on the map) follows minor roads generally running parallel to the N-634 for 4.4km. ◄ The **Tapia de Casariego** albergue is situated in an incredible position, overlooking the Atlantic, as you enter the village (all facilities, **Albergue de Peregrinos** – donativo, 30 beds, 985 628 080).

Those looking for an even more scenic approach can follow the E-9's red/white stripes, making for a longer walk closer to the coastline.

Unfortunately, the return trip from Tapia to the official camino is poorly marked and more than a little frustrating. A detailed overview of what seems to be the 'official' route follows below. However, it involves a lot of backtracking. A second option is to follow the E-9 closer to the coast, via Villamil, to Ribadeo, a distance of roughly 13km. Eric Walker advocates a third possibility in the CSJ's guidebook, an 11km-long route that passes through Calambre, Villamil, Santa Gadea, and San Román. Check the CSJ guide for more details (see Appendix C).

For the 'official' route, follow the road into the center of Tapia, curving left uphill. Climb the steps and pass through the plaza. Turn left before the church, turn left again on the road, and then right on Calle Conrado Villar. Keep straight on for 1.8km through the end of town, continuing under the N-634. At the fork after the N-634, veer right downhill.

At the next fork, turn left uphill towards the small community, following the road as it curves left, after 700m. At this point, you will encounter some camino waymarks pointing in exactly the wrong direction. Ignore these! Proceed 3.2km along the winding road, crossing the A-8 expressway and continuing into Brul. Rejoin the

Map continues on page 173

171

camino here (the route description continues above), but take care as the connection can be a little tricky. Make a sharp right, near a palm tree, with the only waymark behind you.

TOL (10.6KM)

Bar, grocery store. **Albergue de Peregrinos** (6€, 16 beds, 982 128 689).

Keep straight on the AS-31, crossing the Río Tol. The camino splits again 700m later, near signs for Castropol/Barres. The 'official' route towards Ribadeo, described here, continues straight along the highway. ◄ Continue on the AS-31 for 3km, pass through **Barres** (bar), cross the N-640, and proceed an additional 1.7km into

The alternative route, following the left fork, proceeds inland towards Vegadeo and bypasses Ribadeo.

FIGUERAS (5.4KM)

Bars/restaurants, supermarket. **Albergue Turístico Camino Norte** (15€, 20 beds, meals available, W/D, 985 636 207), **Hostal Casa Venancio** (Crta de Figueras, 985 623 072).

The 16th-century **Palacio de los Pardo de Donlebún** has been declared a national monument.

Waymarks in town are white stickers with red Xacobeo 2010 logos on traffic poles.

◄ Fork right as you enter town. Turn right at T-junction 100m later. Proceed 500m, pass through a roundabout, under the N-634, and then turn left at the next roundabout. Continue 600m, then join the N-634 across the Ría de Ribadeo. Turn right off the highway then right again, descending back towards the river. At the T-junction, turn left for the albergue or right to continue into

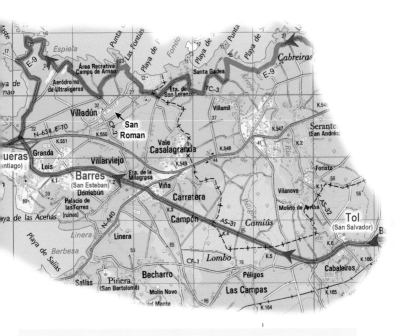

RIBADEO (2.6KM)

All facilities. **Albergue de Peregrinos** (6€, 12 beds, kitchen, 659 942 159), **Hostal Galicia** (singles 15€, doubles 25€, Calle Virgen del Camino 1, 982 128 777), **Hotel Rosmary Ribadeo** (doubles 22–35€, pilgrim discount, Calle San Francisco 3, 982 128 678).

The camino's routing through Ribadeo is a modern development, thanks to the construction of the highway bridge. Medieval pilgrims would have cut south, through Vegadeo. It is a fortunate development for today's walkers. Although Ribadeo was founded by Fernando II in 1183, it was taken by the French knight Pierre de Vaillanes and not fully integrated into the larger region until the 19th century. The nearby beach of **As Catedrais** is a major tourist stop and worth an afternoon taxi ride. Within the city, the **Plaza de España** features many interesting buildings, including the ayuntamiento and the 20th-century **Torre de los Moreno**. The tower is a modern structure, blending multiple styles, but it has fallen into a state of disrepair.

STAGE 25
Ribadeo to Lourenzá

Start	Albergue de Peregrinos, Ribadeo
Finish	Albergue de Peregrinos, Lourenzá
Distance	27.5km
Total ascent	710m
Total descent	695m
Difficulty	terrain: 4; waymarking: 2
Albergues de Peregrinos	Vilela, Gondán, Lourenzá

The walk from Ribadeo leaves the coast behind as a series of modest climbs foreshadow the steeper mountains awaiting in later stages. Dense eucalyptus groves line much of the camino, filling the air with their unmistakable fragrance. Throughout Galicia, anticipate smaller, decentralized villages and many little-used roads. Road signs are now in Gallego, although the changes are modest and easily decoded. Conditions today are particularly rural, with very few opportunities to refuel. Fortunately, arrival in Lourenzá brings all necessary facilities and a beautiful monastery.

Note Galician waymarks need to be read differently from those in Asturias. Up to now, the direction of the route was indicated by following the lines of the scallop shell as they converged. But in Galicia, the opposite is true. Turn in the direction that the lines diverge. Cement waymarks also indicate the distance remaining to Santiago.

The route through Ribadeo is poorly marked. Turn left out of the albergue and proceed straight, passing under the expressway. Turn right on Avenida Leopoldo Calvo Sotelo y Bustelo. At the

T-junction, turn right on Rúa San Roque and then left after the Capela da Virxe do Camiño on Rúa Luz Pozo Garza. Turn right on Rúa San Lázaro. Then, at the soccer field, 1.9km from the albergue, turn left and leave town. From this point, waymarks are very reliable. Proceed along a mix of paved and unpaved roads, including a long stretch along LU-5207, into

VILELA (7KM)

Bar, **Albergue de Peregrinos** (6€, 34 beds, located behind bar, 659 942 159).

Fork right into town. Turn right at the bar/albergue. Continue straight into **O Vilar**. Turn right onto a dirt road, and proceed 5km to **A Ponte de Arante**. Descend to the small bridge and pass the

Map continues on page 177

175

Map continues on page 178

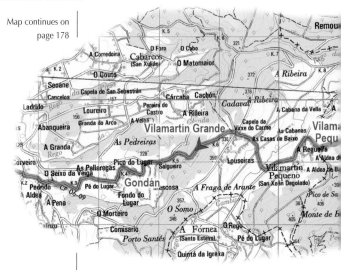

church. Turn right at the end of town, proceeding first on a road, then a dirt road, and then a footpath. Soon after, turn left onto a dirt road; a strong ascent follows.

Once again, the mix of minor paved roads and smooth dirt roads so characteristic of walking in Galicia follows. Proceed 4.5km to **Villamartín Pequeño**, 1.9km

A Ponte de Arante

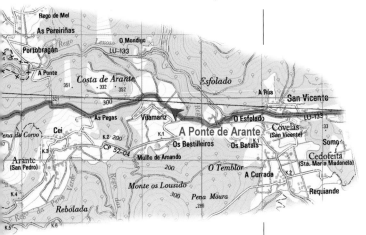

into **Villamartín Grande** (which doesn't seem any bigger than its little brother), and 2.5km into

GONDÁN (13.9KM)

Albergue de Peregrinos (donativo, 30 beds, kitchen, 982 144 072). This albergue may be closed – check before you rely on it.

Keep straight on the road. Turn right onto dirt road. Rejoin the highway into

SAN XUSTO (2.1KM)

Bar/restaurant. **Albergue de Peregrinos** (donativo, 14 beds, 982 144 072).

Continue along the road over a brief climb, followed by a longer descent into

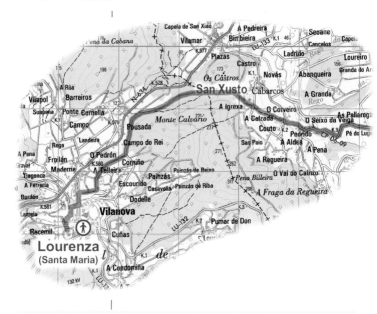

LOURENZÁ (4.5KM)

Bars, supermarkets. **Albergue de Peregrinos** (6€, 20 beds, kitchen, Calle Campo de la Gracia, 652 18 67 31), **Hostal La Unión** (Avda do Val 25, 982 121 028).

The town's undisputed highlight – and reason for being – is the 10th-century **Benedictine Monasterio de San Salvador**, a national historical monument. The Baroque façade, made by the architect Casas y Novoa (also responsible for the Cathedral of Santiago's façade), is highly regarded, as is the sarcophagus of the cathedral's founder, Don Osorio Gutiérrez. Today, it houses a museum of religious art.

STAGE 26

Lourenzá to Gontán

Start	Albergue de Peregrinos, Lourenzá
Finish	Albergue de Peregrinos, Gontán
Distance	24km
Total ascent	740m
Total descent	300m
Difficulty	terrain: 4; waymarking: 2
Albergues de Peregrinos	Mondoñedo, Gontán

Today's walk into the mountains brings with it such fantastic views that you'll hardly notice the ascent. The route climbs into the hills and down to Mondoñedo; once one of the seven capitals of the Kingdom of Galicia, its old town has since been declared a national cultural-historical site. The walk out of Mondoñedo winds uphill for the next 11km, bringing stunning views as you proceed through a series of villages dotting the mountainside. A short and welcome descent leads into Gontán.

Turn right out of the albergue. Turn right uphill onto a small footpath. After a short climb, fork left onto a gravel track. Cross under the A-8 expressway and continue on a brick path through **Arroxo**. After 2.4km turn right onto N-634a. Keep straight

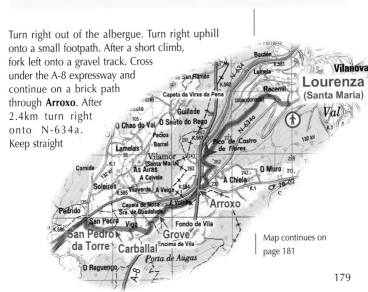

Map continues on page 181

179

View of Mondoñedo

on for 1km into **Grove** (restaurant), then continue 800m. Turn left at the cemetery onto a footpath. Turn left just before the Capela da Virgen de Guadalupe in **Carballal**. Proceed uphill, fork left past a group of houses, then turn right after 1.3km onto a small paved road (fountain on left).

Continue 500m. Turn left onto a footpath into **San Pedro da Torre**. Proceed past a church, then turn right onto a paved lane through town. Turn left on N-634 and proceed 1km. Turn right across the bridge into the outskirts of Mondoñedo, following the LU-123.

Rejoin the N-634 then fork left onto LU-124. Keep straight on for 1.5km into the main plaza of

MONDOÑEDO (8.5KM)

All facilities. Stock up here; it's your only opportunity to purchase supplies during this stage. **Albergue de Peregrinos** (6€, 28 beds, kitchen, Calle Alcántara, 629 469 561), **Hotel Montero I** (doubles 50€, Calle Eladio Lorenzo 7, 982 521 751), **Hospedería del Seminario de Santa Catalina** (doubles 28–42€, located inside 18th-century seminary, 982 521 000).

Nestled in mountains and full of historical charm, Mondoñedo is one of the nicest cities on this stretch of the camino. Bronze Age remains have been found in the vicinity, including an altar once used for human sacrifices. Bronze busts of Marcus Aurelius and Hadrian bear witness to the former Roman presence as well. The 13th-century **cathedral** was declared a national monument in 1902, and is known as the *catedral arrodillada* ('kneeling cathedral') for its perfect proportions and short stature. Its frescos are among Galicia's oldest, the walnut choir stalls are Gothic masterpieces, and the 5m rose window is especially stunning on a sunny day.

Cross the main plaza in front of the cathedral and turn right onto Calle Fonte Vella. Fork left uphill onto Rúa Rigueira. Follow this road for the next 8.3km, passing through **Barbeitas** (1.1km), **Maaríz**, where a private home is open for pilgrims (**O Bisonte de Maaríz**, donativo, 4 beds, communal breakfast and dinner, 626 766 235) and a fountain is available (1.4km), **Paadín** (1.8km), **San Vicenzo** (2.2km), and **Lousada** (1.8km). Turn left onto a gravel track as you leave Lousada. Climb

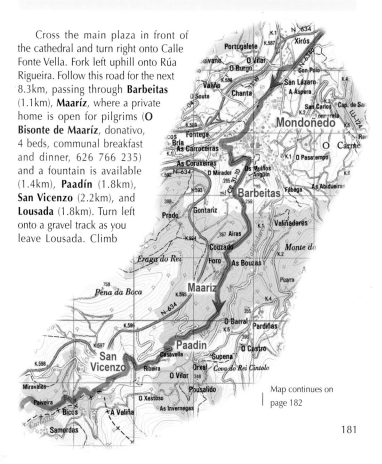

Map continues on page 182

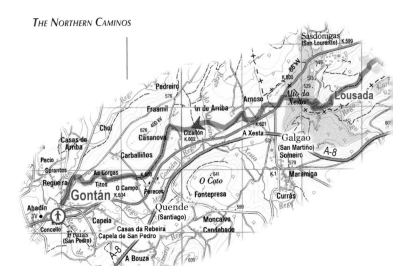

2km sharply uphill. Construction has necessitated a well-marked detour, following temporary waymarks across the N-634. Follow a series of gravel tracks 2.1km before rejoining the camino proper on a minor road. Continue 3.1km downhill into

GONTÁN (15.5KM)

Bar, restaurant. **Albergue de Peregrinos** (6€, 26 beds, kitchen, Crta de Labrada, 616 251 462).

A small community dwarfed by neighboring Abadín, situated 500m further along the camino (and offering a wider array of facilities). Gontán is home to many fiestas and special markets, including the annual **Feria de Santos**.

STAGE 27
Gontán to Baamonde

Start	Albergue de Peregrinos, Gontán
Finish	Albergue de Peregrinos, Baamonde
Distance	40km
Total ascent	320m
Total descent	400m
Difficulty	terrain: 2; waymarking: 2
Albergues de Peregrinos	Vilalba, Baamonde

Although today's walk is long, it passes quickly as the camino meanders easily along rural roads through forested paths and farming villages. Halfway through the walk, Vilalba provides the only large city you'll pass through for the next few days. Those wishing to split the long the day in two can remain in Vilalba for the night. Be sure to stop here and resupply before continuing to the impressive albergue in Baamonde – the largest on the Norte.

Keep straight on through Gontán, passing a fountain on the left before forking right uphill. Join the N-634 and proceed into

ABADÍN (0.5KM)

Bars, restaurant, grocery store, pharmacy. **Pensión Goas** (singles 24–27€, doubles 36–39€, Avda de Galicia 23, 982 508 005).

Waymarking is patchy along the exit from Abadín. Follow the main road through town. Turn right towards the Correos and then left in front of it. Proceed 1.2km out of town. Fork right onto a footpath downhill. Keep straight on for 1.2km, crossing a bridge over the Río Abadín. Turn left onto a paved road through **Ponterroxal**.

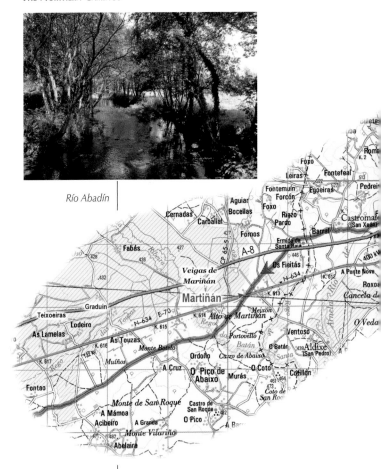

Río Abadín

Map continues on
page 187

Continue straight when the road turns into a dirt/gravel track. After 2.8km cross the highway. Turn right onto a footpath. After 900m, turn right onto a minor road and cross Pontevella de Martiñan. Keep straight on through **Martiñán**. Continue onto a gravel track and proceed 2km. Turn left through an underpass, cross the

184

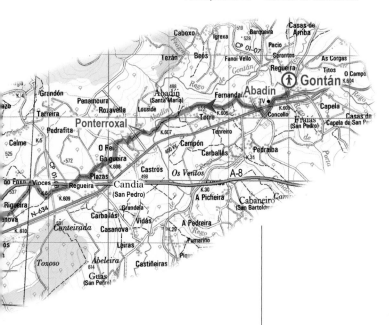

N-634, and continue along a mix of minor paved and gravel roads for 6.7km. Cross the N-634 into

GOIRIZ (14.8KM)

Bar/restaurant. **Hostal Helvetia** (Campo de Cristo 20, 982 511 062).

Cross the N-634 onto a footpath. Proceed 1.7km, transitioning to pavement and then a dirt track. Turn left onto a paved road through **As Casonovas**. Fork right after 300m and continue 1km through **A Casilla** and onto the highway, joining the N-634. Keep straight on for 400m to

Map continues on
page 188

VILALBA ALBERGUE (3.4KM)

Bar/restaurant. **Albergue de Peregrinos** (6€, 48 beds, kitchen, 982 523 911).

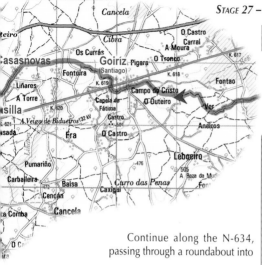

Continue along the N-634,
passing through a roundabout into

VILALBA (1.6KM)

All facilities. **Albergue Turístico Castelos** (10€, 38 beds, kitchen, W/D, Rúa das Pedreiras 16, 982 100 887), **Hotel Vila do Alba** (singles 35€, doubles 45€, free breakfast for pilgrims, Calle Campo del Puente 27, 982 510 245), **Casa Seijo** (doubles 35€, Calle Plácido Peña, 982 510 719).

Vilalba's medieval emergence was closely linked to the Andrade family. A tower from the family castle, the 15th-century **Torre de los Andrade**, has since been converted to use as a Parador hotel. In the 20th century, the town experienced a cultural boom, emerging as a surprising hotbed of intellectual and literary activity.

▶ Follow the main road 400m. Turn right on Calle Alférez López García (watch for the large tree in the middle of the intersection) and proceed 100m to the **Church of Santa María**. In the plaza, find bronze shells leading out of town. Turn left from the church onto Calle Concepción Arenal and then left again, proceeding 100m uphill. Turn right to cross the LU-6513. Fork right onto a dirt track 800m later.

The way through Vilalba is marked by signs on lampposts and bronze scallop shells in the sidewalks.

187

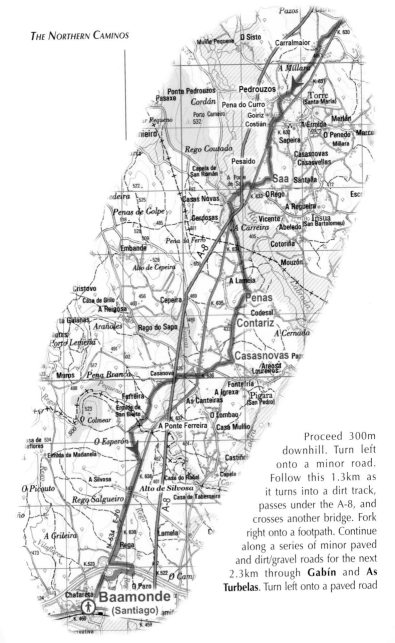

Proceed 300m downhill. Turn left onto a minor road. Follow this 1.3km as it turns into a dirt track, passes under the A-8, and crosses another bridge. Fork right onto a footpath. Continue along a series of minor paved and dirt/gravel roads for the next 2.3km through **Gabín** and **As Turbelas**. Turn left onto a paved road and re-cross the A-8. After 900m turn right onto the N-634, then turn right into

SAN XOÁN DE ALBA (6.2KM)
Bar with provisions just off the camino.

14th-century **Iglesia de San Xoán**.

Shortly after the church, fork right onto a footpath and proceed 1.4km. Follow a paved road for 300m, turn left onto a minor road, continue an additional 700m, and cross the N-634. Keep straight on a dirt track for 600m, then turn right onto a footpath prior to **Saa**. Proceed 400m to

PONTE DE SAA (3.4KM)
Bar.

Medieval bridge.

Cross the N-634 onto a dirt track. Proceed 600m under the A-8, across the medieval bridge over the Río Labrada, and onto a footpath. Cross a paved road, join a gravel track, then follow another minor road back under the A-8. After 700m cross the N-634, onto a footpath.

Ponte de Saa

Keep straight on for 3.4km as the path becomes a minor road and passes through **Penas**, **Contariz**, and **Casanovas**. Fork right across the N-634. Pass under the A-8 (again) after 200m.

Follow a series of dirt and paved roads for 2.1km through **Ferreira** and back to the N-634. Continue straight for 1km. Fork left onto a dirt track. Pass under the A-6 and turn right. This feels counter-intuitive, but is correct. Follow the waymarks through a neighborhood, then turn right onto the N-VI. Arrive 2.1km later in

BAAMONDE (10.1KM)

Bars, restaurant, grocery store, pharmacy. **Albergue de Peregrinos** (6€, 94 beds, kitchen, 628 250 323), **Hostal Ruta Esmeralda** (doubles 32–40€, on the N-VI, 982 398 138).

The Romanesque **Church of Santiago** dates to the 14th century. Baamonde was the birthplace of acclaimed sculptor Victor Corral; his home has been turned into a museum, documenting his life and containing his works.

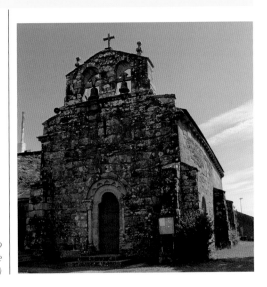

Church of Santiago in Baamonde (14th century)

STAGE 28
Baamonde to Miraz

Start	Albergue de Peregrinos, Baamonde
Finish	Albergue de Peregrinos, Miraz
Distance	14.5km
Total ascent	110m
Total descent	70m
Difficulty	terrain: 1; waymarking: 2
Albergues de Peregrinos	Miraz

Today's short walk to the village of Miraz is pleasant, although not particularly exciting. At the pilgrim stop located just after Raposeira, you'll find extremely friendly owners and a good bar for breakfast. Look forward to an afternoon spent in the fantastic albergue in Miraz – relaxing in the garden, drinking afternoon tea, and speaking English with the hospitaleros. This albergue is run by volunteers from the British Confraternity of St James. Be prepared: food is extremely limited en route today. Stock up before leaving Baamonde.

Follow the N-V1 for 3km. Fork left onto a dirt track and cross over the railroad and the Río Parga. Pass the 14th-century **Chapel of San Alberte**. After

Map continues on page 192

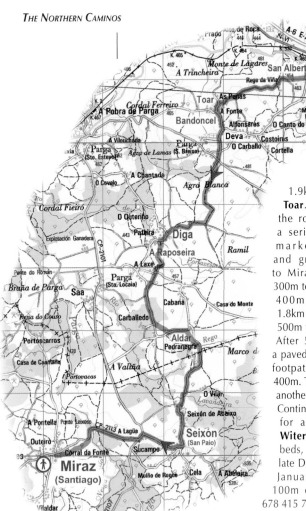

1.9km arrive in **Toar**. From here, the route follows a series of well-marked paved and gravel roads to Miraz. Proceed 300m to **Bandoncel**, 400m to **Deva**, 1.8km to **Diga**, and 500m to **Raposeira**. After 500m, cross a paved road onto a footpath. Continue 400m. Turn left onto another minor road. Continue past a sign for an **Albergue Witericus** (12€, 9 beds, café, closed late December and January, located 100m off Camino, 678 415 728).

Continue 1.3km, passing through **Aldar**. Fork right onto a footpath and then back onto another minor road. Turn right. After 2.1km, turn right onto LU-P-2101 and proceed into **Seixon** (bar and 12th-century church).

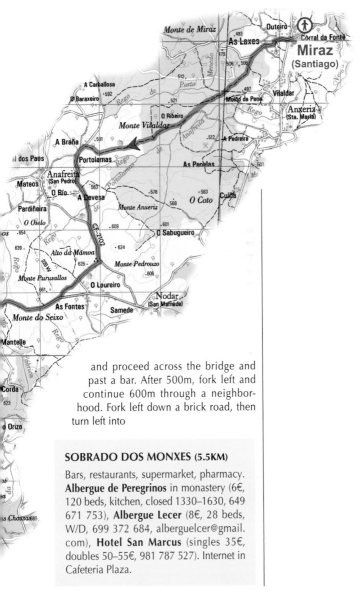

and proceed across the bridge and past a bar. After 500m, fork left and continue 600m through a neighborhood. Fork left down a brick road, then turn left into

SOBRADO DOS MONXES (5.5KM)

Bars, restaurants, supermarket, pharmacy. **Albergue de Peregrinos** in monastery (6€, 120 beds, kitchen, closed 1330–1630, 649 671 753), **Albergue Lecer** (8€, 28 beds, W/D, 699 372 684, alberguelcer@gmail. com), **Hotel San Marcus** (singles 35€, doubles 50–55€, 981 787 527). Internet in Cafeteria Plaza.

The **Monasterio de Santa María de Sobrado** was founded in 952 and soon rose to prosperity in the late 10th century when the then abbot of Sobrado became a bishop in Santiago. In 1142 it became the first monastery in Spain to join the Cisterian order – a good thing for pilgrims, as it was the Cisterians who established a pilgrim hospital within the monastery. The monastery features an impressive Baroque main church with a dominating façade, built in the 17th century by Pedro de Monteagudo, as well as two 17th-century cloisters, a 12th-century chapter house, a Renaissance sacristy, and multiple chapels, including the early Romanesque Chapel of John the Baptist, built in the mon astery's pre-Cisterian history.

Sobrado dos Monxes Monastery

STAGE 30
Sobrado dos Monxes to Arzúa

Start	Albergue de Peregrinos, Sobrado dos Monxes
Finish	Albergue de Peregrinos, Arzúa
Distance	22km
Total ascent	220m
Total descent	320m
Difficulty	terrain: 2; waymarking: 2
Albergues de Peregrinos	Boimorto, Arzúa

Today, the Camino del Norte joins the densely populated Camino Francés. Prepare yourself for pilgrim culture shock when you arrive in Arzúa; it can feel jarring to suddenly find yourself among not 50, but 500 other pilgrims. Enjoy the relative solitude of the morning as you weave your way through medium-sized towns and small villages into bustling Arzúa.

Leave Sobrado on the main street, and proceed 1.3km. Fork left onto a paved road. Continue on a mix of minor paved/gravel roads for 3km, passing through **Vilarchao** and **O Peruxil**, then rejoin the highway and continue through **Castro**. Fork left onto a gravel track. Pass through

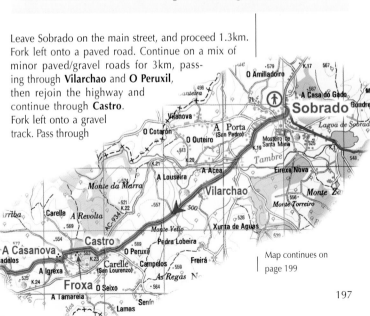

Map continues on page 199

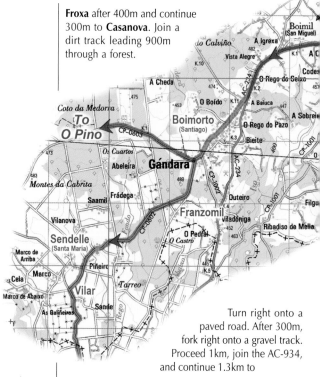

Froxa after 400m and continue 300m to **Casanova**. Join a dirt track leading 900m through a forest.

Turn right onto a paved road. After 300m, fork right onto a gravel track. Proceed 1km, join the AC-934, and continue 1.3km to

Map continues on page 200

AS CORREDOIRAS (8.5KM)

Bar, restaurant, small grocery. **Turismo Rural Casa Boada** (doubles 36–45€, located on AC-540, 981 516 187).

Cross the AC-840, proceed 700m, and fork right onto a paved road. Pass a church on your left, turn right onto the AC-234, and proceed 600m into **Boimil** (bar). Follow the highway for 1km, then fork right onto DP-1002. Continue 900m into

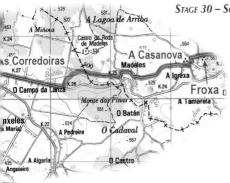

BOIMORTO (3.2KM)

Bar, restaurant, grocery store, pharmacy. **Albergue de Peregrinos** (6€, 32 beds, kitchen, 638 392 024), **Turismo Rural Casa Sobreira** (doubles 54€, 1km from the camino, 670 052 704).

Proceed 1km on Lugar de la Gándara/AC-0603. Fork left onto AC-0602.

Farm near Santa María de Sendelle

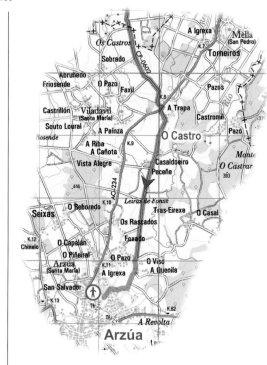

Route to O Pino

An alternative route makes it possible to join the Camino Francés in **O Pino**, roughly 17km after Arzúa. To do this, continue on the AC-0603. This route covers roughly 22km, from Boimorto to the Camino Francés, joining the route shortly before **Santa Irene**, which has two albergues. The route is simple, following the AC-0603 most of the way, then joining the N-547 near **Brea**.

Keep straight on the AC-0602 1.8km through **Franzomil** to **Santa María de Sendelle** (bar and 12th-century church), 1km to **Vilar**, and 2.3km to the AC-234. Cross the highway and continue on a small paved road towards **Castro**

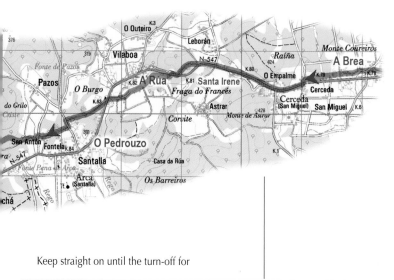

Keep straight on until the turn-off for

PEDROUZO (0.6KM)

All facilities. To reach the town, turn left on the N-547 and proceed 500m. Waymarks allow you to reconnect with the camino without backtracking. **Albergue de Peregrinos** (6€, 120 beds, kitchen, W/D, @, 660 396 826) and three private albergues: **Porta de Santiago** (981 511 103), **Edreira** (981 511 365), and **O Burgo** (630 404 138). **Pensión Bule-Bic** (singles/doubles, 981 511 222), **Pensión Compas** (singles 20–25€, doubles 25–35€, Avda Lugo 47, 981 511 309).

Continue across the N-547 and proceed on a footpath. Transition onto minor roads along the outskirts of Pedrouzo. After 1km, arrive at a bar on the far edge of town, immediately before turning left onto a broad, heavily shaded trail. Far removed from the highway, this is the last best stretch of Galician walking – unpaved footpaths, tall trees, stone bridges, and gurgling creeks. After 2.9km, pass a small bar, and then continue towards modern

civilization, eventually passing to the right of Santiago's Labacolla airport before arriving in

LABACOLLA (7.7KM)

Bars, **Hotel Ruta Jacobea** (doubles 59€, Calle Lavacolla 41, 981 888 211), **Hotel Garcas** (singles 35€, doubles 50€, Calle Naval 2, 981 888 225).

In the Middle Ages, pilgrims paused here to clean themselves in the river, prior to arrival in Santiago. The translation of the name Labacolla highlights a particular concern: 'wash scrotum'.

Keep straight on for 2.2km, and then cross under the N-634, passing a bar and supermarket. Soon after, cross the Labacolla river, washing as needed. Join a road leading steeply uphill and continue through the open countryside, making occasional well-marked turns and eventually passing the local television station's headquarters. Pass through the small town of **San Marcos** (bars, grocery) 4.8km later, before turning left and making the gentle ascent of

MONTE DE GOZO (7.8KM)

Bars, restaurants, grocery. Massive **Albergue de Peregrinos** (6€, 370 beds, kitchen, W/D, @, 981 558 942). An unfortunate cross between an army bunker and summer camp, this is your last possible stopping point before Santiago.

Proceed downhill 100m, cross the A-8, and let loose a cheer when you see the road sign announcing your arrival in Santiago! But, you're still a fair bit from the cathedral. The route follows busy streets through modern Santiago for 3km before crossing into the old town. Only 1.4km now separates you from the Plaza del Obradoiro and the end of your pilgrimage in

SANTIAGO DE COMPOSTELA (4.5KM)

Congratulations! Upon arrival in Santiago, you have two main pilgrim destinations remaining. First and foremost is the **cathedral** (open 0700–2100 daily). Access to a statue of the apostle St James (for hugging purposes) is limited to 0900–1400 and 1600–1900 daily. Pilgrims may visit the apostle's relics

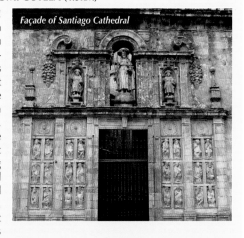

Façade of Santiago Cathedral

all day. Confessions (possible in multiple languages) are heard 0800–1300 and 1700–2100 daily. Pilgrim mass takes place from 1200–1300 daily; arrive early. Second is the brand new **Pilgrim's Office**, which issues Compostelas (0900–2100, shorter winter hours, Rúa do Vilar 1). You are not required to pick this up on the day of arrival; pilgrims continuing to Finisterre may prefer to obtain their Compostela upon return.

Santiago has a wide range of accommodation. **Albergue** options include **Acuario** (10–12€, 52 beds, W/D, San Lázaro Valiño 2, 981 575 438), **San Lázaro** (10€, 80 beds, kitchen, W/D, Rúa San Lázaro, 981 571 488), **Seminario Menor** (10–15€, 199 beds, W/D, Rúa de Belvís, 881 031 768), and **Mundoalbergue** (12–17€, 34 beds, kitchen, W/D, Calle San Clemente 26, 981 588 625). In most cases, reservations are accepted and pilgrims can stay multiple nights. **Hostal Suso** (doubles 40–49€, Rúa del Villar 65, 981 586 611), **Hotel Real** (singles 43–50€, doubles 50–80€, Calle Calderia 49, 981 569 290), **Pensión Badalada** (singles 35–40€, doubles 47–66€, Rúa Xelmírez 30, 981 572 618), **Pensión Con Encanto** (doubles 60–80€, Rúa de Abril Ares 1, 981 576 765), **Hostal Santo Grial** (doubles 55–65€, Rúa do Vilar 76, 629 515 961). For a splurge, consider staying in Santiago's Parador, the **Hostal de los Reyes Católicos.** Once upon a time, this structure was a pilgrim hospital, founded by Ferdinand and Isabel (Plaza del Obradoiro, 902 547 979). Alternatively, many pilgrims are approached in the plaza by older locals, offering comfortable private rooms at very good prices.

Buses to Labacolla airport run daily every 30mins between 0610 and 0010. The trip takes 25mins. The central bus station is located roughly 2km from the cathedral in Praza Camilo Díaz Baliño. The RENFE station is a similar distance in the opposite direction. Those hoping to visit Finisterre as a daytrip may find it more convenient to arrange this through their albergue, as minibus tours cut down the drive time significantly and offer a competitive price.

Head south of the cathedral for Santiago's most lively areas. Rúa do Franco, Rúa do Vilar, and Rúa Nova offer popular restaurants, bars packed full of celebrating pilgrims, souvenir shops, and bookstores. The Correos is located just off Franco on Travesa de Fonseca. If city life is too much after so many peaceful days, keep straight on along Franco, cross out of the old town, and proceed into the Alameda, a large, green park with many quiet corners.

Although there is much to see and do in Santiago, many pilgrims are drawn back to the Plaza del Obradoiro many times, reliving the moment of arrival as new waves of pilgrims surge in front of the cathedral and reuniting with many friends from the walk. For those having walked the Northern Caminos, it can be more than a little overwhelming, encountering so many other pilgrims. But, it is a powerful reminder of the larger community to which you all now belong, pilgrims on the Camino de Santiago, owners of the Compostela.

THE CAMINO PRIMITIVO
Sebrayo to Arzúa

Walk to El Acebo (Stage 8)

THE CAMINO PRIMITIVO

The Camino Primitivo is where it all began. This first major pilgrimage route to Santiago originated in Oviedo; even after the Camino Francés emerged, many pilgrims viewed Oviedo to be a mandatory detour. Today, the Primitivo feels largely untouched, enjoying long stretches of rugged countryside dotted with occasional small villages and towns. While the route traditionally begins in Oviedo, this guide picks up the trail near Villaviciosa, where the Primitivo splits from the Camino del Norte. All told, the Primitivo spans roughly 300km between Villaviciosa and Melide, where it joins the Camino Francés for the final 50km to Santiago. Along the way, the Camino Primitivo enjoys two striking cities, Oviedo and Lugo, numerous medieval villages, and some of the most dramatic views of any camino.

STAGE 1
Sebrayo to Pola de Siero

Start	Albergue de Peregrinos, Sebrayo
Finish	Albergue de Peregrinos, Pola de Siero
Distance	34km
Total ascent	550m
Total descent	320m
Difficulty	terrain: 4; waymarking: 3
Albergues de Peregrinos	San Salvador de Valdediós, Villaviciosa, La Vega, Pola de Siero

Today, the Caminos del Norte and Primitivo split; the Primitivo forks inland, leading to the heart of Asturias. As it leads into the hills, the Primitivo splits again. One route descends to the Monastery of San Salvador, while the high-level option continues uphill through Arbazal. The monastery is stunningly situated in a narrow valley and easy to appreciate, regardless of which route you choose. From San Salvador, a sharp ascent brings you closer to villages dotting the hillside before the two routes rejoin and lead down suburban streets into Pola de Siero.

The walk to Villaviciosa is a bit wiggly, including three different crossings (two under, one over) of the A-8. Although frustrating, the route is well marked, eventually joining Calle Cervantes into

VILLAVICIOSA (5.9KM)

All facilities. Stock up on food here. **Albergue Villaviciosa** (11–15€, 18 beds, kitchen, W/D, c/Marqués de Villaviciosa, 985 891 555), **Hotel Carlos I** (doubles 30€, pilgrim discounts, breakfast, Plaza Carlos I, 985 890 121), **Hostal Café del Sol** (Singles 25€, Doubles 35€, pilgrim discounts, Calle Sol 27, 985 891 130), **Hotel Casa España** (singles 38–53€, doubles 48–66€, Plaza Carlos I, 985 892 030). Internet in Hotel La Ria.

Although its best years are a millennium in the past, Villaviciosa remains a pleasant commercial town, and is known as the 'apple capital' of Spain. Many of those apples end up in the town's dozen cider distilleries. It was the first Spanish town to welcome the new king Charles V when he arrived via boat from Flanders in 1517. The 13th-century **Church of Santa María de la Oliva** is worth a visit.

Pass to the right of the Parque Infantil. As the road curves right, turn left on Calle Valle Ballina y Fernández. Take the next right. Turn left after the church on Calle Cabanilles. Fork right at the end of town, cross through the parking lot, climb the steps, and

Map continues on page 213

211

follow a footpath. Cross a bridge 1km from Villaviciosa and join the AS-255. Fork right past **Sidreria la Regatina**. After 1.7km turn left onto AS-267. Fork right before **Bar Caso**. Just past **Casquita**, 1km later, the Caminos del Norte and Primitivo split. ◄

The Camino Primitivo splits off at Stage 18 of the Norte.

Turn left to follow the Primitivo. Continue on a series of minor roads and dirt tracks for 2.7km, passing through **El Ronzón**, **Camoca**, and **San Pedro de Ambás**. Join the AS-267 and arrive at a rest area.

The split in the Caminos del Norte and Primitivo

Map continues on page 215

Grases de Norte s

Grases de Arriba
El Llano
178

Xiana   El Castañéu   La Riega
141

145   Castro   Castiello

Ambás ás (San Pedro) ro)   K7   AS-113   K6

La Rivera   Sar

Valeri   Peredal   Lloses   Daja K1

Valdediós   K8   Fuente Pipina

Monasterio de Santa María de Valdediós   Lloses   Mogovío
478   454   397

Valdediós   Fta. de San Salvador   435   448
La Viña   Polledo   Fta. de Sta. María

Luaria   Santi   Arbazal
veru   802   Villarrica   K10   395   397
Pico 607   Vallinaoscura   Casa del Monte
598   K11
591   El Mariñág   482   474
Alto de Vallovero   Alto de la Campa   491
Solapeña   Figares   Valvidares   K9   475
K14   AS-113   K13   Pico Torres
568
guera   Pedrosa   El Cuetu   San Román
La Carcava   San Román K8   301
15   291
Berros   301   Granda
284

Oratory of
San Salvador

At this point, the camino splits again. The recommended route remains on the AS-267, continuing 2.9km downhill into

SAN SALVADOR DE VALDEDIÓS (9.3KM)

Bar/grocery. **Albergue de Peregrinos** (5€, 22 beds, kitchen, 670 242 372).

The religious center of Asturias and an important spiritual destination for millennia. The small **Oratory of San Salvador** dates to 893, when Alfonso III ordered its construction. The **Cistercian monastery** was added several centuries later, around the Basilica of Santa María. Only the Romanesque portal and apse survive from the original; the interior, including a Santiago Matamoros, is newer and in the Baroque style.

Follow a paved road out of town. Fork left onto a gravel track. Pass through **Vallinaoscura**, enjoying great views of the monastery below. After 2.8km, arrive on the hilltop. Turn left and walk 700m into **Alto de la Campa**, where the routes reunite.

High-level variant

This route bypasses the monastery, and some pilgrims report poor route conditions, although the views are impressive. From the AS-267, turn left towards **Arbazal**. The initial climb is quite sharp, along a narrow footpath through brambles. As the route flattens and passes through Arbazal, the only village along this stretch, the walking conditions improve. From there, minor roads take you the rest of the way to **Alto de la Campa**, where the routes rejoin. This route is 1.3km shorter than the San Salvador option.

ALTO DE LA CAMPA (3.5KM)

Bar/restaurant. Basic provisions in petrol station.

Cross the AS-267 and join a minor road uphill. Re-cross the AS-267. Turn left onto a dirt track and proceed 1.1km. Turn right onto the AS-267. Fork left after 100m into **Figares** and continue 500m. Turn right onto

a gravel track, ignoring conflicting waymarks. Fork right onto a paved road. Proceed 1.3km through **Pedrosa** and across the AS-267. Continue through **La Cárcava** (bar), then keep straight on the SR-1 for 1.5km into

LA VEGA DE SARIEGO (4.5KM)

Bars, grocery, pharmacy. **Albergue de Peregrinos** (donativo, 16 beds, keys from Supermercado Camín de Santiago, 985 748 402).

Follow the SR-1 for 3.1km, passing through **Barbechu**, **Aramanti**, and **El Castru**. Fork right onto a gravel track. After 1.3km turn right onto a footpath and then right onto a dirt road. After 1.1km, bear right onto the AS-331. Turn left onto a gravel track, then turn right down a dirt track. Proceed 1.6km, passing through **Hermita**. Bear left onto a paved road. Continue 400m, then turn right on dirt track. Keep straight on for 700m and join the AS-331. Continue 800m. From here waymarking is limited. Fork right on Calle Rebollar. Turn left on Calle de Torrevieja, then right on Calle Florencio Rodríguez. This becomes Calle Celleruelo as you pass through town, continuing to the albergue on the far side of

POLA DE SIERO (10.6KM)

All facilities. **Albergue de Peregrinos** (5€, 18 beds, Calle Celleruelo, 666 612 002), **Hostal Siero** (Plaza Campes 33, 985 720 013), **Hotel Loriga** (singles 33–44€, doubles 44–54€, Calle Valeriano León 22, 985 720 026).

STAGE 2
Pola de Siero to Oviedo

Start	Albergue de Peregrinos, Pola de Siero
Finish	Albergue de Peregrinos, Oviedo
Distance	16.5km
Total ascent	80m
Total descent	100m
Difficulty	terrain: 1; waymarking: 4
Albergues de Peregrinos	Oviedo

Today's short walk allows you to make the most of your time in Oviedo – a major pilgrimage site in its own right and the 'official' starting point of the Camino Primitivo. Unsurprisingly, the approach to the city brings long stretches of highway walking and little of interest to see. However, arrival in Oviedo is well worth it. With its amazing architecture, historical sights, and modern conveniences, the city has something to offer every pilgrim.

Turn right onto a minor road,

Map continues on page 218

then fork left onto a gravel road. Turn left onto the AS-246, then right on Avenida de Oviedo into

EL BERRÓN (3.1KM)
All facilities.
A crossroads town, where major highways and railroad lines converge.

Fork right at the end of town. Cross the A-8. Turn right onto the AS-17 and then turn left off it onto another minor road. After 4.2km, fork left onto a dirt track. Proceed 300m to

MERES (4.5KM)
The 15th-century Palacio de Meres has a beautiful chapel, **La Capilla de Santa Ana** (M–F 1000–1400, 1600–1900).

Keep straight on for 3.4km across the highway and railroad, and through **El Campo**. Turn left onto the N-634. Fork left off the highway, cross a medieval bridge and proceed 0.7km to

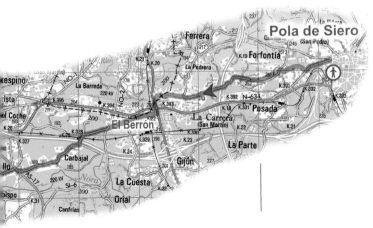

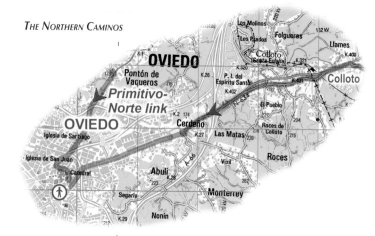

Gothic arches in Oviedo Cathedral

COLLOTO (4.1KM)

Bars, supermarket. **Hotel Palacio de la Viñona** (singles 73–94€, doubles 90–120€, Calle Julian Clavería 14, 985 793 399).

Romanesque bridge.

Rejoin the N-634. Waymarks virtually disappear from this point until Oviedo's cathedral. Keep straight on for 2.4km, passing under the A-66 and through a roundabout. Continue straight as this becomes Calle Tenderina Baja. At the next major intersection, fork left onto Calle Postigo Bajo. Follow this uphill, as it becomes Calle Postigo Alto. To reach the cathedral, turn right on Calle Mon (just before the Plaza de Sol), which turns into Calle Santa Ana. To reach the albergue, turn left on Calle Padre Suárez, and then left in the Plaza Santo Domingo onto Calle San Pedro de Mestallón. Follow this through a busy intersection, and take the next left on Calle Adolfo Posada. The albergue is on the left.

OVIEDO (4.7KM)

Romanesque capitals in the Cámara Santa

All facilities. **Albergue de Peregrinos El Salvador de Oviedo** (5€, 51 beds, kitchen, opens at 1300 May–September at other times call to check, credenciales available, c/Leopoldo Alás 20, 985 228 525), **Villa Cecilia** (private albergue, 10€, 14 beds, private rooms available for 15–20€, kitchen, W/D, Calle Emigrante 12, 657 853 334), **Hostal Albino** (doubles 24€, Calle Gascona 15-17), **Hostal Arcos** (doubles 45€, Calle Magdalena 3, 985 214 773), **Hostal Fidalgo** (doubles 40€, Calle Jovellanos 5, 985 213 287), **Hotel Ovetense** (singles 30–35€, doubles 40–50€, triples 57–63€, Calle San Juan 6, 985 220 840). Internet available in Biblioteca Municipal. Credenciáles available in the cathedral.

Founded in 757 by Fruela I as a fortress to guard the central road linking the coast to the interior, Oviedo became the capital of Christian Spain a half-century later when Alfonso II 'The Chaste' built his palace here.

The construction and expansion of Oviedo's **cathedral** spanned eight centuries, consequentially combining a broad range of architectural styles. The original 9th-century church – oddly designed, with fine carvings of the apostles on the capitals and disembodied heads on the walls – survives as the **Cámara Santa**, accessed by a door in the right transept. The **Capilla de San Miguel**, situated within, houses the cathedral's greatest treasures, including the Cruz de la Victoria (carried by Pelayo at Covadonga), the Cruz de Los Angeles (a gem-studded cross said to have been created by angels), and a silver reliquary chest (contains a vial of the Virgin Mary's milk and one of Judas's 30 pieces of silver). The new cathedral was started in 1388, and its ten chapels range in style from early Gothic to Baroque. The **Capilla Mayor** has an acclaimed, enormous retablo on the Life of Christ.

Oviedo is also home to three pre-Romanesque churches, identified by UNESCO as the finest examples of 9th-century Christian European architecture. **San Julián de los Prados** is the largest and most central, built during Alfonso II's reign. It has two long porches, a wide transept which is also the highest part of the building, and tunnel-vaulted chapels. The interior is filled with frescoes that, while faded, speak to its original beauty. The other two churches are roughly 3km from Oviedo's center. **Santa María de Naranco**, started shortly after the completion of San Julián, is nearly perfectly preserved. Only one-third of **San Miguel de Lilo** survives, but the Visigothic influence remains starkly apparent. The original plan called for a 21m-long basilica, a three-bay nave with tall, circular columns, and impressive stone latticework in the windows and doors. The use of buttresses around the exterior is particularly advanced for the time.

STAGE 3
Oviedo to San Juan de Villapañada

Start	Albergue de Peregrinos, Oviedo
Finish	Albergue de Peregrinos, San Juan de Villapañada
Distance	29.5km
Total ascent	360m
Total descent	300m
Difficulty	terrain: 3; waymarking: 2
Albergues de Peregrinos	Venta del Escamplero, Grado, San Juan de Villapañada

Now the Primitivo begins for real! Departure from Oviedo is nearly painless; after several kilometers of urban sprawl, you escape into quiet countryside. Although the route follows paved roads for much of the morning, the walking is easy and relaxing, with frequent views as you continue into the hills as well as sufficient bars to stop at along the way. Grado is the day's major town, an excellent place to enjoy a good meal and restock before continuing on to the Albergue in San Juan for the night.

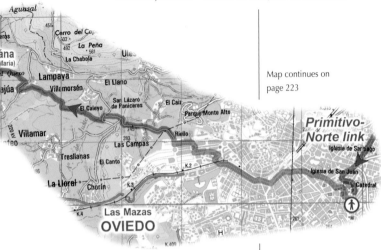

Map continues on
page 223

▸ Leaving the albergue, proceed 800m to the cathedral. Pass in front of it, heading north on Calle Águila. Turn left onto Calle Schultz, then right through the Plaza de Juan. Cross Argüelles Jovellanos onto Calle La Luna, and fork left through the busy intersection onto Calle Covadonga. This becomes Calle Melquiades Álvarez and then Calle Indepencia. Yellow arrows reappear at this point. After 1km, Calle Indepencia merges with the N-634. Cross it and continue through Plaza de la Liberación. Fork left at the roundabout onto Calle Argañosa. After 400m, cross the metal footbridge over the railroad.

Construction has temporarily rerouted the camino on the other side. The detour is well marked, however, and rejoins the camino near a park after 1.5km. Pass through the park and then turn right on a minor road. Proceed 1km along a series of minor roads to

Small bronze shells in the sidewalk mark the camino out of Oviedo.

SAN LÁZARO PANICERES (4.7KM)

A *malatería* is documented here in 1331, providing care for sick pilgrims.

Waymarks in San Lázaro Paniceres

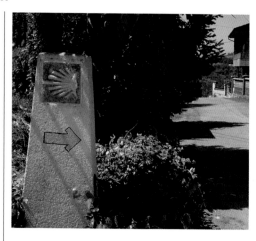

Keep straight on for 2.4km to the **Capilla del Carmen** (sello on porch), 900m to **Santa María de Loriana**, and 700m downhill to **La Bolguina** (bar). Turn right onto the AS-232. Proceed 1.5km through **Fabarín** and **Gallegos**.

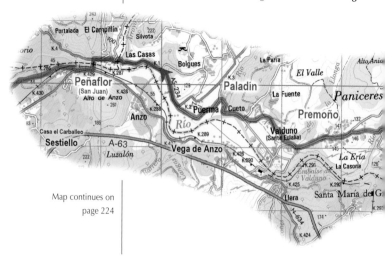

Map continues on page 224

Fork right onto a footpath leading down towards a ravine and back uphill. Follow residential streets 1km to the AS-232. Fork left and proceed 700m into

VENTA DEL ESCAMPLERO (7.2KM)

Bar/restaurant. *Carnicería*/shop with basic provisions. **Albergue de Peregrinos** (4€, 14 beds, kitchen, keys at Bar El Tendejón, 985 799 005).

Follow the road for 400m. Fork left onto a paved lane, then fork left again onto a footpath, returning to the highway. Turn left off the highway, then turn left again onto a paved

Hórreo near Escamplero

223

lane just after an hórreo. Follow a mix of minor roads and dirt tracks into

PREMOÑO (4.2KM)

Bar.

The chapel and **Casona de la Portalada** remain from the former pilgrims' hospital, which operated until the 18th century.

Continue 500m through town, then fork right onto a footpath before an hórreo. Proceed 1.1km, then fork left onto a paved lane. Turn right onto a paved road. Pass through **Paladín** after 1km, cross a bridge, and join a dirt track. After 1.7km, cross another bridge and turn left onto the AS-234. Keep straight on for 1km into

PEÑAFLOR (5.3KM)

Bar, grocery store.

Romanesque bridge. As a strategically significant location, Peñaflor was the site of brutal clashes between the French and Spanish in the Peninsular War.

Cross the Peñaflor bridge and turn right onto the N-634. After 300m, fork right into the town proper. Make a sharp right towards and under the railroad, passing onto a gravel track. Keep straight on for 2km, then fork right onto the road. Cross the railroad, turn left, then turn right towards Bar Gijón on Calle Jove y Valdés. Turn right onto the N-634, cross the bridge, and join Avenida Valentín Andrés. Fork left onto Cerro de La Muralla in

GRADO (3.6KM)

A busy commercial town offering all facilities, with markets on Wednesday and Sunday; supermarkets are closed on Mondays. **Albergue Villa de Grado** (donativo, 16 beds, kitchen, breakfast, W, open March-October, located in La Morantina), **Hotel Palper** (N-634, 985 750 039), **Hotel Autobar** (singles 22–24€, doubles 36€, Avda Flórez Estrada 29, 985 751 127). If you plan to sleep in San Juan de Villapañada, buy your food here.

Waymarks are limited in Grado. Proceed through Plaza Ayuntamiento and Plaza General Ponte, then continue straight on Calle Marqués Vega de Anzó, which turns into Calle Cimadevilla. Turn left onto the N-634 (Avenida Flórez Estrada). After 800m fork left at the supermarket. Fork right uphill and proceed 2.7km, following a mix of paved and gravel roads. Finally, the camino splits. Proceed uphill to continue walking, or turn right and walk 800m to

SAN JUAN DE VILLAPAÑADA (4.3KM)

Albergue de Peregrinos (donativo, 22 beds, kitchen, 670 596 854). Purchase food in advance. The hospitelero, Domingo Ugarte, is friendly and helpful; he may provide a basic dinner to pilgrims without food.

A major battle occurred here in the Peninsular War for control of the village.

STAGE 4
San Juan de Villapañada to Bodenaya

Start	Albergue de Peregrinos, San Juan de Villapañada
Finish	Albergue de Peregrinos, Bodenaya
Distance	24.5km
Total ascent	660m
Total descent	340m
Difficulty	terrain: 4; waymarking: 2
Albergues de Peregrinos	Santa Eulalia de Dóriga, Cornellana, Salas, Bodenaya

Today the climb through the Cordillera Cantabrica begins in earnest. The route continues yesterday's walk uphill into Fresno before dropping into Cornellana, then following undulating tracks along the hillside through two small villages en route to Salas. From Salas, one last long ascent awaits you. The camino gains 500m in elevation as it climbs past the village of La Pereda and into today's destination, the wonderful albergue in Bodenaya.

From the albergue, return 800m to where the route splits and continue uphill 1.4km to **El Fresno**. ◀ Turn left downhill onto a steep gravel road. Proceed 1.2km, crossing over the A-63 and joining a highway. Before the roundabout, turn left onto a footpath. Keep straight on for 1.6km into

Turn right here and walk 1.5km to reach **Albergue Cabruñana** *(5€, 18 beds, kitchen, W/D, 985 750 068).*

SANTA EULALIA DE DÓRIGA (5KM)
Albergue/Bar Cá Pacita (10€, 10 beds, 684 613 861).
12th-century Romanesque church.

Follow the road for 600m, then continue uphill onto a gravel road. On the hilltop, turn left downhill onto a footpath. Keep straight on for 700m, cross the AS-15, and continue 800m. Join the N-634 and cross the Río Narcea. After the bridge, turn left to follow the 'official' camino along the river, proceeding 1km to the albergue. This bypasses all facilities in Cornellana. Alternatively, it is possible to proceed straight, through the center, and continue to the monastery via Calle José María Caballero.

CORNELLANA (3.1KM)

Bars/restaurants, grocery stores, pharmacy. **Albergue de Peregrinos** in the old monastery (5€, 24 beds, kitchen, W/D, 635 485 932), **Hotel Cornellana** (singles 42€, doubles 48€, Avda Fernández Pello, 985 588 356).

The semi-ruined monastery was founded in 1024 and passed to Cluniac rule a century later. It was the major economic force in the region, until it was stripped of its holdings in 1835. Its Romanesque church still preserves its 12th-century interior, but the façade was renovated in the 17th century.

Follow a road along the river for 200m. Turn left uphill on a gravel track. Proceed 1.7km on minor roads. After passing a construction area, turn left onto a minor paved road. Keep straight on for 3.2km, then fork uphill onto a footpath.

Proceed 2.3km, passing through **Villazón**. Turn right

Map continues on page 229

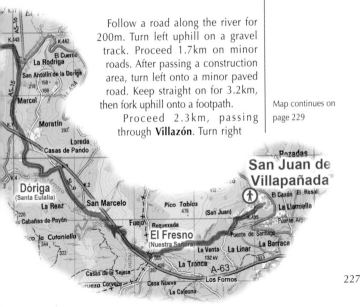

227

under the A-63. Cross a highway and join a footpath. Continue 2km into

SALAS (9.4KM)

All facilities. **Albergue de Peregrinos** (5€, 16 beds, kitchen, Plaza la Veiga 8, 985 832 279), **Albergue Privado La Campa** (10€, 35 beds, kitchen, W/D, 679 390 756), **Hotel Rural Castillo de Valdés-Salas** (singles 49–73€, doubles 61–91€, Plaza de la Campa, 985 830 173), **Hotel Soto** (Calle Arzobispo Valdes, 985 830 037).

Although Queen Urraca granted a castle here in 1120, the town wasn't founded for another 150 years. It promptly became a major stopping point on the camino. The **Valdés-Salas Palace** was the birthplace of Fernando Valdés-Salas, founder of Oviedo University, an Inquisitor General, and the Archbishop of Seville. Across the plaza from the palace is the 16th-century **Santa María la Mayor Collegiate Church**, which features a square nave and pentagonal roof and is generally acknowledged as a masterpiece of Asturian Renaissance architecture.

Follow the main street through Salas and under the arch. Fork right on Calle Ondinas. After 500m, transition to a gravel track. Keep straight on for 2.7km, crossing two bridges. Turn right onto the N-634 and proceed 500m. Turn left onto a dirt track uphill. Continue

1.9km, then turn left up a steep footpath. Turn left onto a paved road. Follow a dirt road and fork right to pass under the highway. Soon fork right onto a paved road, passing a church. After 1.2km, arrive in

The camino to Salas

BODENAYA (6.8KM)

The private **Albergue de Peregrinos** offers wonderful hospitality (donativo, ring to check availability in winter, 21 beds, communal meals, 609 133 151).

STAGE 5
Bodenaya to Campiello

Start	Albergue de Peregrinos, Bodenaya
Finish	Casa Herminia, Campiello
Distance	24.5km
Total ascent	320m
Total descent	310m
Difficulty	terrain: 3; waymarking: 2
Albergues de Peregrinos	La Espina, Tineo, Campiello

Today's walk provides a welcome rest between yesterday's hills and tomorrow's mountains. The route leads along quiet country roads and forested footpaths, but beware that after rain the route into Tineo can turn from a pleasant stroll into a slow and muddy slog. A short detour to the 8th-century Santa María de Obona Monastery is only 500m off the camino, and provides a pleasant highlight and rest stop before following the highway into Campiello.

Cross the N-634 and proceed above the highway. Turn left before the church, then right on the N-634 into

LA ESPINA (1KM)

Bar, grocery store. **Two private albergues: El Cruce** (donativo, 12 beds, kitchen, W/D, 639 365 210) and **El Texu** (8€, 16 beds, kitchen, communal meals, W/D, @, 669 016 667), **Vista La Espina** (doubles 20–25€, 985 837 172), **Pensión El Dakar** (doubles 21–24€, 985 837 062).

Another long-important pilgrim stop, with a legendary 13th-century hospital and malatería founded by the Inquisitor General, Fernando Valdés-Salas, and funded by Santiago's archbishop.

After 300m fork right onto a dirt track. The route to Tineo is well marked, following minor roads through a series of small villages. Pass through **La Pereda** and

Bedures, descend to the AS-216, and arrive in **El Pedregal** (bar) after 3.7km.

The route to Tineo

Follow the AS-216 for 200m. Turn right uphill onto a minor road. Follow dirt roads for 5.6km. Turn right onto a paved road. To enter Tineo, or continue walking, keep straight on the main road downhill into the town center. To sleep in Tineo's albergue watch for waymarks descending left on

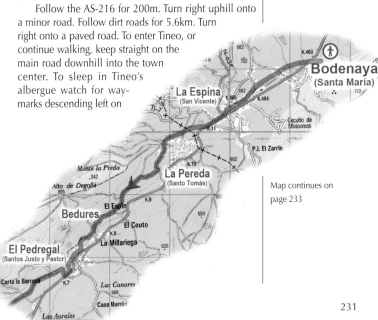

Map continues on page 233

231

a footpath. Turn right onto a paved road and proceed to the albergue in

TINEO (11.1KM)

All facilities. **Albergue de Peregrinos Mather Christi de Tineo** (5€, 32 beds + 6 mattresses, W/D, 985 801 067), **Hostal Don Miguel** (doubles 40–50€, Avda de Oviedo 6, 985 800 325). Internet at Tera Sistemas (Calle Eugenia Astur 48).

Founded by Rome, Tineo experienced its peak in the late medieval period, during which a castle, Franciscan monastery, and pilgrim hospital were all built, none of which survives. King Alfonso IX made Tineo a compulsory pilgrimage stop in 1222. The **Iglesia de San Pedro**, formerly part of the Franciscan monastery, still preserves its Romanesque tower. The highlight is the Merás Chapel, built in 1613, which includes double doors made out of single pieces of oak. Other well-preserved buildings in Tineo include the 16th-century **Palacio de Merás**, another excellent example of Asturian Renaissance architecture, and the **Palacio de los García de Tineo**, originally a Gothic structure but overhauled in the 18th century. Today, Tineo is known as a great trout-fishing area.

The route through Tineo is well marked. Pass through the center, proceed 1.5km, and continue uphill when the road becomes a gravel track. Pass the house of 'El Último de Filipinas' (sello available) and proceed 1.4km. Follow a footpath 1.6km uphill with good views of Tineo behind you. Turn left onto a paved road, then right onto a dirt track. Follow this downhill for 1.4km. Turn left onto a paved road, then turn right at the bottom of the hill. After

600m turn right onto AS-350. Fork left onto a footpath and proceed 1.5km.

The house of 'El Último de Filipinas'

Visit to Santa María de Obona Monastery

The optional detour (1km round-trip) to Santa María de Obona Monastery is marked to the right. Founded in the eighth century, the monastery experienced its peak during the 13th and 14th centuries, when a royal privilege ordered all pilgrims to visit. The monastery was badly

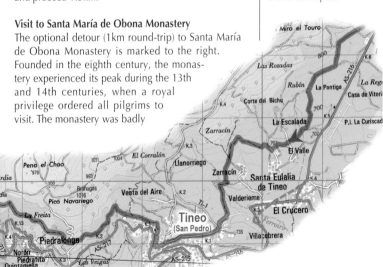

damaged during the *desamortización* (privatization of church property) in 1835, but the church remains in use today.

Turn left to continue on the camino. After 1.5km, pass through a farm. Bear left through the grass and onto a paved road. Turn right on the TI-3 and keep straight on for 2.8km to

CAMPIELLO (12.3KM)

Bar/grocery. **Albergue Privado Casa Herminia** (13€, 23€ for bed, breakfast and dinner, 26 beds, meals, W/D, 985 800 011). This quiet town has, in recent years, become the site of Herminia's growing empire, built largely around providing excellent service to pilgrims. She runs a comfortable albergue, which includes some private rooms, offers a very good pilgrim menu, and serves the largest *cafés con leche* on the camino.

STAGE 6
Campiello to Berducedo

Start	Casa Herminia, Campiello
Finish	Albergue de Peregrinos, Berducedo
Distance	27km
Total ascent	990m
Total descent	800m
Difficulty	terrain: 5; waymarking: 2
Albergues de Peregrinos	Borres, Berducedo, Pola de Allande, Peñaseita

The camino splits soon after Borres. Regardless of which route you choose, today involves a significant ascent and ranks among the pilgrimage's most strenuous stages; it also has the potential to be one of the most memorable. After Borres, at the waymarked intersection, turn right for the Hospitales route or continue straight for Pola de Allande. The Hospitales option, the recommended choice, leads into the mountains and away from civilization for most of the day. While this is one of the most demanding walks on any camino, made more so by the lack of resources, it is strikingly beautiful with expansive mountain vistas unfolding in all directions. The Pola de Allande option provides opportunities to restock or break the journey in half if tired, while still enjoying a pleasant walk with impressive views (although it is a far cry from the Hospitales route).

▶ Follow the TI-3 700m through **El Fresno**. Fork left onto a smaller road, then right onto a dirt track. Keep straight on for 1.6km to

BORRES (2.3KM)

Bar (open at 0600). **Albergue de Peregrinos** (5€, 18 beds, keys and credenciales from bar, historically quite dirty but reportedly better cared for now, 985 800 232).

Be warned that fog settles thickly in this area overnight and can restrict visibility in the morning. Although waymarking is excellent on the Hospitales route, pilgrims are strongly advised to walk through Pola if the weather is bad.

Map continues on page 237

After 500m pass a fountain on your left and ascend a gravel track. After another 500m, the camino splits. ▶ The recommended option, the Hospitales route, passes several ruined former pilgrim hospitals. Turn right at the fork and proceed 2.7km into the mountains. Pass through a fence and find a **fountain** straight ahead – your last chance to refill for 16.5km. Follow footpaths another 2.7km to the ruined **La Parodiella hospital**, 2.2km to **Fanfarón hospital**, and 1.6km to **Valparaiso hospital**.

For the Pola de Allande option, see below.

Fanfarón hospital

After 2km, cross the highway at **Alto de La Morta**, then continue 2.9km up to Puerto del Palo (1146m elevation). The descent begins immediately: 1.4km of steep downhill, cutting a straight line through the zigzagging AS-14, leading into

Map continues on
page 239

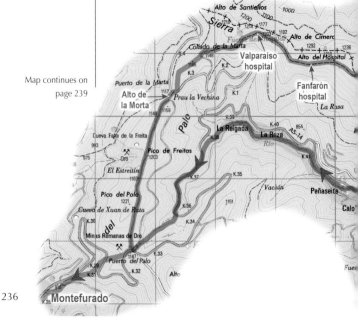

236 Montefurado

MONTEFURADO (16.5KM)

The chapel remains from an earlier pilgrim hospital and features a carving of an apostle.

The Hospitales and Pola de Allande routes rejoin at Montefurado.

◀ Keep straight on the footpath through Montefurado, skirting a rock wall around a house. After reaching a shell positioned before a tree, climb over the rock wall and join a footpath. Pass through a fence after 900m and follow the footpath for 2.6km. Join a paved road, turning left at conflicting arrows. Continue straight past a church. Turn left atop a steep hill, following the AS-14 into

LAGO (4KM)

Bar.

The church has a 16th-century bell.

Cross the AS-14 and fork right uphill onto a footpath. After 1.1km, rejoin the AS-14. Keep straight on for 900m, then fork left onto a dirt track, marked with red/white stripes. Proceed 1.4km to the albergue in

BERDUCEDO (3.4KM)

Bar/grocery, restaurant. **Albergue de Peregrinos** (5€, 12 beds, kitchen, keys from Bar El Cafetín, 985 923 325), **Camín Antiguo** (private albergue, 15€, 10 beds, kitchen, W/D, 696 929 164) also offers private rooms (30€, breakfast).

A pleasant small town with a lot of livestock, a 14th-century church, and the last chance to buy food before Grandas. The former pilgrim hospital is now the doctor's house.

Pola de Allande variant

Keep straight on from **Borres**, proceeding roughly parallel to the AS-219 for 1.3km to **La Mortera** (bar) and then joining the highway before arriving, 3.3km later, in **Porciles** (grocery). Fork left off the AS-219, but rejoin it soon after, for the final ascent to **Alto de Lavadoira**, 1.5km later. It's all downhill to Pola, following 3km of dirt roads and highways.

Berducedo
(Sta. María)

POLA DE ALLANDE (10.1KM)

All facilities. **Albergue de Peregrinos** (5€, 24 beds, kitchen, Avda de América, 646 832 425), **Hotel Lozano** (doubles 40€, Avda de Galicia 5, 985 807 102).

The route from Pola to Montefurado involves a challenging climb (roughly 600m gained) and abrupt descent. Leave Pola on the AS-14, keep straight on for 1.3km, then fork left onto a minor road. Soon after, waymarks return you towards the highway in

PEÑASEITA (3KM)

Bar. **Albergue de Peregrinos** (5€, 12 beds, keys from Bar Viñas, 985 807 116).

Return to the dirt road, where the ascent intensifies. Proceed 3.8km along footpaths uphill, cross the AS-14, and continue 1.1km more to the top, the **Puerto del Palo** (1146m elevation), where the two routes reunite. The descent begins immediately: 1.4km

of steep downhill, cutting a straight line through the zigzagging AS-14, leading into **Montefurado**.

STAGE 7
Berducedo to Grandas de Salime

Start	Albergue de Peregrinos, Berducedo
Finish	Albergue de Peregrinos, Grandas de Salime
Distance	20km
Total ascent	650m
Total descent	820m
Difficulty	terrain: 5; waymarking: 1
Albergues de Peregrinos	La Mesa, Grandas de Salime

Following yesterday's difficult stage, a shorter walk is certainly in order. Be advised, however, that this walk – dropping 800m in 6km – has the potential to devour tired knees. Take your time and enjoy the stunning 360° views from the windmill-lined ridge above La Mesa. The dammed Río Navia below shines like an over-sized sapphire, surrounded by rugged hillside. The final climb to Grandas de Salime proceeds largely along the highway, but the paved ascent comes almost as a relief after the extended downhill.

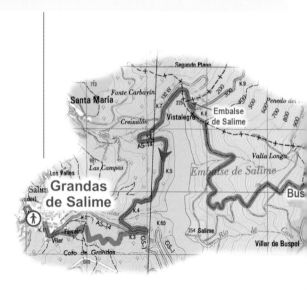

Pass Berducedo's church, joining a footpath after 1.3 km.
After 1km, turn left onto a paved road leading 2.2km
downhill into

LA MESA (4.5KM)

Albergue de Peregrinos (5€, 30 beds + 4 mattresses, kitchen, limited groceries for sale in the summer, 633 148 071). Grocery and produce food trucks
stop at La Mesa on Tuesdays and Fridays around 1600. Those staying here
should consider buying food in Berducedo. Be sure to fill water here before
leaving; it may be your last chance to refill before Grandas.

A small, peaceful village with a 17th-century church dedicated to St María
Magdalena.

Follow a paved road 2.2km uphill. Fork right onto a
gravel track. Continue 200m to **Buspol**, then join a footpath. A long 5.8km descent follows, eventually joining a
dirt road. At the bottom, turn left on AS-14 and proceed
1.5km, crossing the dam and arriving at the restaurant near

EMBALSE DE SALIME (9.7KM)

Bar/Restaurant/**Hotel Las Grandas** (35€ single, 45€ double, meals available,
985 627 230).

The construction of the dam in 1954 flooded old Salime; its abandoned
buildings line the hillside.

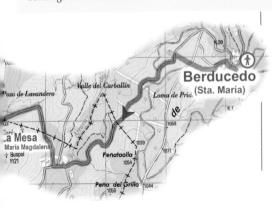

View of Embalse de Salime

Keep straight on the highway 3.5km uphill. Fork left onto a footpath. Bear right after 900m, following the camino waymarks. Join the road leading into Grandas. Turn right in front of the church and arrive at the albergue in

GRANDAS DE SALIME (5.6KM)

All facilities. **Albergue de Peregrinos El Salvador** (5€, 28 beds + 22 mattresses (+30 additional mattresses in August), kitchen, W/D, 633 148 071), **Hotel La Barra** (singles 40–45€, doubles 50–55€, Avda de la Costa 4, 985 627 196). Internet above Turismo/library.

Established in the 12th century following a donation by King Fernando II, Grandas later enjoyed success thanks to gold mining. The **Collegiata de El Salvador**, built around the time of the town's founding, has a huge porch and preserves its original Romanesque front. The **Ethnographic Museum**, located in the former rector's house, provides an excellent introduction to rural Asturian life.

STAGE 8

Grandas de Salime to Padrón

Start	Albergue de Peregrinos, Grandas de Salime
Finish	Albergue de Peregrinos, Padrón
Distance	26.5km
Total ascent	520m
Total descent	260m
Difficulty	terrain: 3; waymarking: 2
Albergues de Peregrinos	Castro, A Fonsagrada, Padrón

Another ascent to hill-top windmills awaits you today. It's an excellent climb from Peñafuente to Alto del Acebo, providing yet more sweeping panoramas and rewarding walking. The route also leads into Galicia, the final region of your walk. That said, the second half of this stage is less interesting, often proceeding alongside the highway, with few opportunities to refuel. Fonsagrada provides a good place to stop for a meal and restock before finishing the walk to Padrón, where an excellent albergue offers a good night's sleep and an outstanding kitchen.

Continue straight through town, generally bearing uphill and away from Grandas. After 500m, fork right onto a dirt track, which soon becomes a footpath. In 600m turn right onto AS-28. Fork right, proceed 400m, then rejoin the AS-28. Fork right onto a footpath, passing a yellow house. Rejoin the highway again and continue 1.1km through **Cereixeira** (bar, grocery). Follow dirt roads 2.2km, then take a paved road 100m into

CASTRO (4.9KM)

Bar/Albergue Juvenil (13€, includes breakfast, 16 beds, meals, W/D, @, 985 924 197).

The **Chao de San Martín**, a well-preserved prehistoric settlement (founded 800BC), was recently excavated.

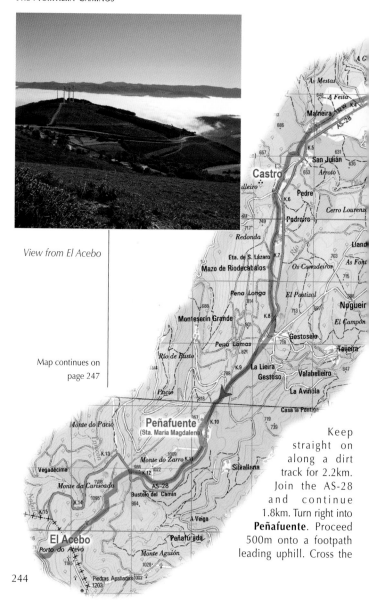

View from El Acebo

Map continues on
page 247

Keep straight on along a dirt track for 2.2km. Join the AS-28 and continue 1.8km. Turn right into **Peñafuente**. Proceed 500m onto a footpath leading uphill. Cross the

highway and continue uphill 2.6km to the windmills.

What goes up must come down: descend 1.2km into Galicia.

EL ACEBO (8.3KM)

Bar (no food).

Located on the Asturias–Galicia border.

Although waymarks thus far have indicated direction based on where the lines in the shell converge, in Galicia the opposite is true. Follow the diverging lines here.

Turn left onto the gravel track behind the bar. Follow this 2.2km to **Cabreira**, crossing and re-crossing the LU-106/LU-701. Keep straight on for 1.8km, turn right onto a road, and pass through **Fonfría**. Follow another gravel track 900m to **Barbeitos** (bar **Catro Ventos**, open 1000). Cross the LU-701 and follow a dirt road 2.5km through **Silvela**, back across the highway, and onto a footpath. Continue 2km. Join and cross LU-701, proceed 500m, and fork right onto a footpath. Continue uphill on a paved road. The route splits many times; following the left-hand waymarking each time brings you 2km on the traditional route into

A FONSAGRADA (11.9KM)

All facilities. **Two private albergues: Cantábrico** (10€, 24 beds, kitchen, W/D, 669 747 560, c/Rúa Ron 5) and **Os Chaos** (10€, 24 beds, kitchen, W/D, 660 011 716, c/Marmoiral 26), **Pensión Casa Manolo** (singles 25–30€, doubles 35–40€, Calle Burón 35, 982 340 408), **Pensión Cantábrico** (singles 25–30€, doubles 35–40€, Rúa Ron 5, 982 350 035). Internet above Casa Cultural.

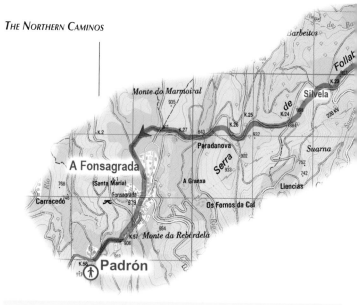

According to legend, St James was attended in this village by a poor widow and, struck by her poverty, turned the village fountain's water into milk – it thus became the *fons sacrata* ('sacred fountain'). Before ever becoming a place of Christian significance, however, the village was frequented by pagans and subsequently held a fourth-century Roman station.

Keep the church on your left and continue uphill through town. Bear left towards the LU-106. Cross the highway onto a side-street downhill, rejoining the highway after 1.2km. Continue 400m through Padrón. Cross the highway one more time to reach the albergue. For a more direct route, saving 600m, follow the highway straight from Fonsagrada.

PADRÓN (1.6KM)

Albergue de Peregrinos (6€, 44 beds, kitchen, W/D, 628 925 037).

Governed by the Knights of St John until 1874, Padrón has a small 18th-century church.

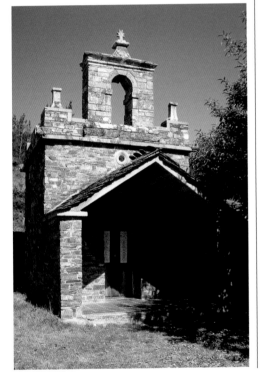

Church in Padrón

247

STAGE 9
Padrón to Cádavo Baleira

Start	Albergue de Peregrinos, Padrón
Finish	Albergue de Peregrinos, Cádavo Baleira
Distance	22.5km
Total ascent	450m
Total descent	580m
Difficulty	terrain: 4; waymarking: 2
Albergues de Peregrinos	Cádavo Baleira

Today's walk offers a variety of walking conditions on small roads and footpaths – including a few surprisingly steep sections – along with some wonderful examples of rural Galician mountain villages. Montouto is a special highlight; the aged village seems to have been carved in whole out of the mountainside. There are a handful of bars to stop at today, including a particularly pilgrim-friendly one just before Paradavella, and another fine albergue awaits in Cádavo. The town has little of interest, however, so enjoy the day, which contains the last significant stretch of higher elevation walking. Those looking for a shorter walk into Lugo tomorrow may consider sleeping another 9km further, at the new Albergue in Castroverde.

Route to Montouto

Cross the highway to rejoin the camino. Turn left onto a dirt road, proceed 800m, and cross the LU-530. Follow a dirt track 400m, then turn left onto LU-530. Fork left onto a dirt road; this becomes a footpath. Cross the highway again onto another footpath uphill. Follow minor roads 4.4km to **Vilardongo**. Fork left downhill, then fork right onto a gravel track. Continue 1.3km to

Hospital de Montouto

HOSPITAL DE MONTOUTO (6.9KM)

Former pilgrim hospital, founded in 1360 by Pedro I 'El Cruel'. Remained open until the early 20th century.

Map continues on page 250

249

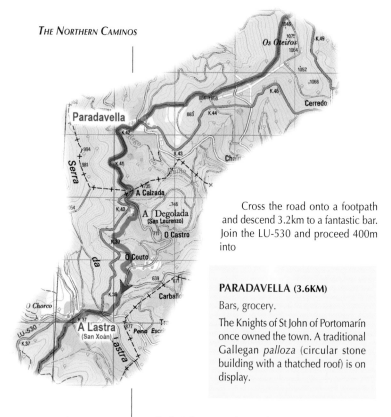

Cross the road onto a footpath and descend 3.2km to a fantastic bar. Join the LU-530 and proceed 400m into

PARADAVELLA (3.6KM)

Bars, grocery.

The Knights of St John of Portomarín once owned the town. A traditional Gallegan *palloza* (circular stone building with a thatched roof) is on display.

Map continues opposite

Fork right onto a footpath, proceeding 2.2km first uphill and then back down to the LU-530. Cross to the footpath and do the reverse: wind downhill and then climb steeply back to the highway 3km later, arriving in

A LASTRA (5.2KM)

Bars.

Formerly owned by the Knights of St John.

Fork left onto a gravel track. Keep straight on for 1.9km. Rejoin the LU-530 and proceed 300m into

FONTANEIRA (2.2KM)

Bar.

The parish church has a Santiago Matamoros.

Continue straight along the highway. Fork right downhill onto a gravel track into

CÁDAVO BALEIRA (4.6KM)

Bars, restaurants, grocery. **Albergue de Peregrinos** (6€, 20 beds, kitchen, 636 947 117), **Hotel Moneda** (singles 25€, doubles 40€, Avda de Baralla 46, 982 354 001).

Like Fonsagrada, Cádavo Baleira features a popular legend, stating that King Alfonso II 'The Chaste' battled a Muslim army here in defense of the pilgrimage road. Excavations in the area have found extensive amounts of armor, and many swords and tombs.

STAGE 10

Cádavo Baleira to Lugo

Start	Albergue de Peregrinos, Cádavo Baleira
Finish	Albergue de Peregrinos, Lugo
Distance	30.5km
Total ascent	310m
Total descent	620m
Difficulty	terrain: 3; waymarking: 2
Albergues de Peregrinos	Castroverde, Lugo

Following a brief ascent out of Cádavo, it's all downhill to Lugo, including a very steep 300m drop in less than 3km between Alto da Vacariza and Vilabade. There are few opportunities to resupply today and long, unbroken stretches with little of significance. But Vilabade, Castroverde, and Santa María de Gondar are all enjoyable places to pause, and Lugo promises some of the greatest sights of the trip. The massive walls surrounding the historic center may be the most impressive work of architecture on the Primitivo, and they are nearly two millennia old!

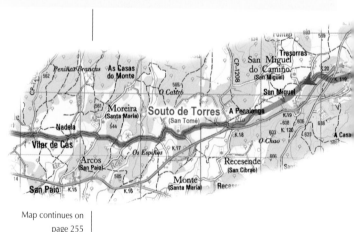

Map continues on
page 255

Take the main road downhill, then fork left. After 1km,
join a gravel road. Keep straight on for 5.6km, following
a paved road into

VILABADE (6.6KM)

Established as a Franciscan community for pilgrims in the 15th century. The
Church of Santa María built in 1457 and restored in the 17th century by the
archbishop and Diego Osorio Escobar, viceroy to Mexico, is a national his-
toric-artistic monument. A Gothic masterpiece, it features a ribbed vault
and a Baroque retablo dominated by an impressive Santiago Matamoros. Next
door is the **Casa Grande de Vilabade**, a 17th-century *pazo* (manor house)
built for Viceroy Escobar.

Continue straight through Vilabade. Turn right on
LU-530. Just before Castroverde, fork left onto a dirt road
skirting the town before finally entering

*Fountain in
Castroverde*

CASTROVERDE (2.2KM)

Bars, grocery. New and modern **Albergue de Peregrinos** (6€, 34 beds, kitchen, 699 832 747), **Pensión Cortés** (doubles 38€, Rúa da Feira 48, 982 312166).

First mentioned in 897AD, this became a major religious center in the late Middle Ages, thanks to the growth of neighboring Vilabade. A pilgrim's hospital existed in the 13th century. One tower survives from the old Lemos castle.

Pass the church and fountain as you leave Castroverde. Continue straight as the road becomes a gravel track, then a footpath. Rejoin the LU-530. After 800m, cross the highway onto a

paved road. Follow minor roads 2.6km to **Souto de Torres** and 5.2km to

SANTA MARÍA DE GONDAR (8.6KM)

Take great care – legend holds that anyone who drinks from the Fontiña de Valiñas will fall in love.

Keep straight on for 3.7km. Turn right onto LU-530 and proceed 1.3km. Construction has marred this route over the past few years, so be prepared for detours. Turn right onto a minor road and soon fork left onto a gravel track. Continue on minor roads 4.2km, passing through **Bascuas** and **A Viña**. Cross the A-6. Continue 2.8km into Lugo. Cross through an underpass, ascend a flight of stairs, and proceed uphill toward the city walls. Enter the Puerta de San Pedro. Turn right for the albergue in

LUGO (13KM)

All facilities. **Albergue de Peregrinos** (6€, 42 beds, kitchen, Nóreas 1, 660 278 926), **Youth Hostel Centro de Ocio Lugo** (9–13€, meals available, private rooms available, kitchen, W/D, @, c/Rúa Pintor Corredoira 4, 982 220 450), **Hostel Roots & Boots** (10€, private rooms available, meals available, W/D, @, Crta Santiago 216, 633 327 550), **Pensión San Roque** (doubles 32–44€, pilgrim discount, breakfast, @, Praza Comandante Manso 11, 982 222 700), **Hostal Parames** (doubles 28€, Rua do Progreso 28, 982 226 251), **Hotel España** (singles 23–32€, doubles 36–44€, Rua Vilalba 2, 982 231 540). Credenciál available in the Cathedral.

Originally a Celtic holding (*lug* is Celtic for 'sun god' or 'sacred forest'), the city is most famous for its Roman years, thanks to its massive walls. However, despite those prominent defenses, the Romans lost Lugo in the fifth century, beginning a period of significant turnover for the settlement. Suevi rule yielded to the Visigoths in 585, only for Lugo to be passed once more to the Moors in the eighth century.

Visitors can ascend the **city walls** and walk around the old town, enjoying excellent views. Declared a UNESCO World Heritage Site in 2000, these are the world's largest surviving Roman walls – 2km long, 8.5m high, and featuring 85 rounded towers.

Other than the walls, Lugo's most impressive sight is the **Cathedral of Santa María**. Although construction began in 1129, the building combines Romanesque, Gothic, Baroque, Rococo, and Neo-classical styles. Indeed, a close inspection of the interior and exterior offers a fine overview of the history of religious architecture. For Romanesque, head to the cathedral's transept and nave. Moving through the nave, the Gothic transition is obvious, particularly in the pointed groin vaulting; this style is also reflected in the main chapel, portico, and ambulatory. The cloister is purely Baroque, while the apse behind the main altar, comprised of five alcoves containing extravagantly ornate chapels, blends Baroque and Rococo styles.

Outside, only the northern façade preserves its Romanesque origins, as seen in the striking Last Supper capitals and the Christ in Majesty. Look to the roof for Gothic flying buttresses, best seen from the city walls.

Lugo city walls

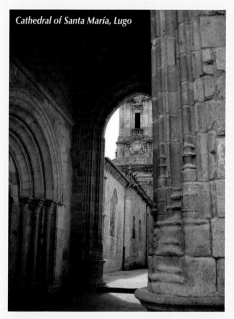

Cathedral of Santa María, Lugo

Finally, the western façade exemplifies the Neo-classical style, inspired by Santiago's cathedral. Lugo's patron saint, San Froilán, is featured here with his wolf. As the story goes, the saint was traveling with his mule when a wolf attacked and devoured it. The saint angrily lectured the wolf until it repented and took up the mule's load.

Lugo's many other interesting sights demand an extra day if your schedule allows the time. Other Roman remains include the 2nd-century **baths** (still open, as a deluxe spa), a **Roman bridge** (modified over the years; you follow this out of Lugo), and the **House of Mosaics** (Calle Doctor Castro 20-22). Next to the cathedral is the **Praza Santa María**, where the 18th-century **Bishop's Palace**, a Baroque structure built by Gil Taboada, is located. The **Convento de San Francisco**, which includes a Gothic cloister, now functions as a provincial museum.

STAGE 11

Lugo to As Seixas

Start	Albergue de Peregrinos, Lugo
Finish	Albergue de Peregrinos, As Seixas
Distance	31.5km
Total ascent	450m
Total descent	310m
Difficulty	terrain: 2; waymarking: 2
Albergues de Peregrinos	San Román, Ferreira, As Seixas

The final 100km to Santiago begins with a long day following peaceful country roads through generally flat, wooded terrain. There isn't a lot to see, but the kilometers pile up quickly and thoughts wander freely as the reality of arrival becomes ever more apparent. There are no large towns between Lugo and As Seixas, although there are a few stopping points, including the opportunity to buy provisions in San Román.

Follow the bronze shells out of Lugo, taking Calle San Pedro through the Plaza Mayor and past the cathedral. Continue straight through the Puerta de Santiago, following Rúa de Santiago as it slopes downhill. Fork right onto Calzada de Ponte and

Map continues on page 261

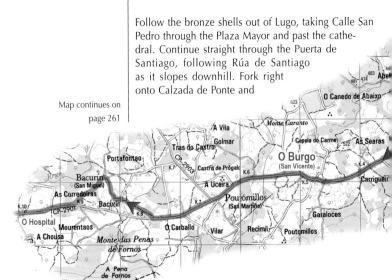

descend under an overpass. After 1.1km, cross a bridge over the Río Miño, then turn right onto Rúa Fermín Rivera. In 2.3km, keep straight on through a highway underpass and ascend 1.1km to join LU-P-2901.

Keep straight on for 4.7km into **Burgo do San Vicente** (bar, fountain). ▶ Follow the highway for 2.8km. Fork right onto a footpath for 2.1km before rejoining the highway. ▶ Proceed 900m to **Hospital**; 550m later, fork right onto another footpath for 250m. As before, this returns to the highway and can also be skipped. Continue 200m to **San Pedro de Baixo**, 850m to **Taboeira** (bar), 100m to **Crecente** (bar, closed Tuesdays), and 800m to the edge of San Román. KSO to continue along the alternate route, or turn right and proceed 50m into the center of

Turn right after 300m for the bar, which offers fantastic bocadillos (100m off-route).

Those in a hurry can remain on the highway.

SAN ROMÁN DA RETORTA (18KM)

Bar/grocery. **Albergue de Peregrinos** (6€, 12 beds, 628 173 456), **Albergue O Cándido** (8€, 21 beds, kitchen, 637 563 755)

Map continues below
on page 261

Another small town with Roman ties: see the Roman milestone opposite the bar. The **Iglesia de Santa Cruz da Retorta** is a 12th-century Romanesque church. Despite extensive renovation, the original floors have been preserved in the apse and nave, as have the original windows and the Trinitarian Christogram carved above the doorway. There have been some odd changes, including a Neo-classical arch and strange corbels on the north wall.

One remains on the highway out of San Román and rejoins the other in Ferreira and is 2.5km longer.

Follow the arrows out of San Román. Two way-marked routes leave San Román. ◀ We recommend following the old Roman road, which passes in front of the bar/grocery store and, 500m later, the albergue. From there, continue on a gravel track. Keep straight on a paved road downhill 2.9km through **Grella**. Continue 800m to **Vilacarpide** and 1km to **Pacio**. Proceed 2km, then fork left onto LU-231. Continue 400m to

FERREIRA (7.6KM)

Albergue A Nave de Ferreira (12€, doubles 40€, meals available, W/D, @, open May–September, 982 173 188, albergue@anavedeferreira.com, located on the Roman route on the way into Ferreira), **Albergue Ponte Ferreira** (11€, 26 beds, W/D, meals available, @, open mid-March–October, 982 036 949, hola@ponteferreira.com, located 200m after the

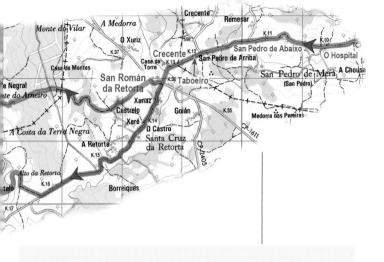

Roman bridge), **Casa Rural da Ponte** (doubles 40–50€, meals, W/D, 616 161 594).

Roman bridge.

Cross the bridge. Turn left onto LU-P-2901, passing the private albergue. After 2.1km fork right onto a dirt track. Join a road passing through **Bouzachás**. Turn left onto LU-P-2901. Proceed 1.4km to **San Xurxo** and 300m to **Montecelo**. Soon after, the route splits. ▶

To remain on the Primitivo, cross the road onto a footpath with a sign for As Seixas/Melide. Continue 900m

To join the Camino Francés before Stage 12, follow the CP-29-01 for 12km into Palas do Rei.

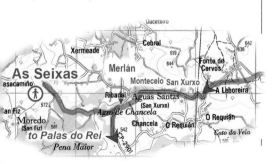

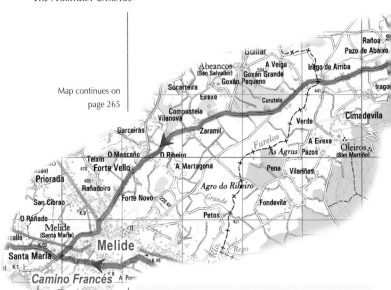

Map continues on
page 265

AS SEIXAS (5.8KM)

A brand new **Albergue de Peregrinos** offering excellent hospitality (6€, 34 beds, kitchen, 609 669 057). A food truck stops here nightly. Bar/restaurant/private albergue **Casa Goriños** (10€, 6 beds; private rooms available for 45€, W/D, 665 022 637).

Route leaving As Seixas

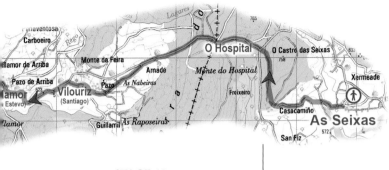

STAGE 12

As Seixas to Arzúa

Start	Albergue de Peregrinos, As Seixas
Finish	Albergue de Peregrinos, Arzúa
Distance	28km
Total ascent	290m
Total descent	480m
Difficulty	terrain: 3; waymarking: 1
Albergues de Peregrinos	Melide, Ribadiso, Arzúa

Enjoy Galicia at its finest! Well-trodden dirt paths pass through aromatic eucalyptus groves, yielding every few kilometers to small stone villages, solemn witnesses to the generations of pilgrims preceding you. Today you join the Camino Francés. Be prepared for some major changes – the number of pilgrims will increase dramatically, there are albergues and provisions in nearly every village, and all route-finding difficulties become a thing of the past. Pause in Melide long enough to sample the regional specialty, octopus, in the town that cooks it best. Sleep in Ribadiso do Baixo, a traditional albergue resurrected from ruin to care for pilgrims once more, or continue on to Arzúa, where accommodation is as plentiful as it is varied.

Return to the dirt track and keep straight on for 1.5km. Turn right (easily missed) uphill through a hamlet, then turn left onto a dirt road. Proceed 1km. Turn left onto a paved road, then right into **Hospital das Seixas**.

Keep straight on for 2.3km. Turn left onto a dirt road. Proceed 1km, entering **Vilouriz**. Walk 200m, then fork left onto a gravel track. Continue 1.6km, crossing a bridge, then fork right onto a paved road. Follow scallop shells 300m through **Vilamor** (bar). Turn left onto a road. Keep straight on for 5.1km. Turn left on DP-4604. Continue 1.8km, turning left toward the church in the center of

MELIDE (14.8KM)

All facilities. **Albergue de Peregrinos** (6€, 156 beds, kitchen, W/D, Rúa San Antonio, 660 396 822). Many albergue privados priced in the 10€/bed range, including **O Palpador** (679 837 969), **O Cruceiro** (616 764 896), **Albergue Pereiro** (981 506 314) and **Albergue San Antón** (698 153 672). **Hotel Carlos** 96 (singles, doubles, Avda de Lugo 119, 981 507 633), **Pensión Berenguela** (singles 30€, doubles 40€, Rúa de San Roque 2, 981 505 417).

The **Iglesia de Sancti Spiritus** contains a number of tombs from the Ulloa family, one of the dominant clans in the 15th century, about which the great Galician novel Los Pazos de Ulloa was written. Octopus is a town gastronomic specialty – Pulperia Ezequiel is famous for serving it.

Romanesque bridge near Melide

Leaving Melide, proceed uphill past the cemetery and then descend along a footpath. Cross the N-547 and then continue along the road. Turn right past a church onto a dirt track. Rejoin the N-547 2.9km from Melide. Keep straight on into

BOENTE (5.1KM)

Bar. **Albergue Boente** (10€ bed, 35€ double, 50 beds, meals available, W/D, @, 981 501 974), **Os Albergues** (11€, 30 beds, meals available, W/D, 629 146 826).

The **Iglesia de Santiago** dates from the 12th century, although little remains of the original. It is very welcoming to pilgrims, with a sello available.

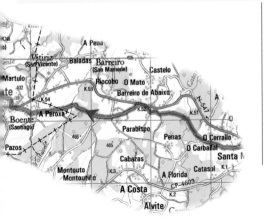

Follow the highway through Boente before turning right 600m later at the Iglesia de Santiago. Follow a dirt track 1.9km to **Castañeda** (bar), passing a small private **albergue** after an additional 300m (10–11€, 6 beds, W/D, @, 981 501 711). Continue along a mix of minor roads before crossing the Río Iso into

RIBADISO DO BAIXO (5.2KM)

Bars/restaurants. **Albergue de Peregrinos** (6€, 70 beds, kitchen, W/D, 981 501 185) in beautiful location along the river, **Albergue Los Caminantes** (10€, 56 beds, kitchen, W/D, @, 647 020 600), **Pensión Rústica Casa Vaamonde** (doubles 36€, 981 500 364).

Follow the road out of Ribadiso, cross the highway, and then turn right through a small neighborhood. Rejoin the N-547 and keep straight on into

ARZÚA (2.7KM)

See information in Camino del Norte Stage 30.

For the route from Arzúa to Santiago de Compostela see Camino del Norte Stage 31.

PRIMITIVO–NORTE LINK
Oviedo to Avilés

Start	Oviedo
Finish	Avilés
Distance	29km
Total ascent	350m
Total descent	495m
Difficulty	terrain: 2; waymarking: 4
Albergues de Peregrinos	Avilés
Note	For the opening section of this route see the map for Primitivo Stage 2, and for the final section see the map for Norte Stage 19.

From Stage 18 of the Camino del Norte it is possible to follow the Primitivo to Oviedo (Stages 1 and 2) and then return to the Norte at Avilés (Stage 19/20) without backtracking. While the route from Oviedo to Avilés is not the 'traditional' way, it provides the opportunity to visit Oviedo, a pilgrimage site in its own right, before returning to the coast. Although this is not the most pleasant of walks – you've only just passed the industrial outskirts of Oviedo before joining the highway into Aviles – it may be a more enjoyable route into Avilés than the walk on the Camino del Norte from Gijón (Stage 19). In many ways, the choice comes down to which city you would prefer to visit: coastal Gijón or Oviedo and its famous cathedral.

From Oviedo's Cathedral continue on Calle de Águila to Calle Gascona. After 600m cross Calle General Elorza onto Avda de Pumarín. Keep straight on for 900m as this becomes Avda de Aureliano San Román. Keep straight on through a roundabout onto Avda del Mar/AS-266. Follow this 900m, then turn left onto a paved road, crossing under a railroad and the AS-18. Follow minor roads 4.6km to Villapérez and cross the Río Nora. In 3.2km turn right onto LL-1. Continue 600m, passing under the AS-17. Turn right, proceed 200m, then turn left onto Calle de Carrión. Keep straight on for 300m into

POSADA DE LLANERA (11.3KM)
All facilities.

Fork right onto Avda Agustín González. Keep straight on for 1km, then turn left onto a dirt road. After 2.3km, cross the AS-17 onto a minor road. Continue along a dirt road for 2km through **La Miranda**, then follow a dirt road for 900m. Turn right onto a minor road. Proceed 1.1km to the AS-17. Keep straight on for 5.7km, passing under the A-8/E-70 into

NUBLEDO (13.1KM)
Bar/restaurant. **Pensión La Estación** (doubles 28€, La Estación 2, 985 505 567).

Keep straight on the AS-17 for 2.8km, then fork left onto Calle del Carmen. Keep straight on for 1km, then turn left onto AS-171. Continue through a roundabout and keep straight on the Calle de Gutiérrez Herreo for 1km.

Turn left on Calle Magdalena to arrive at the albergue in

AVILÉS (4.8KM)
See information in Camino del Norte Stage 19.

Central Avilés

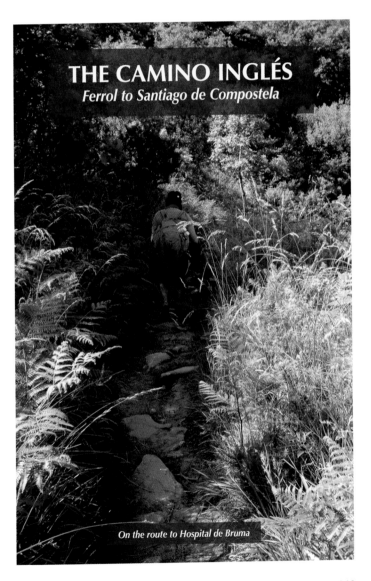

THE CAMINO INGLÉS
Ferrol to Santiago de Compostela

On the route to Hospital de Bruma

THE CAMINO INGLÉS

For many pilgrims in earlier times, the beginning of the Camino Inglés would have marked the end of their pilgrimage's most dangerous section. This is where many seafaring pilgrims, especially from England, would have made landfall and started their trek. Few, if any, of today's pilgrims will face such a journey. Instead, the biggest question is where to begin, as the Camino Inglés offers two different starting points. A Coruña is the more famous option, noted for its ancient lighthouse, the Tower of Hercules. However, the route from A Coruña to Santiago is less than 100km, making pilgrims who start there ineligible for the Compostela. As a result, many pilgrims start in Ferrol, another major port town, from where the route is long enough to gain them a Compostela. The two branches of the Inglés unite in Hospital de Bruma (at the end of Stage 3), 40km from Santiago.

Unlike the Caminos del Norte and Primitivo, the Inglés does not join the Camino Francés prior to arrival at Santiago; instead, the Camino Inglés follows its own distinctive route to the city's walls. Those seeking peaceful Galician countryside and few pilgrims will find both here. Despite its proximity to Santiago and its excellent waymarking, the route remains little used.

STAGE 1
Ferrol to Pontedeume

Start	Curuxeiras docks, Ferrol
Finish	Albergue de Peregrinos, Pontedeume
Distance	29km
Total ascent	365m
Total descent	315m
Difficulty	terrain: 2; waymarking: 2
Albergues de Peregrinos	Neda, Pontedeume

The Camino Inglés begins at ocean's edge at the port of Ferrol. Begin your walk at the dock of Curuxeiras and countinue through the center of town before returning back towards the water. Enjoy the views of the beach and the sea before heading inland, when the walk leads through the industrial and suburban outskirts of Ferrol on the way to Neda. The end of today's walk returns to the coast once again; the beach is just 200m off the camino as you walk through Cabañas and follow the long bridge into Pontedeume, where the new albergue enjoys a waterfront location.

FERROL

All facilities. RENFE/FEVE station. **Hospedaxe da Madalena** (singles 15€, doubles 25€, Calle Magdalena 98, 981 355 615), **Hostal Porta Nova II** (singles 18€, doubles 30€, Calle Naturalista López Seone 33-35, 981 359 772), **Hotel Silva** (singles 31€, doubles 38€, Río Castro, 981 310 552). Credenciál available from the Tourist Office (Praza Camilo José) Cela, 981 311 179).

A long-important port city, given its strategic military position, naval academy and its major shipbuilding facilities. Ferrol was the launch-point for the (ultimately unsuccessful) Spanish Armada in 1588. General Francisco Franco was born here, and from 1938 to 1982 the name of the city was officially changed to 'El Ferrol del Caudillo'.

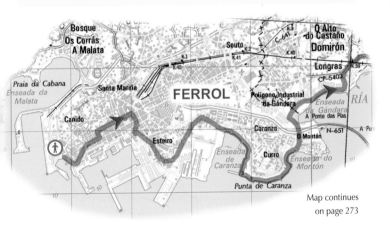

Map continues
on page 273

271

The port in Ferrol

The Camino Inglés begins from Ferrol's central port. The first stone waymark is opposite the tourist booth (opens at 1000) prior to the arch leading to Calle de Carmen Curuxeiras. The route through the city is well marked. Continue onto Calle Virxe, turn right onto Calle Real, and proceed into the Plaza de Armas. Turn right onto Calle Terra, pass through the Plaza da Constitución, cross the street and proceed through the Plaza das Angustias. Keep straight on along Rúa Taxonera, following this road as it turns into Rúa Mac Mahon, then Calle de Circunvalación, Calle de Caranza, and Avenida de Esteiro.

Continue straight through the roundabout onto Avenida Telleiras, which turns into Avenida del Mar. Follow this near the water. After 5.4km diverge from the water towards the N-651. Cross under the highway and continue 500m. Turn right before the factories, then turn right again. After 200m join a pedestrian path. Proceed 1.2km then turn right onto Avenida del Mar. In 100m turn left at the roundabout. 100m later turn right to cross the FE-11.

Waymarks by the sea

Turn right onto a footpath near the railroad. Follow this for 400m, then turn left to pass under the railroad and onto a paved road. Follow a series of minor roads, continuing under the FE-11. After 1.2km pass the 12th-century **San Martín de Xubia**. Turn right onto a small paved road, which soon turns into a dirt path. Proceed 1.5km, passing under the E-1/AP-9. Fork right onto a paved road, turning right after 300m to cross a metal footbridge over the FE-11. Turn right onto a footpath. When that ends, join a minor road, then turn right onto a gravel track which leads 700m to the dam.

Cross over the dam and follow the path. Proceed 500m to a pedestrian walkway. Continue into and through the park, for 1.7km, heading toward the prominent bridge. Cross over the bridge and walk 200m to

NEDA ALBERGUE (14KM)

Albergue de Peregrinos (6€, 28 beds, kitchen, 629 224 622).

Turn right after the bridge, proceed 1.1km on a pedestrian walkway, then turn left onto a small paved road. In 400m turn right, and continue around the **Church of Santa María.** Pass through a playground and between houses onto Calle Paraíso, which turns into Rúa Real. Proceed 300m into the center of

Map continues on page 274

273

NEDA (1.8KM)

Bars, grocery store, pharmacy. **Pensión Maragoto** (singles 14–21€, doubles 25–38€, Avda do Xubia 12, 981 347 304). Internet and sello in the Casa da Cultura, on the main road, just upstairs from the camino.

Medieval pilgrim hospital.

After 300m turn left and continue 400m past a cemetery. Fork left. Cross the N-642 and continue 100m onto the Camino de Regueiro. Turn left onto a dirt track. Proceed 300m onto a small paved road, pass under the AP-9/E-1, and continue 600m on minor roads to **Silva**.

Follow a series of paved roads 2km to **Fene** (bars). Cross the N-651, and continue 200m on the other side, passing the Casa do Concello on your right (sello). Turn left, then right onto Calle del Alcalde Gerardo Díaz. Keep straight on for 1.1km through **Perlio** and **Mundín**, following the road as it bends left uphill. Turn onto a footpath and proceed 500m. Turn right onto a dirt track. Continue 700m under the Viaduct Romariz. Turn right onto a small paved road. Proceed 300m across a main road and join a gravel track, proceeding uphill to the highway.

Turn left across the road, then left again towards the roundabout. After 500m, follow the road marked for 'Pontedeume/Betanzos'. Walk 300m then fork right onto a footpath. Proceed 900m, then turn right onto a small paved road and across the E-1. Turn left onto a dirt track, then right onto a footpath after 300m. Keep straight on for 800m, then join a minor road. Follow a series of minor roads for 1.5km, then turn onto a footpath. Cross over a bridge before rejoining the road after 100m.

Cross the AC-122, pass down the steps, and turn left under the railroad bridge. After 800m enter **Cabañas** (bars). Continue on Paseo de Magdalena alongside the park for the next 800m. Turn left at the roundabout, then right onto the N-651. Proceed 800m on the AP-9/E-1, then cross over the bridge. Turn right immediately after the bridge and proceed 100m to the albergue in

PONTEDEUME (13.4KM)

All facilities. **Albergue de Peregrinos** (6€, 20 beds, W/D, @, hours vary: open weekdays 1630–1830; Saturday (1100–1400, 1630–2100); Sundays (1100–1400, 1730–1930) Avda de Marina, 981 433 039), **Hostal Allegue** (Calle Chafarís 1, 981 430 035), **Hostal Luís** (doubles 25–42€, Calle San Augustín 12, 981 430 235), **Hotel Eumesa** (45–60€, breakfast, Avda da Coruña, 981 430 925).

A picturesque city situated between hills and the River Eume. The powerful Andrade family originated in Pontedeume in the Middle Ages, influenced the town's development, and commissioned many of the city's architectural gems.

The 14th-century **Pontedeume Bridge** leads pilgrims into town and was commissioned by Fernán Pérez de Andrade. It orignally had 116 arches and a chapel located between arches 21 and 22. The **Andrade Tower**, located in the center of town, is all that remains of the grand 14th-century Pazo dos Condes. Currently the tower houses Pontedeume's tourist office and the Andrade Interpretation Center. The 12th-century **San Miguel de Breamo** is an impressive early Romanesque church situated 3km outside of town.

STAGE 2

Pontedeume to Betanzos

Start	Albergue de Peregrinos, Pontedeume
Finish	Praza de Constitución, Betanzos
Distance	19.5km
Total ascent	220m
Total descent	240m
Difficulty	terrain: 2; waymarking: 2
Albergues de Peregrinos	Miño, Betanzos

Today leaves the beaches and port towns of the coast behind, turning inland towards green hills and rural villages. Prepare yourself for a steep climb out of Pontedeume, for which you will be rewarded with great views of the city below. Those who have time could consider making the 6km round-trip detour to the early Romanesque church of San Miguel de Breamo, nestled on the hillside above Pontedeume. The route continues through the countryside, eventually leading to the medieval town of Betanzos. While there isn't an albergue in Betanzos, the city offers accommodation and an enjoyable place to spend the night.

Camino under grapevines near Pontedeume

Continue uphill through town on Calle Real. Pass through a plaza towards the Church of Santiago. Turn left just before the church, then right onto Calle San Augustín, then fork left onto Souto da Vila. Keep straight on past (or take) the detour to **San Miguel de Breamo**, and after 1km turn right between two houses. Continue uphill 1.5km, then turn left downhill, passing a picnic area. Turn right onto a dirt track, and proceed 600m under an arbor, through a field, and into the trees. Turn left, then right onto a gravel track. In 1.1km, cross a paved road onto a footpath that runs 300m through the golf course. Turn left and cross over the AP-9/E-1.

Turn right onto a gravel track, follow this for 1.2km, then turn left onto a small paved road. At the next intersection turn right into **Viadeiro**. Continue through the village onto a series of small paved roads leading 1.8km downhill to **Bañobre**. Cross the Baxoi Bridge and turn right onto a footpath along the river. Pass under the bridge, fork right, and proceed 1km. Pass under the AP-9/E-1, then keep straight on for 600m through three more highway flyovers and then parallel to the highway. Turn

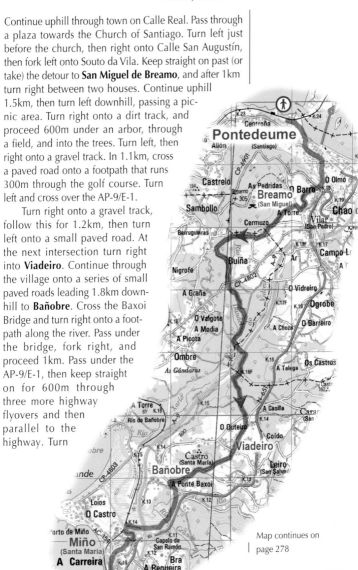

Map continues on page 278

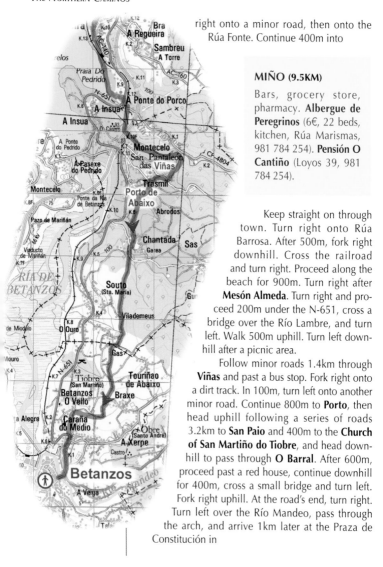

right onto a minor road, then onto the Rúa Fonte. Continue 400m into

MIÑO (9.5KM)

Bars, grocery store, pharmacy. **Albergue de Peregrinos** (6€, 22 beds, kitchen, Rúa Marismas, 981 784 254). **Pensión O Cantiño** (Loyos 39, 981 784 254).

Keep straight on through town. Turn right onto Rúa Barrosa. After 500m, fork right downhill. Cross the railroad and turn right. Proceed along the beach for 900m. Turn right after **Mesón Almeda**. Turn right and proceed 200m under the N-651, cross a bridge over the Río Lambre, and turn left. Walk 500m uphill. Turn left downhill after a picnic area.

Follow minor roads 1.4km through **Viñas** and past a bus stop. Fork right onto a dirt track. In 100m, turn left onto another minor road. Continue 800m to **Porto**, then head uphill following a series of roads 3.2km to **San Paio** and 400m to the **Church of San Martiño do Tiobre**, and head downhill to pass through **O Barral**. After 600m, proceed past a red house, continue downhill for 400m, cross a small bridge and turn left. Fork right uphill. At the road's end, turn right. Turn left over the Río Mandeo, pass through the arch, and arrive 1km later at the Praza de Constitución in

BETANZOS (10KM)

Detail of the Church of Santiago in Betanzos

All facilities. The newly opened **Albergue de Peregrinos** (6€, 35 beds, 981 687 001), **Pensión Betanzos Chocolateria** (singles 15€, doubles 30€, Pintor Seijo Rubio 1, 981 774 495), **Pensión Cheiño** (singles 15€, doubles 30€, Rúa Venezuela, 981 773 128).

The town originated as a Galician port town in the 13th century, but the port subsequently silted up. The town has since become a bustling market town. The 14th-century **Church of San Francisco** was commissioned by Fernán Pérez de Andrade and contains his tomb. The 15th-century **Church of Santiago** features a Santiago Matamoros above the main portal. Attached to the church is a 16th-century clock tower. Much of Betanzos is still surrounded by its medieval wall.

STAGE 3
Betanzos to Hospital de Bruma

Start	Praza de Constitución, Betanzos
Finish	Albergue de Peregrinos, Hospital de Bruma
Distance	27.5km
Total ascent	480m
Total descent	140m
Difficulty	terrain: 3; waymarking: 2
Albergues de Peregrinos	Presedo, Hospital de Bruma

Today's walk brings you into the heart of rural Galicia. Plan to enjoy breakfast in Betanzos – the only sizable city on the itinerary – before climbing out. Wind through a series of farms and small villages to Bar Julia, a good place to stop for lunch and fill your water before one of the steepest ascents of the Inglés. Once you've made it to Vizoño, you've completed the most demanding part of the walk. The last 7km leads to Hospital de Bruma – a historically important pilgrim stop on the Camino Inglés, as the meeting point of the routes from Ferrol and A Coruña. The albergue is fantastic, although there are no facilities in the town – plan to carry food from Betanzos.

San Estéban de Cos

Cross the Praza de Constitución towards the **Church of Santo Domingo**. Keep the church on your left, and continue onto Rúa do Rollo. Proceed 700m, cross a bridge, then continue 1.4km along minor roads leading uphill from Betanzos. Cross the railroad, proceed 500m, cross the A-6, then turn right downhill. Follow minor roads 2.3km to **Liminón**, and transition onto a dirt track. Keep straight on for 1.2km, then turn right onto a minor road. Walk across the river, then bear left. Proceed 1.2km into

COS (7.3KM)
Church of **San Estéban de Cos**

Follow a series of minor roads 800m, then fork right onto a gravel track. Fork right again. Keep straight on for 800m, then turn left onto a minor road. Proceed 1.5km on paved roads, then continue 800m on a dirt track. Turn left onto a paved road and continue 100m to

PRESEDO (3.2KM)
Albergue de Peregrinos
(6€, 16 beds, kitchen, 608 616 533)

Cross the bridge and turn left after 200m onto a footpath.

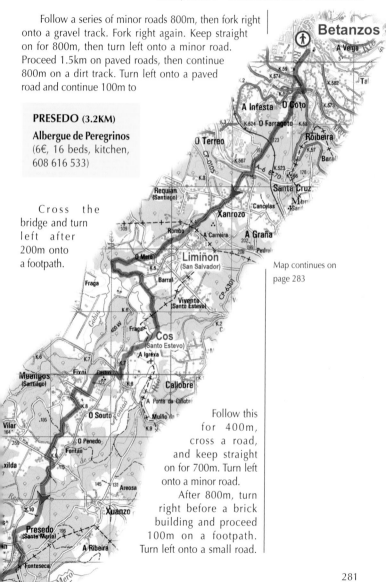

Map continues on page 283

Follow this for 400m, cross a road, and keep straight on for 700m. Turn left onto a minor road.

After 800m, turn right before a brick building and proceed 100m on a footpath. Turn left onto a small road.

Continue 800m through **Leiro**. Join a dirt track and proceed 1.3km. Turn left onto a minor road and keep straight on for 1km. Turn left. After 100m, fork right onto a footpath. Proceed 400m, then turn right at a house. After 100m turn left, then right downhill. Continue 200m along a minor road to **Bar Julia**. ◄ Walk 200m to the bottom of the road and prepare for a steep ascent.

Turn right uphill. Walk 900m. Turn left onto a smaller and steeper road. After 300m, join a footpath, continuing 900m to the hilltop.

Top up your water supplies here.

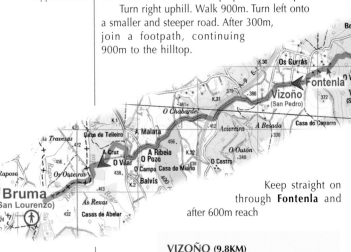

Keep straight on through **Fontenla** and after 600m reach

VIZOÑO (9.8KM)
Bar.

Continue 400m to a footpath. Follow this for 500m, then turn right towards the highway. After 100m turn right, crossing the E-1. Proceed 2km along rural dirt roads and paved roads through a group of farm buildings. Turn right onto a minor road and proceed 800m. Turn right after passing a red house. After 400m cross a larger road and then fork left onto a dirt track. Continue 600m, then fork right over a stream. After 400m, near farm buildings, turn right, then left onto a dirt track. Continue 900m to a stream crossing. Soon after, see the 'Albergue, 1km' sign. Walk 400m, then turn left onto a road. Keep straight on for 600m to

HOSPITAL DE BRUMA (7.1KM)

Albergue de Peregrinos (6€, 22 beds, kitchen, 981 692 921). No facilities in town, but **Bar La Ruta** delivers (981 692 754).

Hospital de Bruma is significant for its position as the junction between the two Inglés routes. The current albergue is located in a renovated medieval pilgrim hospital.

STAGE 4

Hospital de Bruma to Santiago de Compostela

Start	Albergue de Peregrinos, Hospital de Bruma
Finish	Plaza del Obradoiro, Santiago de Compostela
Distance	40km
Total ascent	350m
Total descent	450m
Difficulty	terrain: 2; waymarking: 2
Albergues de Peregrinos	Sigüiero, Santiago de Compostela

Prepare yourself for arrival in Santiago! Although today's walk is long, following minor country roads before hitting the industrial and suburban outskirts of Santiago – the anticipation of completing your pilgrimage will make your walk go by quickly. Buscas provides an ideal stopping point for breakfast. Pilgrims who don't feel comfortable with the length of this walk can stay in Sigüiero, 24km after Bruma, while others can continue the last 16km to the cathedral.

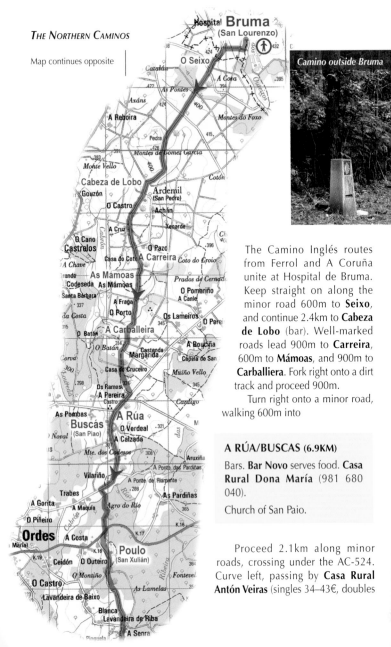

Camino outside Bruma

The Camino Inglés routes from Ferrol and A Coruña unite at Hospital de Bruma. Keep straight on along the minor road 600m to **Seixo**, and continue 2.4km to **Cabeza de Lobo** (bar). Well-marked roads lead 900m to **Carreira**, 600m to **Mámoas**, and 900m to **Carballiera**. Fork right onto a dirt track and proceed 900m.

Turn right onto a minor road, walking 600m into

A RÚA/BUSCAS (6.9KM)

Bars. **Bar Novo** serves food. **Casa Rural Dona María** (981 680 040).

Church of San Paio.

Proceed 2.1km along minor roads, crossing under the AC-524. Curve left, passing by **Casa Rural Antón Veiras** (singles 34–43€, doubles

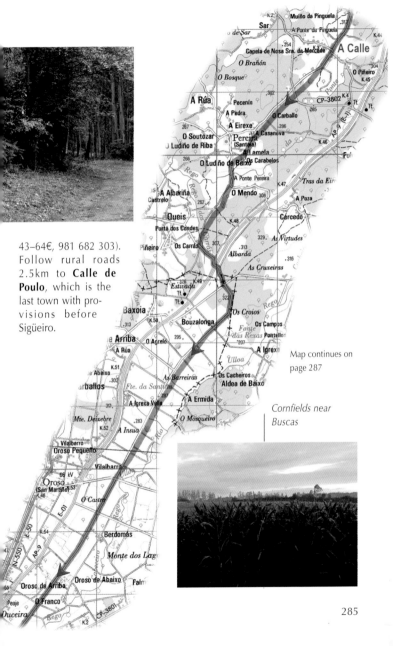

43–64€, 981 682 303).
Follow rural roads
2.5km to **Calle de
Poulo**, which is the
last town with pro-
visions before
Sigüeiro.

Map continues on
page 287

*Cornfields near
Buscas*

285

Keep straight on through town. Cross under AC-3802 and onto a small paved road. Follow another well-marked mix of dirt and paved roads 5.5km, then cross under the E-1 and continue 500m. Turn right onto a dirt road. Continue straight on for 5km, rejoining pavement next to a factory. In 600m bear right onto Calle Ulloa. After 200m, turn left onto a footpath. Turn left at the swimming pool, then continue 500m into

SIGÜERO (16.9KM)

All facilities. Two albergue privados: **Albergue del Delia** (15€, includes breakfast, kitchen, W/D, 687 279 398, c/Portifiño 21, 687 279 398) and **Albergue O Fogar da Chisca** (16€, includes breakfast, 12 beds, kitchen, W/D, @, Rúa do Campo, 4, 626 592 444), **Hostal Miras** (singles 15€, doubles 30€, meals, 981 694 508).

13th-century Romanesque bridge.

Continue 400m through Sigüero, cross over the Río Tambre and turn left. In 100m pass the **Igrexa de Barciela** on your right. Continue 800m meters, then fork right onto a small road. Follow a series of minor roads for 1.45km, continuing straight when you approach the E-1. After 600m descend under the freeway and soon after turn left

A TORRE (4.4KM)

Bar. **Hotel San Vicente** (doubles 67€, c/Marantes 12, 981 694 571, www.hotelsanvicente.com).

Map continues on page 288

onto a gravel road. 750m later, turn left onto a paved road and continue into

Continue another 400m, passing the church of **Nosa Señora da Agualda** on your left, before turning left onto a paved road running parallel to the N-550 and then joining the N-550. After 200m turn left, then right onto a paved road running parallel to the highway, then pass under it. After 200m, turn left onto a dirt road. Follow a series of dirt and paved roads 1.2km to pass under a rail bridge, and another 4.1km to the village of **O Barral** (bar). Continue 1.5km, then turn left onto a highway, passing by another bar. Continue

straight through two roundabouts, then turn right after 500m. In 350m, turn left at the crest of the hill, onto Rúa do Tambre. At this point, if you look carefully, you may be able to catch a glimpse of the cathedral's spires.

Follow this road as it slopes gently downhill. 1km later, turn left, then follow the left fork, in 200m continue straight across the road, and onto a pedestrian track, passing by a medieval bridge on your left. After 300m, turn right across the Avenida de Castelao and turn right onto Rúa dos Basquiños. From this point, the route to the cathedral spans just 1.6km through the city. Fork right onto Rúa Santa Clara as you pass by the Convento de Santa Clara. Follow the road as it winds through the old town, continuing as the road becomes Rúa dos Loureiros, then Rúa da Troia. Turn right to proceed into and through the Plaza Immaculada, down the steps and through the arch, to arrive in the Plaza del Obradoiro in

SANTIAGO DE COMPOSTELA (16.4KM)

See information in Camino del Norte Stage 31.

ALTERNATIVE START
A Coruña to Hospital de Bruma

Start	Church of Santiago, A Coruña
Finish	Albergue de Peregrinos, Hospital de Bruma
Distance	32.5km
Total ascent	420m
Total descent	60m
Difficulty	terrain: 2; waymarking: 3
Albergues de Peregrinos	Hospital de Bruma

A Coruña was historically the favored starting point for pilgrims walking to Santiago. The busy port city is only 73km from Santiago; while this made the A Coruña a popular starting point in the Middle Ages, it is a deterrent for pilgrims today, who must walk 100km to Santiago in order to receive the Compostela. The route begins from the Church of Santiago, located in the historic center of A Coruña, and traditionally the first stopping point on the pilgrimage. The visit to A Coruña may be the highlight of today's route; after leaving the old town, the camino passes through industrial areas and suburbs for most of the walk. The route improves gradually following rural roads past farms towards today's destination in Hospital de Bruma.

The port in A Coruña

A CORUÑA

All facilities. RENFE station. Airport located 8km from the city, offering domestic and international connections. **Pensión Residencia Nogallas** (doubles 22–48€, Calle Julio Rodriguez Yordi 11, 981 262 100), **Pensión Las Rias** (doubles 36–39€, San Andres 141, 981 226 879), **Hotel Santa Catalina** (singles 30€, doubles 44€, Fernando Arenas Quintela 1, 981 226 704). Credenciál available from the Church of Santiago.

A prosperous and strategically located port city, A Coruña has been important since the Romans established it as a

Church of Santiago in A Coruña

trade center in the first and second centuries. Traces of Roman rule can be found in the **Tower of Hercules**, built during Trajan's reign. Located on the edge of the peninsula, it is the oldest functioning lighthouse in the world (open 1000–1800).

In 1589, Sir Francis Drake embarked on a mission to sack A Coruña. A 13-day battle ensued, during which María Pita's husband was killed. When she heard this news she took to arms in his stead and killed one of the English soldiers scaling the city walls, inspiring the women of A Coruña to join the battle and seize victory for the city. The **Plaza María Pita** is named after her and features a dramatic 20th-century Neo-classical Municipal Palace.

The 12th-century Romanesque **Church of Santiago** is the oldest church in A Coruña. The church has been renovated over the centuries and now features Gothic arches, a Baroque altarpiece, and two 18th-century rose windows. A Coruña is sometimes called the 'Crystal City' because glass-enclosed galleries on the seaside promenade (**Dársena de la Marina**) reflect sunlight back towards the sea.

Pilgrims walking from A Coruña to Santiago will not qualify for the Compostela, because the route does not exceed 100km.

◄ From the Church of Santiago's west door, follow Rúa de Santiago through the right side of Prazuela Angeles onto Avenida Angeles and into the Plaza de María Pita. On your right is a tourist office; stop here and ask for a map to follow out of town. Continue diagonally through the plaza, leaving it on Calle San Augustín. Continue

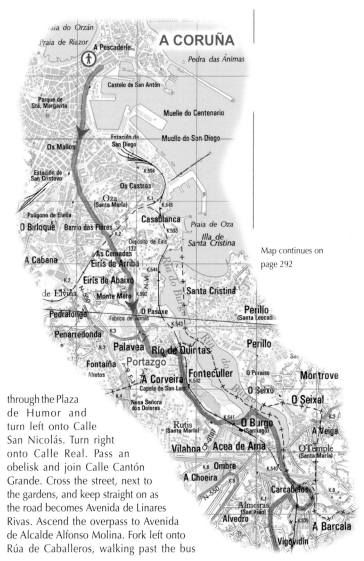

A CORUÑA

Praia do Orzán
Praia de Riazor
A Pescadería
Pedra das Ánimas
Castelo de San Antón
Parque de Sta. Margarita 61
Muelle do Centenario
Os Malios
Estación da San Diego
Muelle do San Diego
Estación de San Cristovo
K.594
Os Castros
K.1
Oza (Santa María)
K.545
Polígono de Elviña
O Birloque
Barrio das Flores
K.2
Casablanca
K.593
Praia de Oza
Illa de Santa Cristina
Depósito de Eiris 132
As Cernadas
A Cabana
Eirís de Arriba
K.544
N-VI
Eirís de Abaixo
K.592
Santa Cristina
de Elviña
Monte Mero
Pedralonga
Fábrica de Armas
O Pasaxe
K.543
Perillo (Santa Leocadia)
Penarredonda
K.3
Perillo
Palavea
Río de Quintas
Fontaíña
Portazo
Abetos
A Corveira
Capela de San Luís
Fontecúller
O Peraiso
Montrove
Nosa Señora dos Dolores
O Seixo
O Seixal
K.4
K.542
Rutis (Santa María)
O Burgo (Santiago)
A Veiga
K.541
A-391
Vilaboa
Acea de Ama
O Temple (Santa María)
K.6
Ombre
K.540
A Choeira
N-550
Carcabelos
Almeiras (San Xián)
K.8
Alvedro
K.939
A Barcala
Vigovidín

Map continues on page 292

through the Plaza de Humor and turn left onto Calle San Nicolás. Turn right onto Calle Real. Pass an obelisk and join Calle Cantón Grande. Cross the street, next to the gardens, and keep straight on as the road becomes Avenida de Linares Rivas. Ascend the overpass to Avenida de Alcalde Alfonso Molina. Fork left onto Rúa de Caballeros, walking past the bus station and under the highway where you'll be able to spot a cement waymark straight ahead. At this point, 2.5km from the center, waymarking becomes frequent and reliable.

Keep straight on along Avenida Molina. Keep left through the roundabout, crossing towards the Eroski and Claudio to continue on Avenida Molina. After 1.5km, fork right off the highway. Make your way 1.1km through the suburb, then turn right onto the highway. Cross the bridge over the N-VI and continue downhill. After 1km turn right into

PORTAZGO (6.1KM)

All facilities. **Hotel El Mesón** (Avda da Coruña 25, 981 660 065), **Casa Julio 2** (Avenida Da Coruña 19, 981 660 089).

The **Bridge of Burgo** was the specific target of Sir John Moore's last mission during the Peninsular Wars.

Proceed 500m through town. Turn onto a promenade, following it 3.2km. At the end, turn right uphill, turning left onto a minor paved road just after the Church of Santiago. Walk through a parking lot, cross Rúa de

Map continues opposite

Pablo Picasso, and continue across the highway. Pass under the AP-9/E-1. Fork right onto Rúa Pelamios. Continue uphill, passing the Church of San Julian de Almeiras 1.4km later. After 1.5km, turn right at the roundabout onto N-550. Follow the highway downhill, turning left then right onto a footpath. Join a road uphill into

SIGRÁS (7.5KM)

Bar/Pensión La Paz (Cuesta de Alvedro 41, 981 650 101).

12th-century **Church of Santiago** featuring a stained-glass Santiago Matamoros and medieval pilgrim hospital.

Keep straight on for 2.2km, crossing the A-6/E-70 on a series of paved roads into **Ancéis**. After 500m turn right onto a gravel track. Proceed 500m. Turn left onto a paved road, then turn left. Follow this gravel track 1km into **Carral** (*panadería*/bakery).

Continue 500m. Turn left onto a paved road and keep straight on for 1.6km to

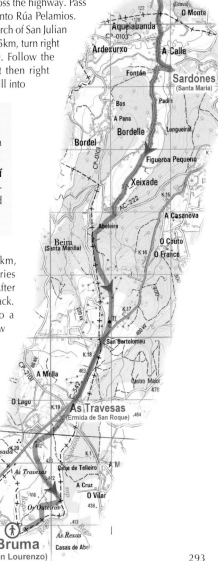

Farmland near As Travesas

Sergude (bar with provisions). Follow a series of minor roads 2km, then join a footpath. Proceed 700m into

SARDONES (9KM)
Bar/grocery.

Capilla de San Júan. King Phillip II of Spain stayed here while traveling to wed Mary, the English queen, in Winchester in 1554.

Keep straight on through town. Turn right onto a paved road and proceed 2.7km to **Cruz de Veira**. Cross the AE-222, then immediately turn left uphill.

Continue 2.6km uphill to **As Travesas**, the highest point on the Inglés (450m). Turn right onto AS-542, then left off it. Follow a path that parallels the highway for 1km, then rejoin the highway, passing **Bar Casa Avelina**. After 1.2km turn left off the highway and continue on minor tracks 2.5km to ◀

For the route from Hospital de Bruma to Santiago see Camino Inglés Stage 4.

HOSPITAL DE BRUMA (10KM)

See information in Camino Inglés Stage 3.

THE CAMINO FINISTERRE
Santiago de Compostela to Finisterre

Waymark en route to Vilaserio (Stage 2)

THE CAMINO FINISTERRE

For many modern pilgrims, the walk does not end in Santiago de Compostela. Instead, they are drawn still farther to the west, as far as the land will permit. They walk to Finisterre, the 'end of the world'.

During Roman times, Finisterre was believed to be the westernmost point in Europe – and therefore the end of the world. (It turns out that Portugal's Cabo da Roca is farther west, and there is more to the world beyond Europe.) While there is no firm evidence about when the pilgrimage to Finisterre began, its perceived geographic position accorded it a certain status that would have carried special meaning for a pagan population. The Christian trek thus ends on a pagan track. Many of today's pilgrims tap into their own primal instincts, burning their clothes at the lighthouse while watching the sunset.

The pilgrimage to Finisterre can be completed comfortably in three days, but the emergence of new private albergues over the last few years makes it easy to take a more leisurely pace. As was the case on the camino, pilgrims should get sellos every day (ideally two per day); upon arrival in Finisterre, it is possible to get a certificate (the Fisterrana), similar to the Compostela. The route is very well marked, the only potential complication being that it is marked in both directions, allowing pilgrims to make the return trip. And, while Finisterre may be the 'end of the world', it doesn't have to be the end of your pilgrimage, as an additional walk to Muxía is possible.

Map continues on
page 301

STAGE 1
Santiago de Compostela to Negreira

Start	Plaza del Obradoiro, Santiago de Compostela
Finish	Albergue Lua, Negreira
Distance	20.5km
Total ascent	435m
Total descent	525m
Difficulty	terrain: 4; waymarking: 2
Albergues de Peregrinos	Negreira

Walking away from Santiago can feel, at first, a bit peculiar, as you shift from arrival at the Cathedral in Santiago and tomb of St James to walking with a new goal – the cliffs of Finisterre and the Atlantic Ocean. The route leaves Santiago on a series of small roads and dirt paths toward Ventosa, which is a good spot to take a break. After stopping, the route continues to one of the prettiest spots on any camino, Ponte Maceira. From there, the last 4km to the albergue in Negreira, a bustling little town, are a fairly easy walk on minor roads.

With your back to Santiago Cathedral, proceed down the steps out of the back-right corner of the Plaza de Obradoiro. Keep straight on for 900m through several intersections until arriving in the Carballeira de San Lourenzo, a small park. Turn right through the park and then left down a minor cement road. After 400m, cross the Ponte Sarela, turn left, and then fork left onto a footpath. Proceed 700m to a T-junction and turn left on a paved road. Fork right uphill. After 1.5km, turn right onto a paved road. Arrive in modest **Piñeiro** 1km later.

Continue through a series of well-marked turns before joining a country highway 2.2km later. Pass through the tiny community of **Villestro** and then cross the bridge over the **Río Roxos** after 800m. Make a sharp right onto a footpath after an additional 800m, before arriving in

VENTOSA (8.7KM)

Brand new bar, with excellent food options.

Turn here for **Albergue Casa Riamonte** (12€, 8 beds, W/D, 981 890 356, located 500m off camino).

Turn right onto the AC-453. After a short stretch on the highway, fork right and proceed through two small neighborhoods. After 1.4km, turn left to rejoin the highway, passing through the small community of **Lombao**. ◄ As you approach a T, turn left past a medieval bridge into

AUGAPESADA (2.8KM)

Bar with small grocery, pharmacy.

Turn right onto a small cement road (or turn left to continue to the bar). Proceed along a mix of dirt tracks and paved roads through a surprisingly sharp ascent. Pass through **Carballo** after 2.2km and **Trasmonte** (bar) after an additional 1.1km. Keep straight on 1.9km into

PONTE MACEIRA (5.2KM)

Bar.

This may be the prettiest town on the whole camino. The medieval bridge over the Río Tambre overlooks boulders on one side and a fortress-like pazo on the other. The river is dammed, and a rope swing on the northwest side has tempted even the most determined of walkers into a lengthy break.

Turn left on the other side of the bridge. Proceed along minor roads and dirt tracks, converging with the Río Tambre and passing under the AC-544 before returning towards the highway. After 1.6km, turn left onto the

AC-544 and enter **Barca**. Cross the highway and fork right, passing through a small neighborhood before returning to the highway once more. Fork left onto a minor road (**Albergue Anjana** – 12€, 18 beds, W/D, 607 387 229), and keep straight on, eventually turning left onto Avenida de Santiago, leading into the center of

Ponte Maceira

NEGREIRA (3.8KM)

A busy little town with all facilities. This is your best opportunity to stock up before reaching the coast. **Albergue de Peregrinos** on the way out of town (6€, 20 beds, kitchen, @, 664 081 498), **Albergue Lua** (10€, 40 beds, kitchen, W/D, @, Avda de Santiago 22, 698 128 883), **Albergue San José** (12€, 50 beds, kitchen, W/D, @, Rúa de Castelao 20, 881 976 934), **Albergue Alecrin** (10€, 42 beds, open April–November, kitchen, W/D, @, Avda Santiago 52, 981 818 286), **Hotel Tamara** (doubles, triples, pilgrim discounts, Avda de Santiago, 981 885 201), **Hostal La Mezquita** (singles 20€, doubles 35€, Calle del Carmen 2, 636 129 691).

STAGE 2
Negreira to Olveiroa

Start	Albergue Lua, Negreira
Finish	Albergue de Peregrinos, Olveiroa
Distance	32.5km
Total ascent	490m
Total descent	375m
Difficulty	terrain: 3; waymarking: 1
Albergues de Peregrinos	Vilaserio, Santa Mariña, Olveiroa

The walk to Olveiroa is longer than yesterday's, and although there are a handful of bars to stop at for food and coffee along the way, the route lacks any sizeable towns or facilities. Instead, it strings together a series of small Galician villages, with rich agricultural fields interspersed. For those seeking more options for food and accommodation, the A Picota variant is recommended, which passes through the small market town of A Picota, your last chance to shop for supplies before the coast. Today's route ends in the small but picturesque town of Olveiroa, which is laden with examples of traditional Gallegan architecture.

Map continues on
page 307

Follow the Avenida de Santiago uphill, curving right past the Gadis supermarket before taking the next left on Carrera de San Mauro (AC-5602). Keep straight on, proceeding downhill across a bridge over the Río Barcala and passing the medieval Pazo de Cotón on your left. After 600m, turn left for Negreira's Albergue de Peregrinos. ▶ Those not staying at the albergue, however, can continue on the highway. After 300m, fork left off the highway and begin an ascent along a tree-covered footpath. Re-emerge on the AC-5603 and proceed into

Waymarks will return you from the albergue to the camino.

ZAS (2.8KM)

Bar with small grocery along the left side of highway (poorly marked).

After passing the bar, fork right off the highway. A combination of footpaths and dirt tracks follows, all well marked and maintained. Pass through **Rapote** after 3.8km and keep straight on to

A PEÑA (5.1KM)

Pilgrim-friendly bar situated off the camino. Those visiting the bar do not need to backtrack, but can instead follow the highway. The camino converges with it soon after.

Upon leaving the town, rejoin the AC-5603 before diverging once again, forking right and then turning left onto dirt tracks. After 2.2km, return to the AC-5603 for a third time.

301

Finally, after a long stretch on the highway, turn left downhill, for the final approach to

VILASERIO (4.2KM)

Bar. Basic **Albergue de Peregrinos** on the road out of town (6€, sleeping pads on floor, 648 792 029), **Albergue O Rueiro** (12€, open March–October, 30 beds, W/D, 981 893 561).

Pass between the bar and private albergue before turning left on the AC-5603. Follow the highway for 1.4km, then turn right into **Cornado**. Turn left at the fountain, then fork left uphill onto a dirt track. After 1.4km, turn right onto a road, and then left onto a dirt road after an additional 300m. The next 3.4km pass quickly, following flat, well-marked roads into **Maroñas**, before joining the AC-400 and continuing into

SANTA MARIÑA (7.5KM)

Two bars. **Albergue Casa Pepa** (12€, 18 beds, meals available, W/D, 981 852 881).

Keep straight on the highway for 500m, then turn right. After 1.9km, pass through **Gueima**. After an additional 700m, fork right in **Vilar de Castro**. Once again, a series of well-marked dirt tracks and minor roads follows. After 2.4km, make a sharp left onto a dirt track. After 600m, arrive in **Lago**. Follow a minor road out of town and then turn left at a T-junction. 1km from Lago, at a minor intersection with a bus shelter and signs for Casa Jurjo and Abeleiroas, the route turns right downhill. ◄

See below for a variant route via A Picota.

Staying primarily on minor roads, pass by the church of **San Cristovo de Corzón** after 2.1km and then continue to the AC-3404 in **Mallón**. Cross the bridge over the Río Xallas and arrive at the bar in **Ponte Olveira** after 1.7km.

A Picota variant

Those unhappy with the limited range of facilities available today should consider this alternative route. At the intersection described above with signs for Casa Jurjo and Abeleiroas, ignore the waymarks and keep straight on. Follow the road for 3km and then turn right at the T-junction into the center of **A Picota**, which offers all facilities, including the pilgrim-friendly **Casa Jurjo** (singles 30–35€, doubles 45–60€, pilgrim discounts, Avda 13 de Abril 91, 981 852 015). At the main intersection in town, turn right onto the AC-3404, rejoining the official route in **Mallón** and continuing into **Ponte Olveira**. This detour is 6.8km, making it 3km longer than the official route.

PONTE OLVEIRA (10.9KM)

Bar/restaurant. **Albergue O Refuxio da Ponte** (10€, 10 beds, W/D, 981 741 706), **Albergue Ponte Olveira** (12€ beds, 30€ doubles, kitchen, W/D, 603 450 145).

Keep straight on the AC-3404 for 1.4km. Fork left off the highway and proceed into the center of

OLVEIROA (1.8KM)

Bars/restaurants. **Albergue de Peregrinos** (6€, 34 beds, kitchen, 658 045 242), **Albergue Hórreo** (12€, 53 beds, kitchen, W/D, @, 981 741 673), **Casa Loncho** (doubles 40€, triples 60€, 981 741 673), **Casa Rural As Pias** (singles 40€, doubles 50–60€, 981 741 520).

The camino has transformed no town more over the last decade than Olveiroa. When the authors first visited it in 2004, it was covered in a thick layer of cow manure, had one bar offering little food, and was in a general state of disrepair. Today, manicured flowerbeds line the camino, new bars and accommodation seem to pop up daily, and the traditional buildings are being restored.

STAGE 3
Olveiroa to Finisterre

Start	Albergue de Peregrinos, Olveiroa
Finish	Albergue de Peregrinos, Finisterre
Distance	31km
Total ascent	350m
Total descent	620m
Difficulty	terrain: 3; waymarking: 2
Albergues de Peregrinos	Cee, Corcubion, Finisterre

Today you walk to the end of the world, Finisterre. After leaving Olveiroa, be sure to stop at the bar in Hospital – the only place with food or water before you reach the coast. The route from here is quite enjoyable, as the majority of the walk follows a footpath through sparse landscape, offering striking views. Descend to the coast at the market town of Cee, another good place to take a break, before walking the final kilometers into Finisterre. Be sure to plan time to walk the 3km from the town up to the lighthouse – these cliffs offer a stunning spot from which to watch the sun set, to reflect on your walk, and to share stories with the other pilgrims congregated on the rocks around you.

Beyond Finisterre, it is possible to extend your pilgrimage to Muxía, another traditional pilgrim shrine. Located north of Finisterre, this can be reached via waymarked routes from Finisterre and Hospital; both options are outlined below.

Continue straight through town, forking left off-road after 300m. Descend to a small river and then curve left back up a modest hill, eventually transitioning from a cement walkway to a footpath. Follow this all the way into and through tiny **Logoso (Albergue O Logoso** (12€, 22 beds, kitchen, W/D, 659 505 399)), 3.4km later. Keep straight on the track for an additional 1.4km. Turn left on the AC-3404 and proceed 300m to the bar at the edge of

HOSPITAL (5.4KM)

Bar offering excellent bocadillos and your last opportunity for food of any kind until you reach the coast. Refill water bottles here.

The camino splits 600m after the bar at a highway roundabout. Pilgrims continuing to Finisterre turn left, while those heading for Muxía should turn right. ▸

For details of the Muxía option, see Extension to Muxía, below.

After turning left, follow the road for 600m and then fork right onto a gravel track. From here to Cee the route is entirely off-road, completely rural, and offers expansive views. Two local shrines offer possible rest stops. After 3.7km, arrive at the 15th-century **Santuario de Nosa Señora das Neves**. There is a sacred fountain here, and a local pilgrimage to the site every year. Continue 3.4km to the **Ermita de San Pedro Mártir**, which has a sacred fountain of its own. The descent to Cee begins soon after, first gradually and then abruptly, with views of the coast, including Cabo Finisterre, unfolding beneath. After 4km, arrive at the edge of Cee, passing by the first of many private albergues (**O Bordón**).

While waymarking is generally excellent on the walk to Finisterre, the route through Cee is problematic. Proceed 300m and turn right on the AC-550. After 600m, fork left off the highway, and then turn right at the next fork. 400m later, turn left and then right. Curve downhill and then keep straight on along a sidewalk past a bar. After 200m, arrive at the *cruceiro* (crucifix) next to the **Igrexa de Nosa Señora da Xunqueira** in the center of

CEE (13.8KM)

Modern beach town with all facilities. Many **Albergue Privados**, including **O Bordón** (12€, 24 beds, kitchen, 981 746 574), **Casa da Fonte** (10€, 42 beds, Rúa de Arriba 36, 699 242 711), **Albergue Moreira** (12€, 22 beds, open late April – early November, kitchen, W/D, c/Rosalía de Castro, 620 891 547) and **O Camiño das Estrelas** (12€, 30 beds, W/D, @, Avda Finisterre 78, 981 747 575). **Hotel Insua** (singles 35–50€, doubles 45–65€, Avda Finisterre 82, 981 747 575), **Hotel La Marina** (singles 30–40€, doubles 40–50€, Avda Fernando Blanco 26, 981 747 381).

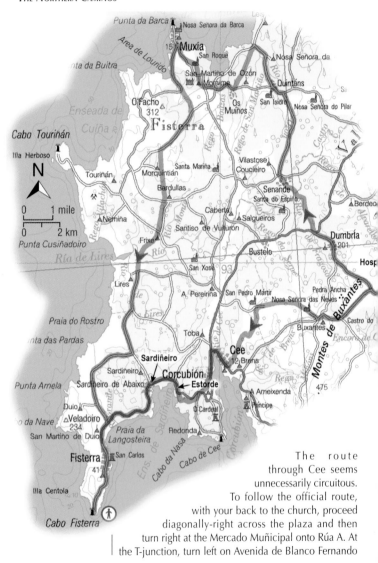

The route through Cee seems unnecessarily circuitous. To follow the official route, with your back to the church, proceed diagonally-right across the plaza and then turn right at the Mercado Muñicipal onto Rúa A. At the T-junction, turn left on Avenida de Blanco Fernando

(AC-550). At the next T-junction, turn left again on Avenida de Fisterra and proceed straight. Alternatively, with your back to the church, pass along the left side of the Carrefour, continue straight until reaching a T-junction, and turn left on Avenida de Fisterra.

After 1.1km, fork right uphill at the road sign for Corcubión. Keep straight on for 700m into the Plaza de Castelao in the center of

CORCUBIÓN (1.8KM)

All facilities. **Albergue de Peregrinos San Roque** on the outskirts of town (donativo, 16 beds, communal meals, 679 460 942), **Albergue Camiño de Fisterra** (10€, Avda Fisterra 220, 981 745 040), **Pensión Beiramar** (doubles 30–50€, Avda Fisterra 220, 981 745 040).

Proceed left uphill out of the plaza. At the 13th-century **Church of San Marcos**, turn right up stairs, and then curve right, proceeding along a footpath between high walls. After 500m, turn left uphill, continuing the surprisingly sharp ascent. Soon after, turn left onto a road, and then right. 900m later, cross the AC-445, passing the Albergue de Peregrinos on your left. At the **Encrucijada de San Roque**, veer right onto a footpath. Descend 600m and return to the highway in **Amarela**. When the road curves hard to the left, fork right off it. Take the next left, then turn right onto a footpath. After 300m, return to the highway, turn right, and proceed into

ESTORDE (2.9KM)

Bars, grocery store in Camping Ruta Finisterre. **Hostal Playa de Estorde** (singles 35–50€, doubles 45–72€, 981 745 585).

Keep straight on the AC-445 into

SARDIÑEIRO (1.1KM)

Bars, restaurants.

Fork right off the AC-445 and then left, proceeding parallel to the highway. Rejoin it once again after 2.2km, crossing to the other side. Descend to the beach and climb back to the highway yet again (those wishing to avoid the up-and-down can easily remain on the road). After 600m, turn left off the highway onto the Corredoira de Don Camilo and descend to the Praia de Langosteira. Once there, you can proceed along the paved walkway or remove your shoes and splash along the beach. After 2.3km, pass by the bar at the end of the beach (with a convenient faucet for rinsing sand off your feet) and return to the AC-445.

Finisterre

Fork left after 400m onto Avenida de A Coruña. Keep straight on for 600m into the center of

FINISTERRE (6.1KM)

All facilities. **Albergue de Peregrinos** (6€, 36 beds, kitchen, W/D, Calle Real 2, 981 740 781). Many **Albergue Privados**, including **Finistellae** (12€, 20 beds, kitchen, W/D, @, Calle Manuel Lago Pais 7, 637 821 296), **Sol** (10€, 29 beds, private rooms, kitchen, W/D, @, Calle Atalaya 7, 981 740 655), **Cabo da Vila** (12€, 48 beds, kitchen, W/D, @, Avda da Coruña 13, 607 735 474) and **Paz** (10€, 30 beds, W/D, @, Calle Victor Cardalda 11, 981 740 332). **Hostal Mariquito** (singles 25–30€, doubles 36–48€, Calle Santa Catalina 44, 981 706 817), **Hotel A Langosteira** (singles 25–42€, doubles 35–52€, Avda de Coruña 61, 981 740 543). The certificate commemorating your pilgrimage to Finisterre, the Fisterrana, is available from the municipal Albergue de Peregrinos.

Buses returning to Santiago depart from the stop situated around the corner from the municipal albergue. The service is run by Monbus, with five departures on weekdays (the first leaves Finisterre at 0820 and the last at 1900), four on Saturdays, and three on Sundays and holidays. The earliest possible departure on weekends is 1145. The trip takes up to three hours and costs 13.1€. Schedules can change, so double-check with Monbus in advance (902 292 900).

Although you have arrived in the town of Finisterre, the lighthouse at the 'end of the world' remains 3.3km away, following the AC-4408. Heading there after an early dinner is recommended, as this gives you a couple of hours of daylight to climb around the point and enjoy the views before watching the sunset. Bring a flashlight for the walk home. Most albergues allow pilgrims to return late, but double-check in advance. It is now possible to sleep next to the lighthouse in the **Hotel O Semáforo** (singles 50–60€, doubles 95–110€, 981 725 869).

Extension to Muxía

Many pilgrims, not ready to go home, are adding Muxía to their itinerary – either before or after they visit Finisterre. Medieval pilgrims are documented as having made the trek to Muxía to visit the Santuario de la Virgen de la Barca, although the current structure dates to 1719. Located on the coast north of Finisterre, Muxía can be reached via waymarked routes from both Olveiroa and Finisterre.

Those visiting Muxía before Finisterre will fork right when the camino splits shortly after **Hospital** (see Camino Finisterre Stage 3), 6km after **Olveiroa**. From there, the route covers 23.9km. The best place for supplies along the way is **Dumbría**, 3.8km from the fork, which has bars, a grocery store, and a new **Albergue de Peregrinos** (6€, 26 beds, kitchen, 981 744 001). Bars are also available in **Senande** (6km), **Quintáns** (5.2km), and **Os Muiños** (5.4km), with several others sprinkled over the remaining 4.5km to **Muxía**.

The route between Finisterre and Muxía spans 27km of rugged Galician countryside. Plan ahead. The only facilities available on this route are in **Lires**, which is nearly halfway between the two towns. Lires has two bars, as well as several places to stay, including **Casa Raúl** (doubles 30–58€, 981 748 156) and **Albergue As Eiras** (12€, 22 beds, W/D, 981 748 180). It is critical to get your credenciál stamped here if you hope either to obtain a certificate or to stay in the municipal albergues.

Muxía has all facilities, including an **Albergue de Peregrinos** (6€, 32 beds, kitchen, Calle Enfesto, 610 264 325) and three private albergues: **Albergue@Muxia** (11€, 40 beds, kitchen, W/D, @, c/Enfesto 12, 651 627 768), **Albergue Bela Muxia** (12€, 52 beds, private rooms available, kitchen, W/D, @, Rúa Encarnación 30, 687 798 222) and **Albergue da Costa** (10€, 10 beds, kitchen, W/D, Avda. Doctor Toba 33, 676 363 820). As was true in Finisterre, there is a certificate given to those who walk this route, available from the albergue. There are two direct buses per day running from Muxía to Santiago, if this is the end of your walk. For more information on the route, including detailed turn-by-turn directions, visit the Confraternity of St James website (www.csj.org.uk), where an online guide is available.

APPENDIX A

Route summary tables

CAMINO DEL NORTE				
Stage	Start	Distance	Total ascent	Total descent
1	Irún	26.5km	710m	720m
2	San Sebastián	18.5km	520m	520m
3	Zarautz	24km	640m	640m
4	Deba	23km	915m	830m
5	Markina-Xemein	25km	440m	515m
6	Gernika	35.5km	835m	825m
7	Bilbao	22km	230m	250m
8	Pobeña	17.5km	235m	235m
9	Castro-Urdiales	30km	410m	410m
10	Laredo	29.5km	280m	200m
11	Guemes	17km	80m	160m
12	Santander	32.5km	180m	100m
13	Santillana del Mar	23km	320m	380m
14	Comillas	28.5km	440m	345m
15	Colombres	23.5km	180m	285m
16	Llanes	30km	150m	160m
17	Ribadesella	31.5km	420m	400m
18	Sebrayo	35.5km	660m	680m
19	Gijón	24.5km	220m	210m
20	Avilés	39km	670m	640m
21	Soto de Luiña	20.5km	370m	320m
22	Cadavedo	15.5km	140m	230m
23	Luarca	31km	340m	280m
24	La Caridad	21.5km	70m	85m
25	Ribadeo	27.5km	710m	695m
26	Lourenzá	24km	740m	300m
27	Gontán	40km	320m	400m
28	Baamonde	14.5km	110m	70m
29	Miraz	25.5km	390m	360m
30	Sobrado dos Monxes	22km	220m	320m
31	Arzúa	39km	290m	450m
	Santiago de Compostela	**817.5km**	**12,235m**	**12,015m**

CAMINO PRIMITIVO

Stage	Start	Distance	Total ascent	Total descent
1	Sebrayo	34km	550m	320m
2	Pola de Siero	16.5km	80m	100m
3	Oviedo	29.5km	360m	300m
4	San Juan de Villapañada	24.5km	660m	340m
5	Bodenaya	24.5km	320m	310m
6	Campiello	27km	990m	800m
7	Berducedo	20km	650m	820m
8	Grandas de Salime	26.5km	520m	260m
9	Padrón	22.5km	450m	580m
10	Cádavo Baleira	30.5km	310m	620m
11	Lugo	31.5km	450m	310m
12	As Seixas	28km	290m	480m
	Arzúa	**39km**	**290m**	**450m**
	Santiago de Compostela	**353.5km**	**5920m**	**5690m**

Primitivo–Norte Link (Oviedo to Avilés)			
Oviedo	29km	350m	495m

CAMINO INGLÉS

Stage	Start	Distance	Total ascent	Total descent
1	Ferrol	29km	365m	315m
2	Pontedeume	19.5km	220m	240m
3	Betanzos	27.5km	480m	140m
4	Hospital de Bruma	40km	350m	450m
	Santiago de Compostela	**116km**	**1415m**	**1145m**

Alternative start (A Coruña to Hospital de Bruma)			
A Coruña	32.5km	420m	60m

CAMINO FINISTERRE

Stage	Start	Distance	Total ascent	Total descent
1	Santiago de Compostela	20.5km	435m	525m
2	Negreira	32.5km	490m	375m
3	Oliveiroa	31km	350m	620m
	Finisterre	**84km**	**1275m**	**1520m**

APPENDIX B
English–Spanish–Euskera glossary

English	Spanish	Euskera
Altarpiece	Retablo	Erretaula
Bakery	Panadería	Okindegia
Bathroom	Baño	Komona
Beach	Playa	Hondartza
Beware of dog	Cuidado con el perro	Kontuz zakurrarekin
Bill (in a restaurant)	Cuenta	Kontua
Blister	Ampolla	Baba
Bridge	Puente	Zubia
Building	Edificio	Eraikuntza
Bull ring	Plaza de toros	Zezen-plaza
Bus station	Estación de autobuses	Autobus geltokia
Butcher's shop	Carnicería	Haretegi
Central plaza	Plaza mayor	Plaza nagusia
Chapel	Capilla	Kapera
Church	Iglesia	Eliza
City	Ciudad	Hiria
Close the gate	Cierren la puerta	Itxi atea
Closed	Cerrado	Itxita
Clothes washing place	Lavadero	Garbitokia
Corn crib/ granary	Hórreo	Garai
Corner	Esquina	Kantoi, izkin
Crucifix	Cruceiro	Kalbario
Dam	Embalse	Urtegi
Detour	Desvío	Desbideratze
Doctor	Médico, doctor	Mediku
Donation	Donativo	Dohaintza
Door, gate	Puerta	Atea

English	Spanish	Euskera
Far	Lejos	Urruti, urrun
Food	Comida	Janari
Fountain	Fuente	Iturri
Goodbye	Adiós	Agur
Good morning	Buenos días	Egun on
Guesthouse	Casa de huéspedes	Ostatu
Help	Ayuda, socorro	Lagundu
Here	Aquí	Hemen
Hermitage	Ermita	Ermita
Highway	Carretera	Errepide
Hill	Colina	Gailur, tontor, gain
Historic center	Casco antiguo	Alde zaharra
Hospital	Hospital	Ospitalea
Hotel	Hotel, hostal	Hotela
How much is it	Cuanto cuesta	Zenbat balio du
Hunting preserve	Coto de caza	Ehiza lekua
Inn	Fonda, hospedaje	Ostatu
Kiosk	Estanco, tabac	Estanko, tabako denda
Left	Izquierda	Ezkerra
Manor house	Pazo	Jauretxe
Mill	Molino	Errota
Monastery	Monasterio	Monasterioa, zenobio
Near	Cerca	Hurbil
Neighborhood	Barrio	Auzo
No	No	Ez
Open	Abierto	Zabalik

English	*Spanish*	Euskera
Pain	*Dolor*	Mina
Path	*Camino, senda*	Bidea
Pelota court	*Frontón*	Pilotalekua
Petrol station	*Gasolinera*	Gasolindegia
Pilgrim	*Peregrino*	Erromes
Pilgrim hostel	*Albergue de Peregrinos*	Erromes Aterpetxea
Plateau	*Meseta*	Goi-lautada
Please	*Por favor*	Mesedez
Post office	*Correos*	Posta
Prehistoric fort	*Castro*	Historiaurreko gotorlekua
Restaurant	*Restaurante*	Jatetxea
Right	*Derecha*	Eskuina
Roadside cross	*Cruce de carretera*	Errepide gurutzea
Sports center	*Polideportivo*	Kiroldegia
St James	*Santiago*	Done Jakue
Stamp	*Sello*	Zigilu
Stepping stones	*Peldaños*	Koska, maila

English	*Spanish*	Euskera
Straight	*Recto, directamente*	Zuzen
Stream	*Arroyo*	Erreka
Street	*Calle*	Kalea
Supermarket	*Supermercado*	Supermerkatua
Telephone	*Teléfono*	Telefonoa
Thank you	*Gracias*	Eskerik asko
Time	*Hora*	Ordua
Tourist office	*Turismo*	Turismo Bulego
Town	*Pueblo*	Herria
Town hall	*Ayuntamiento*	Udaletxea
Valley	*Valle*	Haran, bailara, ibar
View point	*Mirador*	Begiratokia
Water (drinkable)	*Agua potable*	Edateko ura
Waymark	*Señal*	Seinalea
Where	*Donde*	Non
Yes	*Sí*	Bai
Youth hostel	*Albergue juvenil*	Gazte-aterpetxe

APPENDIX C
Suggestions for further reading

Although an overwhelming amount of literature has been produced about the Camino Francés, very little is available in English on the Northern Caminos. Many of the websites and guides below are in Spanish; all other books are in English.

Friends of the Camino de Santiago websites
Amigos del Camino de Santiago de Guipuzcoa: Provides up-to-date information on the first leg of the Camino del Norte, from Irún to Markina-Xemein. www.caminosnorte.org

Asociación Astur-Leonesa de Amigos: Has route information on the Camino Primitivo and runs Oviedo's albergue. www.caminosantiagoastur.com

Amigos del Camino de Santiago Astur-Galaico del Interior: Based in Tineo, this group also provides information on the Camino Primitivo. www.caminotineo.es

Asociación Galega de Amigos: Includes route descriptions and albergue information for all of the Caminos de Santiago through Galicia. www.amigosdelcamino.com

The Confraternity of St James: Based in London, this continues to be the pre-eminent source for English-language information on the Caminos de Santiago. www.csj.org.uk

Other recommended guides
El Camino de Santiago del Norte, Madrid: El País Aguilar, 2010. An excellent Spanish-language guide to the Camino del Norte and Camino Primitivo, recently updated with detailed maps.

El Cuaderno del Peregrino: Camino Norte de Santiago, Madrid: Anaya, 2010. A very clever concept: a moleskine-style compact journal with route maps interspersed.

CSJ Guides. Available from the Confraternity of St James, individual guides to the Camino del Norte, Camino Primitivo, and Camino

Inglés are available for purchase (the Inglés guide can be downloaded). Be warned that although these are often very useful, the route descriptions are sometimes outdated.

Books on pilgrimage
RA Fletcher, *Saint James's Catapult: The Life and Times of Diego Gelmírez of Santiago de Compostela*, Oxford: Clarendon Press, 1984. An introduction to the other man responsible for transforming Santiago de Compostela into a sacred Christian site.

Nancy Louise Frey, *Pilgrim Stories: On and Off the Road to Santiago*, Berkeley: University of California Press, 1988. An anthropologist's study of the modern pilgrim's experience.

Michael Gaches, *Valiant: A Pilgrim on the Camino del Norte*, London: CSJ, 2010. This pilgrim diary of the Camino del Norte won the first prize in the second International Pilgrim Diary Competition.

Cees Nooteboom, *Roads to Santiago: A Modern-Day Pilgrimage Through Spain*, New York: Harcourt Brace, 1997. Although this is not written by a walker, and it does not follow the pilgrimage road explicitly, it serves to nicely place Santiago within the larger context of Spanish history.

Landon Roussel, *On the Primitive Way*, Louisiana: Communitas Press, 2015. An account of two brothers on the Camino Primitivo.

Jonathan Sumption, *The Age of Pilgrimage: The Medieval Journey to God*, Mahweh: HiddenSpring, 2004. A detailed survey of the pilgrimage boom in the medieval Christian world.

APPENDIX D
Useful sources of information

Updated information on albergues
Eroski/Consumer Camino de Santiago Site:
The best resource online for up-to-date albergue information, on all of the major caminos.
caminodesantiago.consumer.es

Mundicamino: Another excellent option. Although the site is not as slick as Consumer's, it is packed with useful material.
mundicamino.com

Transport
For additional information see 'Getting there and back' in the Introduction.

Bus
Movelia: www.movelia.es
ALSA: www.alsa.es
Vibasa: www.vibasa.com
(Basque Country) Chronoplus: www.chronoplus.eu
Ekialdebus: www.ekialdebus.net
Bizkaibus: www.bizkaia.net
Pesa Bus: www.pesa.net
(Galicia) Empresa Freire: www.empresafreire.com
Arriva: www.arriva.es
Castromil: www.monbus.es
ASICASA: www.autoscalpita.es

Train
Renfe: www.renfe.com
FEVE: www.feve.es
EuskoTren: www.euskotren.es
SNCF: www.sncf.com/en/passengers#

Air
RyanAir: www.ryanair.com
EasyJet: www.easyjet.com
Vueling: www.vueling.com

Iberia: www.iberia.com
TAP Portugal: www.flytap.com
Air Berlin: www.airberlin.com

Baggage Transport
On the Camino del Norte
Le P'tit Bag: 635 730 852,
g.car.trans@gmail.com
Peregrine Express: 644 589 217,
christel.langeveld@gmail.com
Jose Luis Pardo Rodríguez (Asturias and Galicia): 606 049 858,
info@caminodesantiago2010.com.es

On the Primitivo
Taxi Camino: 619 156 730,
trastinos@gmail.com (taxi and bag transfer)
Jose Luis Pardo Rodríguez: 606 049 858,
info@caminodesantiago2010.com.es

Credenciál
Before departure, you can obtain the credenciál from Camino-related groups including:
Confraternity of St James (CSJ): www.csj.org.uk
American Pilgrims: Colo www.americanpilgrims.com
Canadian Company of Pilgrims: www.santiago.ca

Once you arrive in Spain, the credenciál can be obtained from Albergues in Irún, Santander, San Sebastián, Avilés, and Oviedo, in the Cathedrals in Oviedo and Lugo, the Church of Santiago in A Coruña, from the tourist office in Ferrol, and may be available at the tourist center in Villaviciosa.

APPENDIX E

Index of principal place names

CICERONE'S EUROPEAN WALKING GUIDES

For full information on all our
guides, books and eBooks,
visit our website:
www.cicerone.co.uk

Walking – Trekking – Mountaineering – Climbing – Cycling

Over 40 years, Cicerone have built up an outstanding collection of over 300 guides, inspiring all sorts of amazing adventures.

Every guide comes from extensive exploration and research by our expert authors, all with a passion for their subjects. They are frequently praised, endorsed and used by clubs, instructors and outdoor organisations.

All our titles can now be bought as **e-books**, **ePubs** and **Kindle** files and we also have an online magazine – **Cicerone Extra** – with features to help cyclists, climbers, walkers and trekkers choose their next adventure, at home or abroad.

Our website shows any **new information** we've had in since a book was published. Please do let us know if you find anything has changed, so that we can publish the latest details. On our **website** you'll also find great ideas and lots of detailed information about what's inside every guide and you can buy **individual routes** from many of them online.

It's easy to keep in touch with what's going on at Cicerone by getting our monthly **free e-newsletter**, which is full of offers, competitions, up-to-date information and topical articles. You can subscribe on our home page and also follow us on **Facebook** and **Twitter** or dip into our **blog**.

Cicerone – the very best guides for exploring the world.

CICERONE

2 Police Square Milnthorpe Cumbria LA7 7PY
Tel: 015395 62069 info@cicerone.co.uk
www.cicerone.co.uk and **www.cicerone-extra.com**